INVENTING CRIMINOLOGY

SUNY Series in Deviance and Social Control
Ronald A. Farrell, Editor

INVENTING CRIMINOLOGY

Essays on the Rise of *Homo Criminalis*

PIERS BEIRNE

STATE UNIVERSITY OF NEW YORK PRESS

Published by
State University of New York Press, Albany

For information, address the State University of New York Press,
State University Plaza, Albany, NY 12246

Production by Bernadine Dawes
Marketing by Lynne Lekakis

Library of Congress Cataloging-in-Publication Data
Beirne, Piers.
    Inventing criminology : essays on the rise of 'homo criminalis' /
Piers Beirne.
        p.   cm. — (SUNY series in deviance and social control)
    Includes bibliographical references and index.
    ISBN 0-7914-1275-X (acid-free paper) : $57.50. — ISBN
0-7914-1276-8 (pbk. : (acid-free paper) : $18.50
        1. Criminology—History.   I. Title.   II. Series.
HV6021.B38   1993
364—dc20   91-46327
                                                                              CIP

10 9 8 7 6 5 4 3 2

To the memory of my father,

Robert Edward S'Bire Beirne

Contents

Illustrations

Figures

Tables

Acknowledgments

Completion of *Inventing Criminology* has incurred more debts than I can ever possibly repay. For their encouragement and for their advice on different aspects of the manuscript I am deeply grateful to many friends and colleagues, who somewhat invidiously and in no particular order include Casey Groves, Jim Messerschmidt, Susan Corrente, Colin Sumner, Alan Hunt, David Garland, Sawyer Sylvester, Rosy Miller, Tom Bernard, Donald Black, Philip Jenkins, Gracme Newman, Lloyd Ohlin, Dario Melossi, Nicole Hahn Rafter, Andrew Scull, Ian Taylor, Jock Young, Emily Broadhead, and Kim Ackley.

A debt of a different sort arises from the fact that, although Maine is undoubtedly blessed with an abundance of natural resources, a well-stocked library for historical research is not yet among them. For responding with unfailing good humor to my unusual dependence on interlibrary loan services, therefore, I am most obliged to Casandra Fitzherbert and James Brady of the Luther Bonney library at the University of Southern Maine. In my travels to other libraries and archives I was warmly welcomed by staff at the following institutions: the Académie Royale de Belgique; the Bibliothèque Royale Albert Premier; the Hawthorne-Longfellow Library of Bowdoin College; the British Library; the British Library of Political and Economic Science; the Cambridge University Library; the Galton Laboratory, University College London; the Library of Congress; the Radzinowicz Library of Criminology at Cambridge University; the Royal Statistical Society; University College London (archives); and the Widener Library at Harvard College. I wish especially to acknowledge the expertise of Stephen Gregory of the Radzinowicz Library of

Criminology at Cambridge University; June Rathbone of the Galton
Laboratory; A. R. Darvall at Cambridge University Library; Liliane
Wellens-de-Donder of the Centre for the History of the Sciences at the
Royal Library of Belgium; and Francesca Emous at the Slade School of
Fine Art.

Several institutions have kindly supplied me with the necessities of
time and financial support during the lengthy process of researching
this book and preparing it for publication. The University of Southern
Maine's College of Arts and Sciences provided me with two summer
stipends, some monies for travel, and release time from teaching, for
all of which I am immensely grateful. The Institute of Criminology at
Cambridge University welcomed me as a Visiting Scholar in the sum-
mers of 1985 and 1989, and I profited greatly there from the good offices of Tony Bottoms and from my long-standing camraderie with
Colin Sumner. The National Endowment for the Humanities generously awarded me a Fellowship for College Teachers and Independent
Scholars that allowed me the luxury of devoting six months in 1989 to
this project.

Thanks too to Pierre DuSautoy in Brussels, to Maurice Herson in
several places, and especially to my brother Nicholas Light and to Jac-
queline Sinclair, who put me up and put up with me on many occasions in London.

Finally, I wish to acknowledge permission to use more or less
substantially revised versions of the following: Beirne, "Inventing
Criminology: the 'Science of Man' in Cesare Beccaria's *Dei delitti e
delle pene* (1764)," *Criminology* 29: 777–820, 1991 (chap. 2); Beirne,
"Adolphe Quetelet and the Origins of Positivist Criminology," *American Journal of Sociology* 92: 1140–69, 1987 (chap. 3); Beirne, "Between
Classicism and Positivism: Crime and Penality in the Writings of Gabriel Tarde," *Criminology* 25: 785–819, 1987 (chap. 5); Beirne, "Heredity versus Environment: A Reconsideration of Charles Goring's
The English Convict (1913)," *British Journal of Criminology* 28: 315–39,
1987 (chap. 6).

Chapter 1

Introduction

To Hegel's remark that all the great events and characters of world history occur twice, so to speak, Marx added in *The Eighteenth Brumaire of Louis Bonaparte* that they occur the first time as tragedy and the second as farce. For those who have trudged through Marx's protracted engagement with Hegelianism in the 1840s, his famous reply to Hegel is not lacking in irony. The tradition of the dead generations always weighs like a nightmare upon the minds of the living! Such a burden is also implicit in the pages of the present book.

The specific contents of *Inventing Criminology* derive from a footnote to an essay that I had intended to write, about ten years or so ago, on the place of the concept of the "average man" in the intellectual history of sociology. That essay has not yet been completed, its aim having been abruptly deflected by my confrontation with an intriguing passage in Emile Durkheim's book of 1897, *Suicide*. In that book Durkheim claimed:

> When Quételet drew to the attention of philosophers the remarkable regularity with which certain social phenomena repeat themselves during identical periods of time, he thought he could account for it by his theory of the average man—a theory, moreover, which has remained the only systematic explanation of this remarkable fact.[1]

What intrigued me about this passage was not so much Durkheim's suggestion—powerful though it might be—that for the origins of certain aspects of their discipline sociologists should look to the theory of social regularities put forward by the Belgian astronomer Adolphe Quetelet in his books *Sur l'homme et le développement de ses*

facultés and *Du système social et des lois qui le régissent* of 1835 and 1848,
respectively. Nor did my attention linger over the discriminatory affront posed by the absence of now-obligatory quotation marks around
the "average man"—I thought at that time, as I still do, that the meaning of such things must initially be excavated in their own cultural
context. Actually, what commanded my interest was the seemingly innocuous fact that in the passage above either his publisher or else
Durkheim himself had chosen to impose an acute French accent on the
first *e* in Quetelet's name, a practice that Quetelet himself never
seemed to favor. In this respect, Durkheim's suggestion about the origins of sociology yields an interesting tale about the cultural dominance of the French bourgeoisie in Belgian intellectual life. I discovered
that on the frontispieces of those of his books that were published in
Brussels the author's name was printed as "Quetelet," but almost always as "Quételet" if they had been published in Paris. To wit, by his
French publishers and later by Durkheim himself it was intended that
Quetelet should be brought down to earth and resurrected with the
more ponderous French nomenclature "Quételet." How and why this
brutal act of cultural imperialism should have been perpetrated on
Quetelet and on his good name at once became a matter of considerable concern to me.

   One thing quickly led to another. A gnawing curiosity about the
different spellings of Quetelet's name prodded me into reading his
book *Sur l'homme*. Here I marveled at Quetelet's extended, presociological commentary on the apparent constancy of crime rates in France
in the late 1820s. Soon I learned that his pronouncements on French
crime rates derived from official data lodged from 1827 onward in the
first set of national crime statistics, the *Compte général de l'administration
de la justice criminelle en France*. The invention in France of the *Compte
général*, I discovered, was facilitated by a variety of social and intellectual forces. The former included, above all, a vast expansion of the
state's surveillance of the population, the rise of a network of carceral
institutions, and middle-class fear of the "dangerous classes"; the latter
embraced the movements in statistics, public health, astronomy, and
cartography. The respective concerns of these forces coincided in the
1820s in the issue of the regulation of the dangerous classes. Specifi-

cally, they coincided in the realm of prison reform which, revitalized, then fed directly into the structure and argumentation of Quetelet's positivist "social mechanics" of crime.

Before I was aware of it, I had gathered enough material for a lengthy essay, not as I had intended on the concept of the "average man," but on Quetelet's contribution to the rise of positivist criminology. Questions raised by this essay, in turn, propelled me to inquire into other concepts and authors who competed for space on nineteenth- and early twentieth-century bookshelves, especially in France, Belgium, Britain, and Italy. Then traveling backward, breathless and almost without pause, I arrived at the point where most intellectual histories of modern criminology begin, namely, Cesare Beccaria's short treatise *Dei delitti e delle pene* ("Of Crimes and Punishments") of 1764.

Inventing Criminology is a preliminary attempt to uncover and to understand certain key aspects of the process of concept formation in the early history of criminology. Its focus is the transformation in explanations of crime that occurred from the emergence of classicism among the Italian *illuministi* to the triumph of positivism in British criminology or, to identify the period somewhat differently, from the appearance in 1764 of Beccaria's *Of Crimes and Punishments* to the publication in 1913 of Charles Goring's celebrated *The English Convict*. As I try to detail, this formative period was increasingly dominated by positivist explanations of crime. I should now admit, therefore, my unwillingness to debate the putative existence of some genuine, correct description of "positivist" relative to the study of crime. This term is nowadays so frequently abused that it tends to be best understood as an epithet, a weapon directed against those with whom one has political or epistemological disagreement. Positivism has several forms, each of which, according to its context and object, can be more or less appropriate as a method of inquiry. By positivist criminology I refer loosely to a discourse about crime that is predicated on the belief that there is a fundamental harmony between the respective methods of the natural and the social sciences, a discourse, moreover, that views its observational categories as independent of theory. Such a description of positivism has its limitations, of course, but it has the singular merit of being the one to which, if not from Beccaria then at least from Quete-let onward, the key authors and texts examined here actually subscribed.

From my brief description of the evolution of the contents of this book the astute reader will already know that, in at least one important respect, the research for it did not proceed according to the conventional canons of historicism. That plan was rudely interrupted by my own sheer ignorance about the history of concept formation in criminology. Allow me to elaborate. For a considerable period of time I have assumed, as have all other scholars to my knowledge, the validity of the hallowed distinction drawn between positivist criminology and the dominant discourse about crime that preceded it, namely, "classical criminology." In unfolding the contents of this distinction, I believed that positivist criminology was originally a multifaceted, nineteenth-century discourse based on economism, biologism, mental hereditarianism, and so on and that its chief objects ("criminal man," "criminality" and "criminal character") were demarcated by pre-given epistemological boundaries dividing the "normal" from the "pathological." Classical criminology, in contrast, has been universally assumed to be a mid- to late eighteenth-century discourse couched in the rhetoric of classical jurisprudence; its chief object, as demonstrated in the works of Beccaria, Bentham, Romilly, and others has been held to be the construction of a rational and efficient penal calculus directed to the actions of the volitional legal subject. Some scholars nowadays suggest, moreover, that because concepts such as "crime," "criminal," and "criminality" were absent from their epistemological universe, classical criminologists such as Beccaria and his followers were not representative of a criminology of *Homo criminalis* as such. As Foucault declared, while referring in *Discipline and Punish* to the era of classical criminology not only in France but also apparently everywhere else, "One will have to wait a long time before *homo criminalis* becomes a definite object in the field of knowledge."[2] Following Foucault, it has been variously suggested that because their concepts were directed to *"Homo penalis,"* the labors of Beccaria and his school should be categorized as either "classical penology" or "administrative penology" or even "a theory of social control."[3]

In Chapter 2 I take issue with such rigid distinctions between classical and positivist criminology, and I do so in part by rejecting the assumption that classical texts should automatically be relegated to criminology's prehistory. My argument engages this issue by reconsidering the merits of the key text in the development of classical criminology, namely, Beccaria's short treatise *Dei delitti e delle pene* of 1764. I focus on this text—rather than, say, on one by Jeremy Bentham—because descriptions of classical criminology invariably concentrate on the life and labors of its anonymous author, Cesare Bonesana, Marchese di Beccaria (1738–94), and because, as I argue here, the discursive objects of Beccaria's famous treatise have by friend and foe alike been persistently misrepresented. However, I do not thereby dispute the momentous practical effects exerted in Europe and colonial America by Beccaria's book, the extent of which is indicated by Durkheim's confident assessment "it is incontestably the case that it was . . . *Of Crimes and Punishments* which delivered the mortal blow to the old and hateful routines of the criminal law."[4] Nor will I suggest that *Dei delitti e delle pene* is to the history of criminology what the Piltdown Man hoax is to the history of physical anthropology.

My thesis about *Dei delitti* unfolds in four stages. First, I claim that in the last two hundred years the predominant images of *Dei delitti* have been constructed more in terms of its practico-juridical effects than in terms of its actual discursive features. Instead, I argue, second, that the persistent misrepresentation of Beccaria's arguments in *Dei delitti* is actively encouraged by the ambiguity of many of the author's own positions and by the obscure and secretive style of much of his prose—common enough textual practices in the dangerous publishing conditions that existed during much of the Enlightenment. Only with considerable difficulty, therefore, can the nature and intended objects of Beccaria's discourse be discerned. Third, I try to show that Beccaria's chief object in *Dei delitti* was the application to crime and penal strategies of the "science of man," a deterministic discourse implicitly at odds with conventional assumption about the exclusively humanist and volitional bases of "classical criminology." In making this claim, finally, I fundamentally challenge the existing interpretations of the context and object of Beccaria's book. It is a corollary of my argument that those modern-day criminologists who adhere to models of human agency based on "free will" and "rational choice" must look to some discourse other than Beccaria's to discover their intellectual ancestry.

Chapters 3 and 4 both demonstrate that the key concepts of positivist criminology developed in France and Belgium from some of the focal concerns of the domains of penality and of the statistical movement. During the Restoration (1814–30) these concerns coincided in the issue of the regulation of the "dangerous classes." This coincidence prompted the emergence of "social mechanics" and of "moral statistics," and it informed much of their conceptual content and explanatory structure. It appeared most forcefully in the positivist discourse of the pioneering thinkers Adolphe Quetelet (1796–1874) and A. M. Guerry (1802–1866). The object of that discourse was the construction of generalizations about the nature of criminal behavior and of criminals. Eventually, in some influential quarters, that object was transformed into a search for *Homo criminalis*, an abnormal being whose characteristics derived from a multiplicity of domains.

My intention in Chapter 3 is chiefly to identify Quetelet's own particular contribution to the rise of positivist criminology. I begin this by means of an outline of the historical context of the genesis of Quetelet's oeuvre, namely, the conjunction of the apparent failure of French penal strategies and the expansion in the scope of the statistical movement to include empirical social research. I then uncover Quetelet's method of inquiry and the structure and content of his criminology. Quetelet, an astronomer, believed that the discourse of celestial mechanics could be used to detect empirical regularities both in criminal behavior and in the personal characteristics of those who committed crimes. The nature of these regularities Quetelet investigated with a panoply of new concepts, including the constancy of crime, criminal propensities, the causes of crime, and the "average man." Implicit in Quetelet's writings is the existence of a full-fledged *Homo criminalis*, a being among whose attributes is a variety of abnormal characteristics that derive from the domains of the social, the body and the mind.

Chapter 4 identifies the influence of the movement in social cartography on concept formation in criminology, especially as this was manifest in the labors of the French moral statistician A. M. Guerry. As the necessary background to Guerry's book *Essai sur la statistique morale de la France* of 1833, the chapter outlines the conceptual and technical innovations of French cartography from the late seventeenth century to the Napoleonic era. Epistemologically akin to Quetelet's positivist "social mechanics of crime," Guerry's "social cartography of crime" was erected on the erstwhile facticity of *cartes thématiques* ("thematic maps"). Guerry believed that these condensed statistical images could serve as aids in the factual presentation of given classes of empirical social phenomena. His analysis of crime, such as it was, involved descriptive commentary based on the use of shaded maps that portrayed crime rates. With the aid of several thematic maps, Guerry developed significant positions on the methodology of official crime data, on economic development and crime rates, and on levels of education and crime rates, the last of which provoked great controversy among British social statisticians during the 1830s and 1840s.

Chapter 5 is a foray into a neglected but nevertheless important area in the intellectual history of criminology. Its primary focus is the writings of Gabriel Tarde (1843–1904), an elusive figure who was tremendously influential in his own time yet whose criminology was quickly lost in the even wider acclaim then accorded his contributions to political philosophy and social psychology. Several consistent lines of inquiry in Tarde's considerable discourse on crime are explained in this chapter. These include his virulent opposition to biological positivism, his attempt to transcend the crude scientism of the Franco-Belgian moral statisticians, and his debate with Durkheim about the putative normality of crime. I suggest that Tarde's engagement in these debates contributed to a protracted, neoclassical compromise in criminology whereby, to a certain extent, the volitional subject of classical jurisprudence was rescued from the dominance of the positivist revolution.

More so in Tarde's case than in that of any other major figure in the early history of criminology, the identification of his criminology has been notoriously susceptible to the tendency to reconstitute past intellectual history according to the dominant concerns and perspectives of the present. This "presentist" tendency has been encouraged, I suggest, both by the inconclusiveness of his debates with Durkheim and, even more so, by Tarde's unwillingness to align his discourse either with the voluntarism or with the determinism that dominated the field of criminology in the late nineteenth century.

In the history of positivist criminology few texts have commanded such gargantuan esteem as *The English Convict,* a lengthy methodological landmark of 1913 written by the English prison doctor Charles Goring (1870–1919), and whose several concerns are examined in Chapter 6. In this chapter I identify the ways in which Goring's methodology and findings were decisively swayed by the British movements in mathematical and evolutionary zoology, in statistics, and in eugenics. In so doing I attempt to reconsider the merits of *The English Convict*'s critical engagement with the Lombrosian notion of the "born criminal." I claim that the effects of *The English Convict* on the subsequent development of the criminological field—especially in Britain and the United States—should not be considered a progressive advance on Lombrosianism. In refuting certain aspects of the notion of the born criminal, while lending support to others, *The English Convict* advanced an ambiguous argument about *Homo criminalis* not in opposition to Lombrosianism but in parallel to it.

In collecting and presenting the material in *Inventing Criminology,* I have tried to steer an appropriate path between the disembodied abstractions of structuralism and the hagiographies of the founding fathers. To put this caveat another way, each chapter opposes two sorts of conventional claims about the understanding of concept formation in criminology, one externalist the other internalist. Against externalist claims, on the one hand, I suggest that the origins of the conceptual content and explanatory structure of criminology cannot adequately be understood either as mere representations of the power relations peculiar to modernity or as unmediated expressions of the epistemological divisions wrought by state practices in the asylum, the clinic, and the prison. The whys, hows, and whens of the invention of concepts and ideas, in other words, can never be understood properly if one approaches them as being parasitic on external events. Against internalist claims, on the other hand, I suggest that the key concepts and discursive techniques of criminology were not invented and did not develop as logical or even inevitable products of scientific development. Nowhere, therefore, do I assume that any of the explanatory claims of criminology—of positivist or any other sort of criminology—necessarily has any objective truth.

Although the present book tries to mine some unexcavated territory in intellectual history, I do not claim that the chapters of *Inventing Criminology* comprise even additively the basis of a coherent account of concept formation in criminology. My intentions here are far more limited than that, my methods too undisciplined, and my interests too eclectic. Moreover, I believe that there is no transcultural, quasi-scientific stock of knowledge about crime and penality whose truth can somehow be identified, agreed upon, and filed away as authoritative. There is an almost endless number of still-to-be-written histories of concept formation in criminology: concepts that were invented in this culture, by thinkers in those strata, in that period of time, for these reasons, and with those effects. What follows here are modest slices carved from those would-be histories.

Notes

1. Durkheim, *Suicide: a Study in Sociology* (1897), p. 300.

2. Foucault (1979), *Discipline and Punish: the Birth of the Prison*, p. 102.

3. For example, David Garland argues that it is altogether misleading to designate the work of writers such as Beccaria, Voltaire, Bentham, and Blackstone as criminology: "Their work is essentially the application of legal jurisprudence to the realm of crime and punishment, and it bears no relation to the 'human sciences' of the nineteenth century that were to form the basis of the criminological enterprise" (1985a, *Punishment and Welfare: a History of Penal Strategies*, pp. 14–15). Similarly, see Taylor, Walton, and Young (1973), *The New Criminology*, pp. 2–3; Foucault (1979), p. 102; Foucault (1988), "The Dangerous Individual"; Pasquino (1980), "Criminology: The Birth of a Special Savoir," pp. 20–21.

4. Durkheim (1901), "Two Laws of Penal Evolution," p. 113. See also *inter alia*, Phillipson (1923), *Three Criminal Law Reformers: Beccaria/Bentham/Romilly*, pp. 89–106; Maestro (1942), *Voltaire and Beccaria as Reformers of Criminal Law*, pp. 124–51; Paolucci (1963), translator's introduction to Beccaria's *On Crimes and Punishments;* Venturi (1971), *Utopia and Reform in the Enlightenment*, pp. 100–116; Young (1984), " 'Let Us Content Ourselves with

Praising the Work While Drawing a Veil Over Its Principles': Eighteenth-
Century Reactions to Beccaria's *On Crimes and Punishments"*; and Young
(1986), "Property and Punishment in the Eighteenth Century: Beccaria and
His Critics."

Chapter 2

Toward a Science of *Homo Criminalis*:
Cesare Beccaria's *Dei Delitti e Delle Pene* (1764)

❖ ❖

On 13 October 1761, Marc-Antoine Calas, the eldest son of the pros-
perous Huguenot cloth merchant Jean Calas, was found dead in his
father's shop at 16 Grand Rue des Filatiers in the Catholic city of Toulouse. The rope marks on Marc-Antoine's neck clearly indicated that
he had died by strangulation. The only suspects in the case were those
members of the household present at the time of Marc-Antoine's
death. They included his father Jean Calas, his English mother Anne-
Rose, a younger brother Pierre, a servant woman Jeanne Viguier, and
François Lavaisse, a guest who happened to be the son of a prominent
Protestant lawyer. Each of these five was arrested, imprisoned, and
charged with the murder of Marc-Antoine. At first the Calas family
claimed that Marc-Antoine had been murdered, ostensibly because
they wished to avoid the public humiliation that would befall the kin of
a successful suicide, whose dead body would be dragged naked
through the streets and then hanged by the neck. Soon, however, the
family admitted that Marc-Antoine had killed himself, as he had often
threatened to do.

The judges of the Toulouse Parliament nevertheless convicted Jean
Calas of the murder of his son, an act allegedly motivated by his anguish at Marc-Antoine's conversion to Catholicism. Having been sub-
jected to the gruesome tortures of interrogation, during which he
steadfastly protested his innocence, Jean Calas was executed on 18
March 1762. The sentence of execution required that Calas

> in a chemise, with head and feet bare, will be taken in a cart,
> from the palace prison to the Cathedral. There, kneeling in
> front of the main door, holding in his hands a torch of yellow

wax weighing two pounds, he must make the *amende honor-able,* asking pardon of God, of the King, and of justice. Then the executioner should take him in the cart to the Place Saint Georges, where upon a scaffold his arms, legs, thighs, and loins will be broken and crushed. Finally, the prisoner should be placed upon a wheel, with his face turned to the sky, alive and in pain, and repent for his said crimes and misdeeds, all the while imploring God for his life, thereby to serve as an example and to instil terror in the wicked.[1]

On 29 March 1762 Voltaire wrote to his good friend the philosopher Jean d'Alembert bemoaning the way in which the "fanatical" city of Toulouse had glorified Marc-Antoine as a martyr, and a Catholic one at that: "For the love of God, render as horrible as you can the fanaticism which would have it that a son has been hanged by his father, or which has caused an innocent man to be placed on the wheel by eight of the king's counsellors."[2] Voltaire claimed that Jean Calas had been the victim of religious persecution. To instantiate this claim he pointed out that no witnesses were called or orally examined at his trial; no advocate was provided for the accused; the evidence of guilt was entirely circumstantial; the proceedings, though lawful, were gruesome; he was convicted only by a majority of eight judges, with five dissenting. Voltaire then orchestrated a campaign for the reversal of Calas's conviction. On 12 July he urged d'Alembert to complain loudly about the horrible events in Toulouse: *"écrasez l'infâme!"*[3] In 1763, in between the execution of Jean Calas and his rehabilitation, in his short book *Traité sur la tolérance à l'occasion de la mort de Jean Calas,* Voltaire professed his strong belief in the innocence of Jean Calas. He argued, for example, that it was impossible for Jean Calas, an old man of sixty-eight years whose legs had long since been weak and swollen, to have strangled and hanged his young and very powerful son of twenty-eight years. Moreover, Voltaire condemned as dangerous and unjust the ease with which the Toulouse judges had treated him. He urged that, Calas having been condemned by eight votes to five,

> when it is a question of parricide and subjecting the father of a
> family to the most horrible punishment, the verdict should be

unanimous, because the evidence of such an extraordinary crime should be so obvious as to be clearly perceptible by everyone. In such a case the least doubt should suffice to unnerve the judge responsible for signing the death sentence. The fallibility in our judgement and the deficiencies in our laws are felt every day. How wretched it is when a majority of a single voice causes a citizen to be placed on the wheel?[4]

In the summer of 1764, two years after the execution of Jean Calas, the first copies of a treatise entitled *Dei delitti e delle pene* ("Of Crimes and Punishments"—henceforth, *Dei delitti*—appeared in Italy. This notoriously misunderstood little book is the focus of this chapter.

Images of *Dei Delitti e Delle Pene*

The first copies of *Dei delitti* were printed in Livorno and circulated anonymously in the summer of 1764.[5] Beccaria's short treatise of 104 pages was an instant and dazzling success. The first Italian edition was quickly followed by two others and then in 1765, through the intercession of the philosophes d'Alembert, Malesherbes, Voltaire, and the Abbé Morellet, a widely read French translation (*Traité des délits et des peines*). By 1800 there had been no less than twenty-three Italian editions, fourteen French editions, and eleven English editions (three printed in the United States).[6] Clearly, Beccaria's proposals for the reform of criminal law appealed to a large cross section of educated society. His disciples included benevolent and not-so-benevolent despots, such as Gustavus III of Sweden, Catherine II of Russia, and Empress Maria Theresa of Austria; lawyers and legal philosophers in England like William Blackstone[7] and Jeremy Bentham;[8] republican revolutionaries in colonial America such as Thomas Jefferson and John Adams;[9] and most importantly, the philosophes in France. Among the philosophes, Beccaria's ideas were highly esteemed by a great many luminaries, including d'Alembert, Diderot, Helvétius, Buffon, and Voltaire. Echoing this esteem was d'Alembert's opinion, written in a letter to the Italian mathematician Paolo Frisi, that in his book Beccaria had successfully combined "philosophy, truth, logic, and precision with sentiments of humanity" for which he would gain an "immortal reputation."[10] An even more visible accolade was bestowed on *Dei delitti* when in 1766, and in many subsequent editions thereafter, Voltaire's glowing *Commentaire sur le livre des délits et des peines* was appended to Beccaria's text.

Although *Dei delitti* was received with rapture by a large majority of the philosophes, some among them greeted it with cautious criticism. While they unanimously endorsed Beccaria's humanitarianism, some disagreed with either the direction or the extent of his specific proposals for reform of the criminal law. Against Beccaria's reticence about the legality of suicide, for example, Voltaire explicitly denied that it was a crime. Against Beccaria's complete opposition to torture, Diderot and others argued that it was justified for the discovery of a guilty party's accomplices; many others protested Beccaria's absolute opposition to capital punishment. Moreover, according to the dour Melchior Grimm,[11] Beccaria's proposals were "too geometrical," a vague and overused term which for Grimm implied a narrow emphasis on probabilism and mathematics. A similar accusation was leveled at Beccaria's work by the Scottish painter Allan Ramsay, a leading figure in the Scottish Enlightenment and Painter-in-Ordinary to King George III. In a letter to Diderot, Ramsay complained that "it is useless to treat penal questions abstractly, as if they were questions of geometry and arithmetic."[12]

Worse still, with many jurists in Italy and France, *Dei delitti* immediately became an object of derision and scorn. Beccaria's novel ideas about torture, capital punishment, and equality before the law were condemned as highly dangerous, for example, by Muyart de Vouglans, Daniel Jousse, and the French Attorney General Louis Séguier.[13] Powerful elements in Roman Catholicism also opposed Beccaria's proposals. For example, in early 1765 the Dominican friar Ferdinando Facchinei, a cantankerous mouthpiece of the Inquisitorial Council of Ten in Venice, published a tract that accused Beccaria of sedition, impiety, and a new heresy that he termed "socialism"; Facchinei derided Beccaria as "the Rousseau of the Italians." The next year

Beccaria's book was condemned for its extreme rationalism and placed on the papal Index Prohibitorum, where it remained for almost two hundred years.

Notwithstanding some retributivist objections to Beccaria's utilitarianism voiced at the end of the German Enlightenment,[15] the initial furor over *Dei delitti* gradually gave way to a stock of complacent assumptions about the intentions of its author. Chief among these assumptions has been the view that the key ideas in *Dei delitti* can be apprehended in terms of their practical effects. An unmediated and necessary association is held typically to exist between Beccaria's intentions, as they were formulated in his text, in other words, and their more or less successful appropriation for the practice of criminal law and criminal justice in the eighteenth century. Since then, most, if not all, sociologists and historians of penology[16] have read backward from the effects of the written word to Beccaria's intentions and have thereby assumed that *Dei delitti:* (1) was primarily a humanist project, inspired by the tradition of the French philosophes and motivated by the author's humanitarian opposition to the arbitrariness and barbaric cruelty of European criminal justice in the mid-eighteenth century, and (2) had as its chief objectives the reform of judicial irrationality (including judicial torture and capital punishment) and the institution of a utilitarian approach to punishment based on a calculus of pleasure and pain. In concert, these assumptions have retrospectively led to another, namely, that Beccaria was the founder of classical criminology,[17] marked as it is by a penal calculus based on the doctrine of the social contract and couched in the rhetoric of the free legal subject.

Recently, during the last decade or so, this Whiggish consensus has been challenged by various studies that have attempted to scrutinize the ideological content of *Dei delitti*. In particular, Foucault has argued that neither Beccaria's classical criminology nor its effects were the projects of genuinely enlightened or humanitarian reform.[18] Instead, he has claimed, they were but two among many artifacts peculiar to a new disciplinary power. Following Foucault, a number of other critical assessments of *Dei delitti* have been voiced. The radical pioneering role usually assigned Beccaria within classical criminology

has been contradicted, for example, and he has been viewed as allegedly far more conservative than other Enlightenment theorists because
he deliberately equivocated on dangerous issues such as materialism
and spiritualism.[19] Beccaria is held to have been a champion of aristocratic values that in his native Lombardy had been deeply penetrated
by the ideology and interests of capitalist agriculture and the new
bourgeoisie.[20] Beccaria's liberalism, it is claimed, responded to a fundamental difficulty of post-feudal societies: how to prevent the criminality of the masses while masking the fact that the criminal law
preserved a class system based on social inequality? Beccaria's solution
to this problem is portrayed as popularization of the legal doctrine
"equality before the law," a bourgeois fiction that, simply by doctrinal
fiat, lodges criminal responsibility at the level of the individual.[21] Even
Beccaria's intervention in judicial history has been dismissed as a fairy
tale, his humanism ridiculed because he did not know that the process
of abolishing judicial torture had already been initiated through a decisive transformation of the medieval law of proof.[22] His attempts to
reform the criminal law have therefore been described as fundamental
only to the myth of rational sentencing replacing arbitrary injustice.[23]

Many of these assessments of the discourse in *Dei delitti* assume
that Beccaria's arguments and ideological presuppositions can be understood more or less exclusively in terms of their manifest effects.
Beccaria's intervention in criminal jurisprudence, for example, continues to be regarded either as "humanist" because it opposed the barbaric practices of the *ancien régime* or as "revolutionary" because it was
in the vanguard of the Italian Enlightenment in exposing religious intolerance or as "conservative" because it did not travel as far down the
road of materialism as others undoubtedly did at that time.

However, *Dei delitti* shares with many Enlightenment treatises the
fact that the meaning of the author's arguments do not always strike
with immediate clarity. To a certain extent, I will suggest, the vivid
humanism in the forty-seven rambling chapters of *Dei delitti* is a mask
behind which some of Beccaria's other arguments lie hidden; these can
only be discerned with some difficulty and not a little speculation. Accordingly, neither the structure nor the content of Beccaria's discourse
should be taken at face value. To understand how and why this is so,

some indication must be given of the conditions of production of *Dei delitti* as a text of the Enlightenment.

Reading *Dei Delitti e Delle Pene* as a Text of Enlightenment

> When you have any thing to obtain of present dispatch, you entertain; and amuse the party, with whom you deal, with some other Discourse; that he be not too much awake, to make Objections.
>
> —Francis Bacon, *Sermones Fideles*

A key feature of the Italian Englightenment was how backward its own practitioners believed it to be compared with elsewhere in Europe. "This backwardness was ascribed," Woolf has recorded, "to the stifling effects of the 'official' counter-reformist culture in Italy, to a conformist mentality which led to acquiescence in the teachings of churchmen and lawyers, an acceptance of scholasticism, superstition and curialism."[24] In matters of religion, science, politics, and economics, the intellectual universe of the *illuministi* was one in which transgressions of the permitted bounds of discourse invited more or less severe censure either from the papacy or from the tiny political cliques that ruled each state.

During the first half of the eighteenth century, in the decade or two prior to the publication of *Dei delitti,* the degree of publicity and openness attending Enlightenment discussion of such matters as religious doctrine, scientific development, and the relationship between them was largely dictated by the ebb and flow of the political interests of the papacy. Concern about the political divisions of Italy, for example, naturally led to a fierce and threatening debate about the sovereign powers of Church and State, raising questions about authority over the clergy, the limitation of mortmain, customs duties, and restraint of trade. In the first decade of Benedict XIV's pontificate (1740–50), Rome opened itself up somewhat to the new culture of science, especially physics and chemistry, in the expectation that these sciences could be applied to the alleviation of chronic economic and social problems in the Papal States.

Then, during the 1750s, the religious and scientific communities engaged in a heated debate on the nature of faith, on the existence of
magic, and on the remedies for witchcraft. This debate was led by Mu-
ratori, the first Italian advocate of scientific history, and it encompassed
both the attack on miracles in the *Encyclopédie* by d'Alembert and Diderot and also the discussion between La Mettrie and Maupertuis on
the scientific calculation of pleasure and pain. Initially, these and other
scientific arguments were couched in the rhetoric of religious doctrine.
Rapidly, however, the antagonists in this debate discovered discursive
weapons even more potent than religion: first Cartesian rationalism,
then enlightenment, and finally "reason."[25]

In Beccaria's Milan, the state of Lombardy was subject to the political and economic dominance of the enlightened Austro-Hapsburg
ruler Maria Theresa. Under Austrian rule, various aspects of social life
in Lombardy were somewhat more liberal than elsewhere in Italy. For
example, Maria Theresa had loosened the influence of the Church
with the *Giunta economale* and the 1762 Pragmatic Sanction, which required royal consent before papal letters and bulls could be entered and
published.[26] In addition, her representative in Lombardy, Count
Firmian—to whom Beccaria would later be indebted for warding off
attempts to prosecute him for his book—had enacted a variety of liberal inroads into social and intellectual life, including toleration of debate and discussion by reform-minded *illuministi*. Beccaria himself was
a member of the Milanese *illuministi*. These were typically government
officials who sought to create a model bourgeois society that combined
spiritual and moral regeneration with and through the materialist advantages of economic growth. However, far from being simple "ther-
mometers of bourgeois opinion," these Milanese reformers envisioned
a well-ordered, hierarchical society whose reconstruction would ema-
nate from an enlightened state administration that, though working in
alliance with other powers such as the papal administration, could
dominate all other power blocs and would include all men of property
and education.[27] For the *illuministi* the problem, both intellectual and
organizational, was how this collective dream could be implemented.

This problem was the chief focus of the group of Milanese reformers with whom Beccaria mixed in the literary club Accademià dei

pugni ("Academy of Fisticuffs"), whose members included the Verri brothers Pietro and Allesandro, the economist Gian Rinaldo Carli, the ecclesiastical law expert Alfonso Longo, and the mathematicians Paolo Frisi and Luigi Lambertenghi. In 1762 the ideas of the Accademià began to be published in its critical literary journal *Il Caffè* which, Beccaria later confided,[28] imitated Joseph Addison's *Spectator* in England. Beccaria himself was undoubtedly motivated to join the Accademià, and then to compose *Dei delitti,* by his discomfort both with the absence of reforms in Lombardy in the domain of criminal law and the administration of justice and also with the continued burden of censorship of the written word.

Throughout the Enlightenment, in Italy especially but also elsewhere and with varying degrees of necessity, its practitioners employed ubiquitous trickery to defeat the censor and the police and, in Beccaria's Lombardy, to avoid the prying eyes of the Inquisitorial Council of Ten. Beccaria was painfully aware of the fates of Machiavelli, Galileo, and the historian Giannone.[29] Thus, Pietro Verri wrote in 1765 that for his friend Beccaria the major difficulty in preparing his book was how to publish "such delicate matters without having trouble."[30] Everyday ruses were devised simply to allow heretical, seditious, or egalitarian ideas to be transmitted to the reading public. As in the case of *Dei delitti,* these included anonymous authorship, frontispieces with phoney places of publication, secret printing presses, and an underground network for the distribution and sale of books and pamphlets. Numerous other ploys were designed to cover the truth with a thin veil that would protect a text from hostile eyes, including the publication of the diaries of imaginary travelers abroad, the translation of imaginary foreign books, and pervasive use of *double entendre* which would allow only the *cogniscenti* the pleasure of piercing its message.[31]

Few works of Italian illuminism were able to escape such textual deformities and both the style and the content of the arguments in *Dei delitti* suffered from them. As a result, a serious difficulty in understanding the arguments of *Dei delitti* is that, like many other Enlightenment texts, it employed an array of devious textual practices which relied on the cautious dictum that it is better to be a secret witness of Enlightenment than a posthumously acknowledged martyr. Thus, the

stated objects of Beccaria's protestations in *Dei delitti* were not the despotic monarchies of contemporary Italy but those of the "state of nature" and of classical Rome and Greece,[32] and his angry remarks on
religious intolerance are utterly devoid of clear temporal and empirical
referent. Moreover, in what was more than simply a casual failure to
document his sources, Beccaria's text is virtually bereft of intellectual
bearings which, had he openly pointed to them, would have allowed
his readers ("the few sages scattered across the face of the earth") the
privilege of observing more clearly the precise mast to which he chose
to nail his colors. Thus, Beccaria referred to no contemporary sources
other than the standard Enlightenment fare of Hobbes, and Montesquieu; even in these two cases, no specific reference is made to any particular work.

The absence of formal acknowledgment to other authors creates an
immediate hardship for anyone attempting to trace a genealogy of
Beccaria's ideas. The voluminous secondary literature on *Dei delitti* has
attempted to solve this thorny problem by declaring that it is not, in
fact, a problem at all. Was not Beccaria casually indulging in the free
trade of current ideas so prevalent among Enlightenment authors in his
day? Can one not read into Beccaria's text the popular views held, if
not by all, then by most members of the Enlightenment, and especially
by the French *philosophes*?

Enlightenment and Darkness

However, it is not easy to generalize about the eclectic ideas of that period from the middle of the seventeenth century to the last quarter of
the eighteenth century, which the philosophes joyously referred to as
l'éclaircissement and which the taciturn English ironically dubbed the
Age of Enlightenment. It can perhaps be said that all members of
the Enlightenment affirmed their belief in the principles of reason, in
the precision of the scientific method, and in the authority of nature,
but because there was enormous disagreement about each one of these
beliefs, this is to say very little of real substance. In response to religious intolerance, for example, Helvétius, d'Holbach and La Mettrie
professed atheism, Condillac Catholicism, and Diderot alternately em-

braced both, "according to the state of his nerves."[33] Some *philosophes* were ardent materialists, others subscribed to spiritualism. Some were Cartesians, others Newtonians. Some looked to the anthropological state of nature with a romantic nostalgia, others detected in it the sorry aftermath of mankind's fall from grace and the onset of original sin. Some, like Diderot, assented to a limited use of judicial torture. Some opposed capital punishment, but others, like Voltaire and Montesquieu, believed that on certain occasions it was an appropriate device. Moreover, there was not just one Enlightenment but several, and in France, Italy, Holland, Germany, Sweden, Russia, England, Scotland, colonial America, and elsewhere, there existed diverse and sometimes quite incompatible notions of the content and direction of enlightenment.

The objects in Beccaria's text naturally reflected this diversity of opinion, and it is unwise to assume that they had some unitary source. As Beccaria himself later suggested, it was in "the choice of expressions and the *rapprochement* of ideas" that the power of his text resided.[34] His attempted *rapprochement* occurred with respect to two chief ideas, each of which exerted different effects on his text and with varying degrees of impact. In concert, both confirmed the fact that the Italian Enlightenment, which set in relatively late, was significantly influenced by foreign authors. One was the humanism of the French *philosophes*; the other was the largely unacknowledged influence of the embryonic "science of man" in Scotland.

The Humanism of the French Philosophes

On more than one occasion Beccaria openly acknowledged his profound indebtedness to the humanist writings of the French *philosophes*. For example, in a letter to Abbé André Morellet, the translator of the first French edition of his book, Beccaria gushed, "I myself owe everything *to French books*," adding that "they developed in my soul feelings of humanity that have been stifled by eight years of a fanatical education."[35] Specifically, he referred to the influence of d'Alembert, Diderot, Helvétius, Buffon, and Hume [sic].[36] Among the *philosophes*, it was Montesquieu who exerted the greatest influence on Beccaria's thinking prior to the publication of *Dei delitti*. Thus, Beccaria declared, in his letter to Morellet, that he had first been converted to the study of philosophy by Montesquieu's *Lettres persanes* of 1721.[37] Moreover, it was on Montesquieu that the only significant textual acknowledgment was bestowed in *Dei delitti:* "Invisible truth has compelled me to follow the shining footsteps of this great man."[38]

Although these few observations are far from conclusive, the influence of the *philosophes* on *Dei delitti* can with reasonable confidence be discerned in the spacious antechamber to Beccaria's edifice, which is lavishly decorated with their humanist rhetoric. It is demonstrated in two ways. First, Beccaria inherited from Montesquieu—and through Montesquieu, ultimately from the secular law tradition of Grotius and Pufendorf—a desire to disentangle and then sever criminal law and justice from religion. In arguing for the supremacy of the rule of law in human affairs, Beccaria thus rejected any claim that the laws that regulate social relationships derive from divine will. For Beccaria, it was imperative that sin be demarcated from crime, spiritual powers from temporal powers, and ecclesiastical bodies from secular courts. The Supreme Being who casually enters the pages of *Dei delitti* is not therefore the omnipotent God the Father of Roman Catholicism but a depersonalized god who has been cast into the nether regions where all other spirits dwell. This god was merely another benevolent despot who could be contemplated "with respect untempered with fear or adoration,"[39] and whose jurisdiction, for Beccaria, encompassed sins ("offenses between men and God") rather than crimes ("offenses between men and men"). For Beccaria, then, crime is not a theological concept ("I do not address myself to sins . . . ") but a *social* one. Thus, "the true measure of crimes is . . . *the harm done to society.* This is one of the palpable truths which one needs neither quadrants nor telescopes to discover."[40]

A second way in which French humanism was manifest in Beccaria's text was in his rejection of the cruel physical pain inflicted by the judiciary on suspects and on convicted felons. At one point, for example, he drew a stark contrast between "the indolence of the judge and the anguish of someone accused of a crime—between the comforts and pleasures of the unfeeling magistrate . . . and the tears and squalid condition of a prisoner."[41] His strictures in this regard, however, were directed almost exclusively at the practices of judicial torture and capital punishment. Thus, "The torture of the accused while his trial is still in progress is a cruel practice sanctioned by the usage of most nations."[42] More dramatic still, in what was likely a macabre comment on the crowd-pleasing manner of disposing of witches and heretics, Beccaria declared that "rational men" object to the distasteful spectacle of "the muffled, confused groans of poor wretches issuing out of vortices of black smoke—the smoke of human limbs—amid the crackling of charred bones and the sizzling of still palpitating entrails."[43] Elsewhere, Beccaria confessed that he would deem himself fortunate if,

> in the course of upholding the rights of men and invincible truth, I should contribute to saving an unhappy victim of tyranny or of equally pernicious ignorance from suffering and from the anguish of death, then the blessings and tears of that one person overcome with joy would console me for the contempt of all humanity.[44]

Not without good reason, then, did Melchior Grimm observe about *Dei delitti* that "M. Beccaria writes in French with Italian words."[45] But although it was a major impetus to the erection of the aims in Beccaria's text, the humanism of the *philosophes* was not at all the sole feature of its discourse. Indeed, at times Beccaria's humanism seems only an incidental feature that was grafted on almost in ad hoc fashion to other, more significant arguments in *Dei delitti*. While, as we have seen, humanism asserted itself in elegant passages that disavow the physical brutality of criminal law and adopt a charitable position bent on ameliorating economic inequality, the depth of its textual penetration must not be exaggerated. This is unremarkable, though, if only because the *philosophes* themselves did not often address in their own writings the issues of penality raised in *Dei delitti*. Even in the case of those *philosophes* who did address issues of criminal law and punishment, such as Montesquieu and the Chevalier de Jaucourt in his *Encyclopédie* entry on "Crime" of 1751, the textual structure of these authors' works resembled unkempt mazes rather than the systematicity to which Beccaria's treatise aspired.

To uncover the principal discursive inspiration behind Beccaria's treatise we therefore need to look elsewhere. It is to be found, I suggest, in the ideas of Enlightenment authors in Britain, especially as they developed in Scotland.

The "Science of Man" in Scotland

I have suggested that, because the publishing conditions in Lombardy were so fraught with danger, Beccaria was forced to conceal some of the intellectual influences on *Dei delitti* and, moreover, some of the arguments within it. Nevertheless, with typical Enlightenment flourish, Beccaria attached to his text a deliberate clue of extraordinary significance for unlocking the aims of his work. Preceding the text, and prominently displayed on the frontispiece of each of the six editions of *Dei delitti* personally authorized by Beccaria, is an epigram from one of the first purveyors of Enlightenment ideas, Francis Bacon (1561–1626): "In rebus quibuscumque difficilioribus non expectandum, ut quis simul, et serat, et metat, sed praeparatione opus est, ut per gradus maturescant." This pious warning, originally delivered to educated Elizabethan souls in his *Sermones fideles, sive Interiora Rerum,* had been rendered in English by Bacon himself as: "In all Negociations of Difficulty, a Man may not look to sow and reap at once; But must Prepare Business, and so Ripen it by Degrees."[46]

It is interesting to speculate why Bacon's advice was so highly esteemed by Beccaria that he actually introduced his text with it. An obvious but perhaps superficial explanation is that Beccaria was declaring his intention to practice a virtue that was decidedly lacking in other *illuministi,* namely, patience. In other words, though fearing that his proposals in *Dei delitti* might arouse stiff opposition from Church and State, Beccaria nevertheless was secure in the knowledge that they would eventually see the light of day, ripen, and bear fruit, and was hereby stating as much. Still, an intriguing question remains. If Beccaria chose to introduce his text with a message for the faithful, then why did he do so with an epigram from Bacon rather than, say, from Montesquieu or Helvétius or Voltaire? Is it only that Beccaria had enormous admiration for Bacon?[47] One of Beccaria's unpublished manuscripts, indeed, reveals that with marginal lines and copious notes he devoured several of Bacon's treatises, including *Sermones Fideles, De Dignitate, De Augmentis Scientiarum,* and the *Novum Organum.*[48] Or is it more likely that Beccaria wished to invite his readers to draw a favorable parallel between what Bacon had attempted to do to English law in Elizabethan times and what he intended to do to Italian criminal law in his day? Indeed, to his eighteenth-century Enlightenment disciples, Bacon was admired not only because he was the founder of empiricism and a great philosopher and scientist. To would-be legal reformers, like Beccaria in Italy and William Blackstone in England, Bacon was also revered for his legal theorizing, for his statute consolidation, and for the attempt in his *Digests* to give the law "light."[49] These very purposes were among Beccaria's own, as well, with respect to Italian criminal law. Beccaria thus had good reason to pay homage to Chancellor Bacon and to England, "a nation whose literary glory, whose superiority in commerce and wealth (and hence in power), and whose examples of virtue and courage leave no doubt as to the excellence of its laws."[50]

The placement of Bacon's epigram must be mentioned not least because of Beccaria's use of it as an introduction to his text. As an introduction, it directs us to another dimension of Enlightenment thinking, the powerful presence of which in *Dei delitti* has largely been overlooked[51] but which was, I suggest, its central thrust and one which Beccaria had very good reason to hide from Catholic censors. This is the drift toward a "science of man" that had been inaugurated by enlightened English philosophers, such as Bacon himself, and by Newton and Shaftesbury and after them by Locke. Later, it was developed even more forcefully in the civic tradition of Scottish authors such as Hutcheson, Hume, John Millar, Adam Ferguson, and Adam Smith.[52] Indeed, in a letter of 6 April 1762, Pietro Verri described his young friend Beccaria as "a profound mathematician . . . with a mind apt to try new roads if laziness and discouragement do not suffocate him."[53] Given the virulent Anglomania which gripped the Italian devotees of the Enlightenment, it is only to be expected that Beccaria should have been compared with some English theorist, but the comparison was not with a legal reformer such as William Blackstone but with the great scientist Isaac Newton. The affectionate and admiring nickname given Beccaria by his friends was *Newtoncino,* "little Newton."[54]

Before I try to demonstrate the influence of certain British authors on Beccaria's arguments in *Dei delitti*, let me offer some anticipatory evidence of this connection from the period just prior to and contemporaneous with its publication in 1764. To begin with, it should be noted that there is nothing exceptional in the fact that Beccaria's discourse drew heavily on the ideas of Enlightenment authors in England and Scotland. Among the Italian *illuministi*, they, of all the authors, exercised enormous influence, the peak of which they enjoyed from the late 1750s to the early 1770s. In much of Italy there was widespread feeling that the economic and political progress of countries like England, France, and Holland was directly linked to the scientific rationalism embedded in the empiricist discourse of the Enlightenment triumvirate of Bacon, Newton, and Locke. Some of the key works in this tradition had been banned in Italy either by state authorities or by the papacy or by both; Locke's *Essay Concerning Human Understanding,* for example, was placed on the Index in 1734 by Pope Clement XII explicitly because its empiricism threatened religious belief. Nevertheless, they were widely available. Bacon and Newton, for example, could of course easily be found in Latin, and a French translation of Locke's *Essay Concerning Human Understanding* and Voltaire's *Eléments de la philosophie de Newton* appeared in 1700 and 1738, respectively. Indeed, the work of British authors dominated the conversations and the literary discourse of Beccaria's group Accademià dei pugni. Members of the Accademià regularly read and discussed works by Bacon, Shakespeare, Swift, Addison, Pope, Dryden, and Locke[55] as well as by the Scottish philosophers, among whom certainly were Hutcheson and Hume.[56]

The subtle complexity of *Dei delitti* cannot be comprehended in all its richness without recognizing the effects on his text of Beccaria's thoroughgoing admiration for enlightened British writings, especially those in the Scottish "civic tradition." Beginning with the writings of Andrew Fletcher in the late seventeenth century, the civic tradition was concerned above all, and to a degree that existed in no other country, with the multifaceted relationship between political institutions and economic progress.[57] This concern, heightened at the turn of the century by the possibility of enforced union with England, was directed to a variety of issues, many of which naturally excited the reformist yearnings of the Italian *illuministi* as well in the middle of the eighteenth century. Chief among these topics were religious toleration, the merits of property and industry, the rule of law, constitutional government, justice, and the conditions of social order. In fact, from 1750 to 1770 the Scottish civic tradition was pivotal in the rise of a presociological discourse about society, and within that discourse a central place was occupied by the attempt to construct a "science of man,"[58] a tendency on whose centrality in *Dei delitti* I will soon remark.

It is instructive now to refer to Beccaria's other early writings which, against *Dei delitti*'s bright reception, have generally been ignored. This is unfortunate because, although none of Beccaria's other writings exerted much influence, they do provide a somewhat broader view of his concerns at the time he wrote *Dei delitti*. Prior to the publication of *Dei delitti,* Beccaria published two short tracts, each of which yields some details as to the direction of his thought. In his first work, in 1762, he addressed the economic problems of the Milanese currency.[59] This essay drew its inspiration from Hume, from Sir William Petty[60] and especially, he admitted, from Locke.[61] Beccaria specifically referred in this work to the influence on his monetary analysis of "Locke's *Nuove considerazioni.*"[62] It is no small coincidence that in his *Essay Concerning Human Understanding*—available throughout Europe in Latin since the 1690s—Locke had argued, in the context of equating the growth of crime with the rise of money as a universal form of exchange, that those who committed crime did so because they were trying either to assuage an immediate pain or to satisfy an absent pleasure.[63] In a second essay of the same year, published in *Il Caffè,* Beccaria creatively used algebraic formulae to analyze the costs and benefits of the crime of smuggling; Beccaria's central question here was "given that a certain proportion of smuggled goods will be seized by the authorities, what is the total quantity that smugglers must move to be left with neither gain nor loss?"[64] Moreover, there is evidence in this work that he had read and been influenced by Jonathan Swift's satirical *Gulliver's Travels.*[65]

It has never been properly acknowledged that, like several other continental adherents of the Enlightenment,[66] Beccaria was inspired

by the ideas of the founder of the Scottish Enlightenment, the Glaswe-
gian philosopher Francis Hutcheson, and by Hutcheson's pupil Hume
(whose "profound metaphysics" Beccaria praised generously).[67] The
same mathematical heresies that led to the condemnation and avoidance
for two decades of Hutcheson's work in France at once endeared it to
various scholars in Italy. However, in the middle of the century the
philosophes revived interest in Hutcheson's mathematical approach to
utilitarianism: Lévesque de Pouilly, Maupertuis, and Duclos wrote of
happiness in Hutchesonian terms, Marc Antoine Eidous published a
French translation of Hutcheson's *Inquiry,* and Diderot described his
aesthetic ideas in the *Encyclopédie*.[68] Beccaria almost certainly had read
Hutcheson's *Inquiry into the Original of Our Ideas of Beauty and Virtue* of
1725, probably in a French translation of 1749.[69] One of Beccaria's *Il
Caffè* essays of 1765 shows the unmistakable influence of Hutcheson's
idea of the beauty of theorems.[70]

This influence of Hutcheson on Beccaria's *Dei delitti* far transcends
the communality of discursive practices often engaged in by Enlightenment writers. When Beccaria introduced *Dei delitti* with the enig-
matic sentence "Mankind owes a debt of gratitude to the philosopher
who, from the despised obscurity of his study, had the courage to cast
the first and long fruitless seeds of useful truths among the
multitude,"[71] he was undoubtedly referring to Hutcheson, who had
explicitly termed himself "an obscure Philosopher."[72] Nearly every
page of *Dei delitti* is marked, I suggest, by Hutcheson's towering influence on Beccaria's thinking. It is found in the common metaphors
of expression used in *Dei delitti* and in Hutcheson's (1755) *System of
Moral Philosophy*.[73] These metaphors are taken from such diverse fields
as theology, law, architecture, Newtonian mechanics, and geometry. It
is found in the extraordinary correspondence between key recommendations in Beccaria's *Dei delitti* and those in Hutcheson's *System*. Careful comparison reveals that whole sections of *Dei delitti* either restate
or develop the proposals for law and criminal justice in Hutcheson's
System. Among the most important of these are those that refer to
property as the basis of the social contract, the definition of crime, the
uniformity of laws, the simplicity of laws, the harm inflicted by cor-
rupt public servants and magistrates, the compensatory use of fines, the

deterrent nature of punishment, the proportionality of punishment to crime, and opposition to judicial torture.[74]

But my chief intention here is not to document in detail the remarkable identity in the respective penal recommendations of Hutcheson's *System* and those of Beccaria's *Dei delitti*. Rather, it is to show that, in the same way much of the specific content of Beccaria's famous treatise is taken from Hutcheson's (1755) *System* so, too, much of the structure of *Dei delitti*'s argumentation also reflects Hutcheson's *System*. As we will see, Beccaria's treatise must thus be placed in a trajectory radically different from the "classical" one conventionally accorded it. In the same way that Hutcheson's *System* contained a progeny of useful truths otherwise known to Beccaria as the new "science of man" so, too, did Beccaria aspire in *Dei delitti* to apply this new science to the field of crime and punishment.

The "Science of Man" in *Dei Delitti e Delle Pene*

Some of the arguments of *Dei delitti* employed a deterministic discourse which, if not for their author then in retrospect, seem decidedly at odds with the classical dependence on free will that is commonly attributed to *Dei delitti*. Among Enlightenment thinkers this discourse was denominated loosely and was signified by such terms as Pascal's *esprit géométrique*[75] and, after midcentury, the Scottish civic tradition's "science of man." Beccaria himself variously referred to it as "geometry," "moral geography," "political arithmetic," "number," and the "science of man." Woven within Beccaria's stylistic eloquence and his passionate humanism is a strong reliance on the discursive use of determinist principles derived from the "science of man."

Several key features of this new science are plainly recognizable in *Dei delitti*. Chief among these are the doctrines of utilitarianism, probabilism, associationism, and sensationalism. The doctrine of utilitarianism operated for Beccaria as a core justificatory argument for establishing "the right to punish," and it is positioned prominently at the very beginning of the text. With it Beccaria attempted to forge linkages, as had Hutcheson before him, among the rule of law, justice, and the economic marketplace. Probabilism, associationism, and sensationalism, Beccaria employed throughout *Dei delitti,* and he wielded these three doctirnes in concert as mechanisms with which to advance the various technical and administrative aspects of his chosen penal strategies (or "how to punish").

The Right to Punish

The point of entry into Beccaria's discourse about penal strategies is provided by his subscription to an economistic form of social contract theory based on utilitarianism and secured through the rule of law.[76]

Dei delitti begins with a utilitarian argument for "the greatest happiness" cast in the specific context of a plea for the supremacy of the rule of law. Whereas in the past, according to Beccaria, law has most commonly been the instrument of the passions of a few persons, "the impartial observer of human nature [would] grasp the actions of a multitude of men and consider them from this point of view: *the greatest happiness shared among the majority of people*" (*la massima felicità divisa nel maggior numero*).[77] The happiness of "a few illustrious persons" is therefore something Beccaria derided as tyranny. To whatever he intended as the content of the otherwise empty utilitarian objective *felicità,*[78] Beccaria attached the condition that, if every individual member is bound to society, then—as opposed to the original, warlike state of nature—society is likewise bound to every individual member by a contract that, owing to its very nature, places both parties under obligation.

> This obligation, which reaches from the throne to the hovel and which is equally binding on the greatest and the most wretched of men, means nothing other than that it is in everybody's interest that the contracts useful to the greatest number should be observed. Their violation, even by one person, opens the door to anarchy.[79]

Beccaria harnessed his declared utilitarianism to two mechanisms, which he tended to elevate to the status of ends. The first of these is the rule of law: "the true foundations of the happiness I mentioned here are security and freedom limited only by law."[80] For Beccaria law is the

condition by which "independent and isolated men, tired of living in a
constant state of war and of enjoying a freedom made useless by the
uncertainty of keeping it, unite in society."[81] As we will soon see in
some detail, Beccaria urged that criminal law, especially, should have
various features of formal and substantive rationality, including clarity,
logical inclusiveness, and predictability. Beccaria's plea for the rule of
law emerged largely *via negativa,* as a result of his disenchantment with
the theocentrism of Rome, with its ecclesiastical courts and its inquisitorial practices. Law and justice must develop apart from the activities
of religious policing:

> It is the task of theologians to establish the limits of justice and
> injustice regarding the intrinsic goodness or wickedness of an
> act; it is the task of the observer of public life to establish the
> relationships of political justice and injustice, that is, of what is
> useful or harmful to society.[82]

Moreover, Beccaria asserted that those who believe that the intention
of the criminal is the true measurement of crimes are in error because
the only true measurement of crimes is "the harm done to the nation"
or "to the public good."

> Given the necessity of men uniting together, and given the
> compacts which necessarily result from the very clash of pri-
> vate interests, one may discern a scale of misdeeds wherein the
> highest degree consists of acts that are directly destructive of
> society and the lowest of the least possible injustice against one
> of its members. Between these extremes lie all actions con-
> trary to the public good, which are called crimes.[83]

For the achievement of his declared utilitarian objective Beccaria
envisaged a second mechanism, namely, the economic marketplace.
For Beccaria, indeed, the free economic agent and the subject of law are
one and the same individual; the atomized individual who "thinks of
himself as the center of all the world's affairs" is an economic agent
simply reconstituted in juridical terms. Thus, Beccaria argued that
while "commerce and the ownership of goods" are not the goal of the

social contract, they can be a means of achieving it; *"common utility,"* in other words, as "the basis of human justice."[84] Beccaria was enthusiastic about the "quiet war of industry [that] has broken out among great nations, the most humane sort of war and the kind most worthy of reasonable men,"[85] and he praised "easy, simple, and great laws . . . that require only a nod from the legislator to spread wealth and vigor throughout the nation."[86] Indeed, the surest way of securing the compliance of individuals with the law of their country is to "improve the relative well-being of each of them. Just as every effort ought to be made to turn the balance of trade in our favor, so it is in the greatest interests of the sovereign and of the nation that the sum total of happiness . . . should be greater than elsewhere.[87]

Given this relationship, Beccaria's concept of crime as "what is harmful to society" is likewise intimately linked to the economic marketplace.[88] For Beccaria, the social contract entails that all citizens must surrender a portion of their liberty to the state, in return for which the state protects their right to security and tranquility. "There is no enlightened man who does not love the open, clear, and useful contracts of public security when he compares the slight portion of useful liberty that he has sacrificed to the total sum of all the liberty sacrificed by other men."[89] The sum of all these portions of liberty is thus a "deposit" which no citizen can ever "withdraw" from the "common store" or from the "public treasury,"[90] and herein lies the basis of the state's right to punish its subjects.

> The mere formation of this deposit, however, [is] not sufficient; it [has] to be defended against the private usurpations of each particular individual. . . . Tangible motives [are] required sufficient to dissuade the despotic spirit of each man from plunging the laws of society back into the original chaos.[91]

Crime is taken as an offense against both law and economic intercourse. Accordingly, when in *Dei delitti* Beccaria referred to particular crimes he only emphasized crimes against property, including theft, bankruptcy, counterfeiting, smuggling, and indolence. He especially condemned political indolence (which "contributes to society neither with work nor with wealth") and "timid prudence" (which "sees only the present moment").[92] At several points in his discussion of punishment, moreover, he invoked a symmetry between the aims and conditions of penal servitude and those of the marketplace. One aspect of this symmetry is described as "the faint and prolonged example of a man who, deprived of his liberty, has become a beast of burden, repaying the society he has offended with his labors."[93] At another point he urged that "the most fitting punishment [for theft] . . . is the only sort of slavery that can be deemed just: the temporary subjugation to society of the labor and the person of the criminal."[94]

How to Punish

It is not my concern here to outline each of Beccaria's chosen penal strategies but to show how his argumentation regarding them again demonstrates his adherence to various aspects of the new "science of man." Chief among these were the loosely defined doctrines of probabilism, sensationalism, and associationism.

1. Probabilism

Beccaria's attempt to apply "probability" and "number" to matters of punishment is explicable precisely in terms of his dependence on the ideas of wise governance held by British authors such as Locke[95] and Hutcheson[96] rather than by the French *philosophes*.

Near the beginning of *Dei delitti* Beccaria asserted his intention of "going back to general principles" to uncover the rampant political and judicial errors "accumulated" over several centuries. In a sense, his search for these principles reflected an abhorrence of uncertainty. He objected to "*arbitrary* notions of vice and virtue."[97] Sometimes, he complained, "despotic impatience" and "effeminate timidity" transform "serious trials into a kind of game in which chance and subterfuge are the main elements,"[98] and he derided "the errors and passions that have successively dominated various legislators."[99] Such errors included the useless tortures "multiplied" with prodigious and useless severity; the punishment of crimes that are "unproven"; and the horrors of a prison, "augumented" by "uncertainty" ("that most cruel tormentor of the wretched").[100] At the same time, Beccaria bemoaned the unhappy fact that, unlike "the symmetry and order that is the lot of brute, inanimate matter," "turbulent human activity" and "the infinitely complicated relationships and mutations of social arrangements" are impossible to reduce to a geometric order devoid of irregularity and confusion."[101]

> It is impossible to prevent all disorders in the universal strife of human passions. They increase at the compound rate of population growth and the intertwining of public interests, which cannot be directed toward the public welfare with geometric precision. In political arithmetic, one must substitute the calculation of probability for mathematical exactitude.[102]

Beccaria's advocacy of probability extended as well to each stage of the criminal justice system, including the clarity of the law itself; judicial torture; witnesses and evidence; jurors; and sentencing practices. In this regard, his remarks were addressed not only to the *illuministi* and *philosophes* but also, especially, to enlightened lawmakers, to "the legislator [who] acts like the good architect, whose role is to oppose the ruinous course of gravity and to bring to bear everything that contributes to the strength of his building."[103] A brief outline of these remarks is now in order.

Beccaria urged that only a fixed and predictable law could provide citizens with personal security and liberate them from judicial arbitrariness. Thus, "the greater the number of people who understand the sacred law code and who have it in their hands, the less frequent crimes will be, for there is no doubt that ignorance and uncertainty concerning punishments aid the eloquence of the passions."[104] The law itself must be unambiguous because only with "fixed" and "immutable" laws can citizens acquire personal "security": "this is just because it is the goal of society, and it is useful because it enables [citizens] to calculate precisely the ill consequences of a misdeed."[105] Moreover,

> when a fixed legal code that must be observed to the letter leaves the judge no other task than to examine a citizen's ac-

tions and to determine whether or not they conform to the written law, when the standard of justice and injustice that must guide the actions of the ignorant as well as the philosophic citizen is not a matter of philosophic controversy but of fact, then subjects are not exposed to the petty tyrannies of many men.[106]

In addition, for minor and less heinous crimes, there should be a statute of limitations that relieves a citizen of "uncertainty" regarding his fate, but such time limits "ought not to increase in exact proportion to the atrocity of the crime, for the likelihood of crimes is inversely proportional to their barbarity."[107]

Beccaria's subscription to the doctrine of probabilism throws more light on the question of how *Dei delitti* viewed judicial torture. We have seen that it was on humanist grounds that Beccaria opposed the practice of interrogating an accused with methods of torture.[108] However, if in this specific context humanism is simply taken to connote a condemnation of the infliction of physical pain on others, then we are left with some difficulty because Beccaria vigorously supported noncapital corporal punishment (*pene corporali*) "without exception" for crimes against persons and for crimes of theft accompanied by violence.[109] However, this apparent paradox can be resolved by stressing that, in addition to his humanism, Beccaria articulated his opposition to judicial torture in another, even more insistent way. This involved the claim that judicial torture is an inefficient method of establishing the "probability" or the "certainty" of the guilt or innocence of the accused. Accordingly, "the problems of whether torture and death are either just or useful deserve a mathematically precise solution."[110] Elsewhere, Beccaria added that it is "a remarkable contradiction in the laws that they authorize torture, yet what sort of interrogation could be more *suggestive* than pain?"[111]

> The outcome of torture, then, is a matter of temperament and calculation that varies with each man in proportion to his hardiness and his sensitivity, so that, by means of this method, a mathematician could solve the following problem better than

a judge could: given the strength of an innocent person's mus-
cles and the sensitivity of his fibers, find the degree of pain that
will make him confess himself guilty of a given crime.[112]

Instead of judicial torture Beccaria recommended "the real trial, the 'informative' one, that is, the impartial investigation of facts which reason demands."[113]

In respect of witnesses and evidence, Beccaria argued that, in order
to determine the guilt or innocence of a defendant, more than one witness is necessary because if one witness affirms the guilt and another
denies it, "there is no certainty."[114] A witness is credible if he is "a rational man" and his credibility increases if his reason is undisturbed by
a prior relationship with either the defendant or the victim; "the credibility of a witness, therefore, must diminish in proportion to the hatred
or friendship or close relationship between himself and the accused."[115]
The credibility of a witness also diminishes significantly as the gravity
of the alleged crime increases or as the circumstances of the crime become more "improbable."[116] The credibility of a witness is virtually
nil in cases that involve making words a crime: "[it is] far easier to
slander someone's words than to slander his actions, for, in the latter
case, the greater the number of circumstances adduced as evidence, the
greater are the means available to the accused to clear himself."[117]
However, and somewhat inconsistently, Beccaria also held that to the
degree that "punishments become moderate, that squalor and hunger
are banished from prisons, and that compassion and humanity pass
through the iron gates . . . the law may be content with weaker and
weaker evidence to imprison someone."[118]

For Beccaria there exists a "general theorem" that is most useful in
calculating with certainty the facts of a crime, namely, the "weight of
evidence." In unfolding the aspects of this theorem, he argued that (1)
when different pieces of actual evidence are substantiated only by each
other, the less certain is any one fact; (2) when all the proofs of a fact
depend upon one piece of evidence, the number of proofs neither aug-
ments nor diminishes the probability of the fact; and (3) when proofs
are independent of each other, then the probability of the fact increases
with each new witness.[119] Moreover, Beccaria considered it ironic that

the most atrocious and the most obscure crimes—i.e., "those that are most unlikely"—are the most difficult to prove. These crimes are typically proved by conjecture and by the weakest and most equivocal evidence; it is as though "the danger of condemning an innocent man were not all the greater as the probability of his innocence surpasses the liklihood of his guilt."[120] That is not to say there are not some crimes that are both frequent in society and difficult to prove—such as adultery and pederasty—and in these cases "the difficulty of establishing guilt takes the place of the probability of innocence."[121] Finally, because the respective probabilities of "atrocious" crimes and of lesser offenses differ greatly, they must be adjudicated differently: for atrocious crimes the period of judicial examination "should decrease in view of the greater likelihood of the innocence of the accused . . . but with minor crimes, given the lesser likelihood of the innocence of the accused, the period of judicial investigation should be extended, and as the pernicious consequences of impunity decline, the delay in granting immunity from further prosecution should be shortened."[122]

Finally, Beccaria offered some brief comments on jurors and on sentencing practices from the perspective of probabilism. About jurors he wrote, without further explanation, that when a crime has been committed against a third party "half the jurors should be the equals of the accused and half the peers of the victim."[123] About sentencing practices, he warned that "certainty" ought to be required for convictions in criminal cases, and that if geometry "were adaptable to the infinite and obscure arrangements of human activity, there ought to be a corresponding scale of punishments, descending from the most rigorous to the slightest."[124]

Many of the strategies in Beccaria's penal calculus, including his key concept of deterrence, are derived not from geometry or probabilism as such but from the doctrines of associationism and sensationalism. To these related doctrines in the "science of man" we now turn.

2. Associationism

Beccaria's penal calculus rested on the view that it is better to prevent crimes than to punish them. This can only occur if the law forces potential criminals to make an accurate "association" of ideas between crime and punishment. "It is well established," Beccaria claimed, along with Hume and Helvétius, "that the association of ideas is the cement that shapes the whole structure of the human intellect; without it, pleasure and pain would be isolated feelings with no consequences."[125] Following Hume, Beccaria urged that associated ideas must be in a position of constant conjunction and that they must comprise a relation of cause and effect. The nexus of the desired association between crime and punishment Beccaria characterized in many ways, such as "deterrence," "intimidation," and "dissuasion."[126] The key properties of the association between crime and punishment are condensed in the following formula, which is the concluding sentence of *Dei delitti,* now appropriately enshrined as the original statement of the principle of deterrence: "*in order that any punishment should not be an act of violence committed by one person or many against a private citizen, it is essential that it should be public, prompt, necessary, the minimum possible under the given circumstances, [and] proportionate to the crimes.*"[127]

Elsewhere in his text, yet still within the context of an associationist framework, Beccaria expanded on several items in this formula, most notably on the need for prompt, mild, and proportionate punishment. About the promptness of punishment, first, Beccaria believed that the shorter the time period between a crime and chastisement for the crime "the stronger and more permanent is the human mind's association of the two ideas of crime and punishment, so that imperceptibly the one will come to be considered as the cause and the other as the necessary and inevitable result."[128] Delay thus serves only to sever the association between these two ideas. Moreover, the temporal proximity of crime and punishment is of paramount importance if one desires to arouse in "crude and uneducated minds the idea of punishment in association with the seductive image of a certain advantageous crime."[129] About the mildness of punishment, second, Beccaria argued that to achieve its intended effect, the intensity of a punishment should exceed the benefit resulting from the crime, and that in its application punishment should be "inexorable," "inevitable," and "certain."[130] Cruel punishments, insofar as they destroy the association between law and justice, therefore undermine the aim of deterrence. Finally, about the required proportion between punishment and crime, Beccaria warned that "the obstacles that restrain men from committing crimes should be stronger according to the degree that such misdeeds are contrary to the public good and according to the motives that lead people to crimes."[131] This is so because, if two unequally harmful crimes are each awarded the same punishment, then would-be miscreants will tend to commit the more serious crime if it presents the greater advantage to them. If punishments are disproportionate to crime by being tyrannical (i.e., excessive), then popular dissatisfaction will be directed at the law itself—"punishments will punish the crimes that they themselves have caused."[132] Further, in arguing that "punishment . . . should conform as closely as possible to the nature of the crime,"[133] Beccaria implicitly attempted to link the argument about the proportionality of crime and punishment with the desired association among the ideas about the type of crime (e.g., theft), the form of punishment (penal servitude with forced labor) and the virtue of industriousness.[134]

It is worth briefly returning at this point to Beccaria's opposition to capital punishment. In the context of his use of the doctrine of associationism, it seems fair to suggest that Beccaria opposed capital punishment as a penal strategy not because he thought it cruel, which he did, but because it did not serve the new penal objective of deterrence.[135] Beccaria argued instead that a life sentence is a sufficiently intense substitute for the death penalty and includes all the necessary ingredients needed to deter the most hardened criminal. "Neither fanaticism nor vanity survives among fetters and chains, under the prod or the yoke, or in an iron cage . . . a lifetime at hard labor."[136] It is thus not the severity of punishment that, for Beccaria, has the greatest impact on a would-be criminal but, albeit in addition to its other characteristics, its duration.

> If someone were to say that life at hard labor is as painful as death and therefore equally cruel, I should reply that, taking all the unhappy moments of perpetual slavery together, it is perhaps even more painful, but these moments are spread out over a lifetime, and capital punishment exercises all its power in an instant. And this is the advantage of life at hard labor: it frightens the spectator more than the victim.[137]

3. Sensationalism

A third hallmark of the "science of man" engraved in *Dei delitti* is the doctrine of sensationalism. In Beccaria's discussion of the nature of honor, for example, the presence of this doctrine is indicated by a Newtonian metaphor:

> How miserable is the condition of the human mind! It has a better grasp of the most remote and least important ideas about the revolutions of the heavenly bodies than of the most immediate and important moral concepts, which are always fluctuating and confused as they are driven by the winds of passion and guided by the ignorance that receives and transmits them![138]

This "ostensible paradox" will disappear, Beccaria continued, only when one considers that

> just as objects too close to one's eyes are blurred, so the excessive proximity of moral ideas makes it easy to confuse the large number of simple ideas that go to form them. Wishing to measure the phenomena of human sensibility, the geometric spirit needs dividing lines. When these are clearly drawn, the impartial observer of human affairs will be less astonished, and he will suspect that there is perhaps no need for so great a moral apparatus or for so many bonds in order to make men happy and secure.[139]

These two passages betray the influence on *Dei delitti* of the doctrine of sensationalism which, in the course of his unheralded book of 1770 on aesthetics, Beccaria explicitly acknowledged having taken from works by Locke and Condillac.[140] Besides the humanism inherent in his noted and widely circulated (in French and German) condemnation of religious persecution and superstition in *Letters Concerning Toleration* of 1689, Locke's sensationalism tended to suggest that all things painful are by definition bad and all things pleasurable good. Interestingly, his original discussion of the doctrine of hedonism—the pleasure/pain principle as outlined in chapter 20 of his *Essay Concerning*

Human Understanding—occurred within the framework of sensational-ism; when Locke discussed the status of hedonism in human affairs, he did so in a radically materialistic way, arguing that "pleasure and pain, and that which causes them, Good and Evil, are the hinges on which our *Passions* turn."[141] Among the philosophes, Condillac (1715–1780) was the most ardent champion of the antimetaphysical, empirical tra-dition of Bacon, Newton, and Locke. In his preparatory *Essai sur l'origine des connaissances humaines* (1746), in his *Traité des systèmes* (1749), and then in his *Traité des sensations* (1754), Condillac developed Locke's doctrine of sensationalism, positing that, at birth, the human mind is a tabula rasa which operates through sensations. Like Locke, Condillac championed the rigidly materialistic conclusion that a per-son is simply what he or she has acquired through sensations.

> It is pleasures and pains compared, that is to say, our needs which exercise our faculties. As a result, it is to them that we owe the happiness that is ours to enjoy. We have as many needs as different kinds of enjoyment; as many degrees of need as degrees of enjoyment. And there you have the germ of ev-erything that we are, the source of our unhappiness or of our happiness. To observe the influence of this principle is thus the sole means to study ourselves.[142]

It is difficult to imagine a doctrine more seemingly hostile to the doctrine of free will than sensationalism. When Beccaria applied it to criminal justice, sensationalism effectively displaced the volitional sub-ject of Catholic theology and, thereby, denied any active role in human society for the Supreme Being. Beccaria was so fearful of the censor precisely because his text implicitly suggested that human agents are no more than the products of their sensory reactions to external stim-uli. His text, replete as it is with probabilism, associationism, and sen-sationalism—all directed to the new objective of deterrence—is resolutely opposed to any notion of free will. *Dei delitti* contains a con-cept of volition, it is true, but it is a determined will rather than a free will. Thus, "sentiment is always proportional to the result of the im-pressions made on the senses."[143] The penal recommendations of *Dei*

delitti are not at all predicated, therefore, on the notion of a rational calculating subject who, when faced with inexorable punishment, will
weigh the costs and benefits and choose to desist from crime. In this
discourse, punishments ("tangible motives") have "a direct impact on
the senses and appear continually to the mind to counterbalance the
strong impressions of individual passions opposed to the general
good."[144]

Sensationalism intersects concretely with Beccaria's chosen penal
strategies in three ways. It appears, first, as an additional ground on
which judicial torture must be rejected. Beccaria insisted that, in terms
of their respective results, the only difference between judicial torture
and other ordeals, such as fire and boiling water, is that the former appears to depend on the will of the accused while the latter depend on a
purely physical act. To this he responded that "speaking the truth amid
convulsions and torments is no more a free act than staving off the effects of fire and boiling water except by fraud. Every act of our will is
always proportional to the strength of the sense impressions from
which it springs."[145]

Sensationalist claims are also inserted by Beccaria into his arguments about the nature of deterrence. In the context of the discussion of
the appropriateness of prompt punishment, for example, he argued
that "that gravity-like force that impels us to seek our own well-being
can be restrained only to the degree that obstacles are established in opposition to it,"[146] and that "remote consequences make a very weak
impression."[147] Effecting a link with probabilism, he argued that "experience and reason have shown us that the probability and certainty of
human traditions decline the farther removed they are from their
source";[148] effecting yet another link, this time with associationist
claims, he reflected that

> the magnitude of punishment ought to be relative to the con-
> dition of the nation itself. Stronger and more obvious impres-
> sions are required for the hardened spirits of a people who
> have scarcely emerged from a savage state. A thunderbolt is
> needed to fell a ferocious lion who is merely angered by a gun
> shot. But to the extent that human spirits are made gentle by the

social state, sensibility increases; as it increases, the severity of punishment must diminish if one wishes to maintain a constant relation between object and feeling.[149]

Finally, Beccaria attached his belief in sensationalism to a variety of nonpenal strategies designed to manipulate and channel sense impressions into law-abiding actions. While penal strategies tend to operate swiftly and dramatically on their subjects, these other strategies are designed as positive mental inducements which operate slowly and calmly at the level of custom and habit, or at what is nowadays known as the domain of socialisation. Thus, Beccaria suggested that in order to prevent crimes, "enlightenment should accompany liberty."[150] What precisely he meant by this recommendation is not very clear, but he possibly had in mind education, an instrument whose importance he also stressed,[151] and which had recently been emphasized by such thinkers as Montesquieu, d'Alembert, Helvétius, Rousseau, and Charles Pinot Duclos.[152] He warned that "the most certain but most difficult way to prevent crimes is to perfect education."[153] By education, a vague term without clear institutional or empirical referent in *Dei delitti,* Beccaria likely intended a process whose outcome, at least, was the gradual inculcation in the citizenry of such attributes as virtue, courage, and liberty—for the encourgement of which he recommended the distribution of prizes.[154]

From the "Science of Man" to *Homo Criminalis*

Morality, politics, and the fine arts, which are respectively the sciences of virtue, of utility, and of beauty, have a greater identity of principles than can be imagined: these sciences all derive from one primary science, the science of man; it is hopeless to think that we will ever make rapid progress in fathoming the depths of these secondary sciences without first immersing ourselves in the science of man.

—Beccaria, *Ricerche intorno alla natura dello stile*[155]

In addition to the contemporary protestations of certain luminaries, such as Grimm and Ramsay, that Beccaria's treatment of penal questions in *Dei delitti* was "too geometrical," other legal scholars and social reformers of the period more or less clearly understood the proto-scientific intentions of *Dei delitti* and valued it for this very direction.[156] To the French mathematician and *philosophe* Condorcet, for example, Beccaria was one of a select group of scholars—which included the Scottish political economists, Rousseau, and Montesquieu—whose works, since the time of Locke, had advanced the moral sciences, or *mathématique sociale* and *science sociale,* as he termed the application of "the calculus of . . . probabilities" to the understanding of human societies.[157] In letters to Beccaria of 1771, Condorcet condemned the injustices of existing criminal jurisprudence and expressed his desire to follow Beccaria's lead in using mathematics to search for rationality in judicial decision-making.[158] Later, he recommended to Frederick II of Prussia the application of the "calculus of probabilities" to Beccaria's ideas on capital punishment and on wise legislation.[159] The influential English legal scholar Blackstone observed in 1769 in his *Commentaries on the Laws of England* that Beccaria "seems to have well studied the springs of human action,"[160] and he emphatically placed Beccaria's "humane" reform proposals within the rubric of a new discourse of crime and penality that emerged in Britain in the 1760s and which stressed investigation of the "causes of crime," deterrence, and the correction of offenders.

It should be noted that, attached to Beccaria's discourse on penal strategies, there is indeed present in *Dei delitti* a very rudimentary attempt to forge some key concepts of an embryonic criminology. These concepts include "crime," "criminal," and "causes of crime." Quite apart from his innovative approach to the understanding of crime (i.e., "the harm done to society"),[161] Beccaria also attempted to identify "the criminal" as something other than a mere bundle of illegalities. This concept of criminal operates in concert with and is burdened by Beccaria's humanism and his advocacy of legal rationality, yet it marks, one might say, a movement away from a single-minded focus with how to punish *Homo penalis* to a wider "criminological" concern with understanding the situation of *Homo criminalis*. An example of this movement occurs when, during an impassioned tirade against unjust laws, Beccaria inserted the following words into the mouth of "a scoundrel":

> What are these laws that I must respect and that leave such a great distance between me and the rich man? . . . Who made these laws? Rich and powerful men who have never deigned to visit the squalid hovels of the poor, who have never broken a moldy crust of bread among the innocent cries of their famished children and the tears of their wives. Let us break these bonds that are so ruinous for the majority and useful to a handful of indolent tyrants; let us attack injustice at its source.[162]

At several other points in his text, as well, Beccaria indicated that criminals and criminal behavior should be understood causally, in material and social terms rather than purely individualistic ones. He suggested, for example, that "theft is only the crime of misery and desperation; it is the crime of that unhappy portion of humanity to whom the right of property . . . has left only a bare existence."[163] It is difficult to know, without indulging in an anachronism, precisely how much to invest in Beccaria's reasoning in passages such as these, other than to say that he seems keen to position illegalities in a quasi-social context. Further, he argues on adultery:

> Adultery is a crime that, politically considered, derives its strength and orientation from two causes: variable human laws and that very strong attraction which impels one sex toward the other. The latter is similar in many respects to the force of gravity which moves the universe; for, like gravity, it diminishes with distance.[164]

On pederasty:

> Pederasty . . . is founded less upon the needs of the isolated and free man than upon the passions of the sociable man. It draws its strength not so much from a surfeit of pleasures as from the sort of education that begins by making men useless

to themselves in order to make them useful to others. It is the result of those institutions where hot-blooded youth is confined.[165]

On infanticide:

Infanticide is . . . the effect of an inevitable contradiction, one in which a woman is placed when she has either submitted out of weakness or been overpowered by violence. Faced with a choice between disgrace and the death of a creature incapable of feeling pain, who would not prefer the latter to the unavoidable misery to which the woman and her unfortunate offspring would be exposed?[166]

It must also be mentioned that *Dei delitti* even contains an adumbration of a "dangerous class."[167] This is visible at several points. Thus, Beccaria spoke philosophically of wanting to disabuse those "who, from a poorly understood love of liberty, would desire to establish anarchy" and who are inclined toward "a desperate return to the original state of nature."[168] These unfortunates he described as "the credulous and admiring crowd," "a fanatical crowd," "a blind and fanatical crowd, pushing and jostling one another in a closed labyrinth" which "does not adopt stable principles of conduct."[169] In crowds there resides, for Beccaria, a "dangerous concentration of popular passions" which is akin to the sentiments in "the state of nature . . . the savage."[170] Its actions include "concealed despotism . . . turbulent mob anarchy"[171] and those events especially

that disturb the public tranquility and the peace of citizens: matters such as tumults and carousing in public thoroughfares meant for business and for traffic, or such as fanatical sermons that excite the fickle passions of the curious crowd. These passions gather strength from the great number of the audience; they owe more to the effects of a murky and mysterious rapture than to clear and calm reason, which never has any effect on a large mass of men.[172]

Ultimately, *Dei delitti* teases its audience with a presociological view of the relation between crime and social organization:

> Most men lack that vigor which is equally necessary for great crimes and great virtues; thus, it seems that the former always coexist with the latter in those nations that sustain themselves by the activity of their governments and by passions working together for the public good, rather than in countries that depend on their size or the invariable excellence of their laws. In the latter sort of nation, weakened passions seem better suited to the maintenance rather than to the improvement of the form of government. From this, one can draw an important conclusion: that great crimes in a nation are not always proof of its decline.[173]

Notes

1. Translated from a French report of the sentence of execution given in Frederic Maugham (1928), *The Case of Jean Calas,* pp. 96–97.

2. Voltaire (1762a), "Lettre à M. d'Alembert", p. 79.

3. Voltaire (1762b), "Lettre à M. d'Alembert", p. 168.

4. Voltaire (1763), "Traité sur la tolérance à l'occasion de la mort de Jean Calas," pp. 22–23. Jean Calas was formally acquitted of the charge against him on 9 March 1765, and his memory was declared to be rehabilitated. The question of whether Jean Calas was innocent or guilty of the murder of his son Marc-Antoine has never adequately been settled. Arguments for both verdicts have been championed by numerous advocates.

5. Although he had received a law degree from the University of Pavia in 1758, Beccaria knew very little about criminal law and punishment when he began to write *Dei delitti* in March 1763. The project itself actually was first suggested to him by Pietro Verri and then developed through discussion with fellow *illuministi* in the *Accademià dei pugni*. Beccaria completed his treatise in January 1764, after working on it for only ten months. Biographical details of Beccaria's career can be found in Cantù (1862), *Beccaria e il diritto penale,* passim; Landry (1910), *Cesare Beccaria: Scritti e lettere inediti,* pp. 7–46; Phillipson (1923), op. cit., pp. 3–26; Maestro (1942), op. cit., pp. 51–55; Maestro (1973),

Cesare Beccaria and the Origins of Penal Reform, pp. 5–12; and Paolucci (1963),
op. cit., pp. ix–xxiii.

6. Which of the several editions of *Dei delitti* represents Beccaria's intended
text is not entirely clear. The first Italian edition of 1764 arguably contains the
text closest to Beccaria's initial thinking, but this was published only after extensive editing by his friend Pietro Verri. The first French edition of 1765 certainly made the greatest impact on intellectual circles outside Italy, and of the
early editions it had by far the largest circulation. However, its translator, the
famous Abbé Morellet, made a variety of changes to Beccaria's manuscript
without his permission, ostensibly for the sake of clarity of presentation but
which perhaps resulted in an undue emphasis on its utilitarian features. For
this, Morellet's translation was castigated by the *philosophe* Melchior Grimm
(1765b, "Examen de la traduction du *Traité des Délits et des Peines de Beccaria par
Morellet,*" pp. 424–25) and scorned as a perversion of the author's meaning by
the anonymous translator of the first English edition of 1767. Yet no compelling evidence exists that Beccaria himself was overly concerned either with
Morellet's rearrangement of the text or with the effects of the translation—*pace*
Venturi (1971), op. cit. pp. 106–8; and Young (1984), op. cit., pp. 164–65. In
one of his letters to Morellet, Beccaria (1766,"Ad André Morellet, le 26 janvier," pp. 862–63) commented on this very issue in the following terms:

> "My work has lost none of its force in your translation, except in
> those places where the essential character of one or the other lan-
> guage has imparted some difference between your expression and
> mine. . . . I find quite without foundation the objection that your
> changing the order of my text resulted in a loss of its force. The force
> consists in the choice of expressions and the *rapprochement* of ideas,
> neither of which has been harmed."

Nevertheless, the edition of *Dei delitti* used here is the sixth Italian edition
of 1766. This is so because all its major arguments are faithful to the original
edition, because it appeared not long after the original, and because it was the
final edition personally supervised by Beccaria himself. This choice is also fa-
vored by the Italian Enlightenment specialist Franco Venturi (1965), *Cesare
Beccaria, Dei delitti e delle pene. Con una raccolta di lettere e documenti relativi alla
nascita dell'opera e alla sua fortuna nell'Europa del Settecento.* Fortunately, it has
been recently made available in an excellent English translation by Young
(Beccaria, 1764, *On Crimes and Punishments*), on which I largely depend here.

7. In his *Commentaries on the Law of England,* Blackstone (1769, 4: pp. 3, 14–18), referred to Beccaria as "an ingenious writer," and he praised Beccaria's humanism and his specific recommendations for rules of evidence, for deterrence ("certainty" rather than "severity" of punishment) and a "proportionate scale" of punishments. On the timeliness of Beccaria's ideas for English reformers, and on Blackstone's indebtedness to them, see Beattie (1986), *Crime and the Courts in England 1660–1800,* pp 555–57; and Lieberman (1989), *The Province of Legislation Determined,* pp. 208–9. Beccaria's influence on other English reformers, such as William Eden, Henry Dagge, and Manasseh Dawes, is discussed in Green (1985), *Verdict According to Conscience: Perspectives on the English Criminal Trial Jury 1200–1800,* pp. 290–303).

8. Upon reading *Dei delitti,* Bentham exclaimed: "Oh! my master, first evangelist of Reason, you who have raised your Italy so far above England, and I would add above France . . . you who have made so many useful excursions into the path of utility, what is there left for us to do?—Never to turn aside from that path" (cited in Halévy, 1928, *The Growth of Philosophical Radicalism,* p. 21; and see Hart, 1982, *Essays on Bentham,* pp. 40–52). Elsewhere, Bentham wrote of Beccaria that "he was received by the intelligent as an Angel from heaven would be by the faithful. He may be styled the father of *Censorial Jurisprudence*" (1776, *A Fragment on Government,* p. 14).

This is the same Bentham who in 1778 recommended "periodical returns on criminals . . . [to] furnish *data* for the legislator to work upon"(quoted in Radzinowicz, *Ideology and Crime,* 1966, p. 31), and who encouraged the use of statistics (Bentham, 1831a, "Untitled Manuscript") and the formation of a "Statistic Society for the collection and publication of facts and reasonings relating to political economy and morals and legislation" (1831b, "Untitled Manuscript").

9. Thomas Jefferson, for example, "copied long passages from it in his *Commonplace Book* and used it as his principal modern authority for revising the laws of Virginia" (Wills, 1978, *Inventing America: Jefferson's Declaration of Independence,* p. 94). In 1770, during his speech in defense of the British soldiers implicated in the Boston Massacre, John Adams pleaded, "I am for the prisoners at the bar, and shall apologize for it only in the words of the Marquis Beccaria: 'If I can but be the instrument of preserving one life, his blessing and tears of transport, shall be a sufficient consolation to me, for the contempt of all mankind' " (quoted in Kidder, 1870, *History of the Boston Massacre,* p. 232).

10. D'Alembert (1765), "Lettera a Paolo Frisi," p. 313.

11. Grimm (1765b), op. cit., p. 424.

12. Ramsay (n.d.), "Lettre à A. M. Diderot," p. 55.

13. Maestro (1942), op. cit., pp. 64–67. Elsewhere, Maestro (1973, op. cit., pp. 38–39) has outlined the attack made on Beccaria in 1771 by the French jurist Daniel Jousse, in the latter's *Traité de la justice criminelle de France*. Maestro asks, "Why these attacks on Beccaria on the part of the jurists?" and responds "[because] the men who had built their lives, their fortunes, and their reputations on the old customs could not bear to see this young idealist suddenly ruin their edifice" (ibid.). This answer, while correct, fails to specify the precise terms in which the jurists of the *ancien régime* recognized Beccaria's book as such a dangerous threat.

14. Facchinei (1765), "Note ed osservazioni sul libro intitolato 'Dei delitti e delle pene,' " p. 173; and see Maestro (1973), op. cit., pp. 35–37.

15. See especially Kant's (1797) *Metaphysical Elements of Justice*, pp. 102–7; and Hegel's (1821) *Philosophy of Right*, pp. 70–71.

16. For example, see Gorecki (1969), *A Theory of Criminal Justice*, pp. 67–68; Jones (1986), *History of Criminology: A Philosophical Perspective*, pp. 33–57; and Mueller (1990), "Whose Prophet is Cesare Beccaria? An Essay on the Origins of Criminological Theory."

17. For example, see Matza (1964), *Delinquency and Drift*, pp. 3, 13.

18. Foucault (1979), *Discipline & Punish: The Birth of the Prison*, pp. 73–103; and Foucault (1988), "The Dangerous Individual."

19. See Jenkins (1984), "Varieties of Enlightenment Criminology"; and Roshier (1989), *Controlling Crime: The Classical Perspective in Criminology*, pp. 16–18.

20. Humphries and Greenberg (1981), "The Dialectics of Crime Control." p. 224.

21. Weisser (1979), *Crime and Punishment in Early Modern Europe*, pp. 133–38.

22. See Langbein (1976), *Torture and the Law of Proof: Europe and England in the Ancien Régime*, pp. 67–68; and Chadwick (1981), "The Italian Enlightenment," p. 98.

23. Hirst (1986), *Law, Socialism and Democracy*, pp. 152–55. See further Young (1983), "Cesare Beccaria: Utilitarian or Retributivist?"; and Newman and Marongiu (1990), "Penological Reform and the Myth of Beccaria."

24. Woolf (1979), *A History of Italy, 1700–1860*, p. 75; and see Gross (1990), *Rome in the Age of Enlightenment*, p. 258.

25. Venturi (1972), *Italy and the Enlightenment*, pp. 103–29; Woolf (1979), op. cit., pp. 83–84.

26. Roberts (1960), "Enlightened Despotism in Italy," p. 38.

27. Klang (1984), "Reform and Enlightenment in Eighteenth-Century Lombardy," pp. 41–46.

28. Beccaria (1766), "Ad André Morellet, le 26 janvier," p. 866.

29. Ibid., p. 863.

30. Cited in Maestro (1942), op. cit., pp. 54–55.

31. Darnton (1979), *The Business of Enlightenment: A Publishing History of the Encyclopédie, 1775–1800*; and Darnton (1982), *The Literary Underground of the Old Regime*.

32. Beccaria (1764), *Dei delitti*, pp. 15, 45, 49, 53.

33. Knight (1968), *The Geometric Spirit: The Abbé de Condillac and the French Enlightenment*, p. 5.

34. Beccaria (1766), op. cit., p. 863.

35. Ibid., p. 862, emphasis added. It is significant that Beccaria received from those schoolmasters of Europe, the Jesuits, training in arithmetic, algebra, and geometry, "a fanatical education" as he described it, and one that he shared with anti-Jesuit intellectuals in France such as Descartes, Montesquieu, Fontenelle, Voltaire, Diderot, Buffon, Condorcet, and possibly Condillac. See further his comments to d'Alembert on the Jesuits in Beccaria (1765a), "A Jean-Baptiste Le Rond d'Alembert," p. 860.

36. Ibid. p. 864. Beccaria added that he derived many of his ideas from Helvétius's *l'Esprit*, which had alerted him to the misfortunes of humanity (and see *infra*, n. 125); from Buffon, who opened up for him the *sanctuaire* of nature; and from d'Alembert: "I know enough about mathematics to appreciate the great discoveries of this celebrated man, and to regard him as the greatest geometer of our century" (ibid., pp. 865–66).

37. Beccaria (1766), op. cit., p. 865. Montesquieu, then chief justice of the provincial parliament of Bordeaux, had written in his anonymously published *Lettres persanes* (1721) that "obedience to law does not depend on whether punishment is more or less cruel. In countries where chastisements are moderate, they are feared no less than if they were tyrannical and horrible" (p. 170). Montesquieu's *Lettres* commented on various other topics of interest to the young Beccaria, including the virtue of treating the families of successful suicides with compassion rather than terror and especially the need for Christian princes to establish a proportion between crimes (*fautes*) and punishments (ibid., p. 212).

But Montesquieu exerted his greatest influence on Beccaria through his *De l'esprit des lois*, a complicated and contradictory treatise that effectively severed the Enlightenment equation of reason with nature, and which was placed

on the Index in 1752 for its rationalism. Here Montesquieu claimed both that
"the law, in general, is human reason insofar as it governs all the peoples of
the earth" and that "the political and civil laws of each nation should only be
the particular cases where human reason is applied" (1748, *De l'esprit des lois,*
1:12). This recognition of the facts of social diversity led him to conclude that,
though justice is a universal principle, the forms of justice vary and are intimately linked to types of political regime. In arguing for the superiority of the
republican and democratic forms of government over monarchic and despotic
forms, Montesquieu suggested that the virtue of a republic is its love of virtue and that the greatest virtue is love of the laws.

    38. Beccaria (1764), op. cit., p. 4. In Book 6 (chap. 1) of *De l'esprit des
lois,* Montesquieu made a number of famous proposals for the democratic reform of the criminal justice systems of Europe. These included the separation
of powers (op. cit., pp. 1622-74); the simplification of criminal law (pp. 83–
84); the use of mild punishments (pp. 91–92); the abolition of violent punishments (p. 93); a just proportion between punishments and crimes—"because
it is essential that a great crime be avoided rather than a smaller one, and that
which harms society more rather than less" (pp. 100–101); the abolition of torture (p. 102); and the moderate use of monetary and corporal punishments (pp.
102–3). In Book 12 Montesquieu classified crimes into those which offend religion, morals, public tranquilty, and the security of citizens (1:203). In a none-
too-subtle attack on the Spanish Inquisition, he argued that criminal law ought
to be distinct from the prosecution of offenses against religion and that great
care ought therefore to be exercised in the prosecution of homosexuality ("offenses against nature"), witchcraft, heresy, and treason (1: 203–11; and see
Book 25, 2: 162–65).

    Montesquieu's great book is full of misgivings and uncertainties about
the thorny problem of free will and determinism. It is instructive, for example, to juxtapose the sort of persistent claim Montesquieu made at the very
beginning of his book that "it is absurd to say that *'a blind determinism' [fatalité]
has produced all the effects that we see in the world:* what could be more absurd
than to say that a blind determinism seems to have produced intelligent beings?" (Book 1, p. 7, emphasis in original) with his materialist analysis of
the geographical distribution of various social events in Book 16. There Montesquieu actually claimed that such factors as climate and soil influence
sexual inequality and the type and content of laws (1748, Book 16, pp.
280–94).

    39. Becker (1932), *The Heavenly City of the Eighteenth-Century Philoso-
phers,* p. 50.

40. Beccaria (1764), op. cit., p. 17.

41. Ibid. p. 36.

42. Ibid. p. 29.

43. Ibid. p. 72. In *Dei delitti* Beccaria argued that capital punishment is justified if (1) an incarcerated citizen is still a threat to society, (2) a citizen's mere existence could produce a revolution dangerous to the state, (3) a citizen's execution deterred others from committing crimes (pp. 48–49).

44. Ibid. p. 23; and see pp. 4, 29.

45. Grimm (1765a), "Sur le traité des *Délits et des Peines, par Beccaria*," pp. 330–31.

46. Bacon (1632), *The Essayes or Counsels Civill and Morall, of Francis Lo[rd] Verulam,* chap. 47 ("Of Negotiating"), p. 283.

47. Beccaria shared his neglected Baconian heritage with the anti-Cartesian humanist Giambattista Vico (1668–1744), professor of Latin Eloquence at the University of Naples and one of the most creative social theorists in the entire Enlightenment. In his books *On the Study Methods of Our Time* (1709) and *The New Science* (1725), Vico audaciously applied Bacon's evolutionary and inductivist analysis of nature to natural law, jurisprudence, and history. Vico anticipated the *philosophes* in arguing that, through the judicious use of rewards and punishments, aristocratic laws can turn private vices into public virtues, and thus ensure civil happiness. Moreover, in *The New Science* his expansive historical analyses suggested that on the "concrete and complex order of human civil institutions, we may superimpose the order of numbers" (Vico, 1725, pp. 339–40; see further the commentary in Berlin, 1960, "The Philosophical Ideas of Giambattista Vico"). However, few of the *philosophes* themselves bothered to pierce Vico's obscure, convoluted, and tormented style, and in his lifetime he exerted almost no influence.

48. Beccaria (n.d. 1), "Estratti da Bacone: Nota al testo, materiali non pubblicati," pp. 459–70.

49. Lieberman (1989), op. cit., pp. 181–86.

50. Beccaria (1764), op. cit., pp. 31–32. Beyond the explanations given above, the remote possibility exists that there is even more to Beccaria's prominent placement of Bacon's epigram than meets the eye; perhaps Beccaria was indulging in another Enlightenment game with his readers, designed not so much to stimulate his readers to seek its textual meaning *between* the lines but *before* them. Perhaps it was not to this particular Baconian passage that Beccaria wished to alert his fellow *philosophes*, but to the one preceding it, which states: "In Dealing with Cunning Persons, we must ever Consider their Ends, to interpret their Speeches; And it is good, to say little

to them, and that which they least look for" (quoting Bacon, 1632, op. cit., pp. 282–83). If Beccaria was inviting his readers to "interpret" his own argument then, given that his opposition to judicial arbitrariness was not hidden in his text, but quite exposed, it is possible that there was some other important, though hidden, feature of his text, to which Beccaria wanted to alert his readers.

51. *Pace* Wills (1978), op. cit., pp. 149–51.

52. In Maestro's *Voltaire and Beccaria as Reformers of Criminal Law* (1942), for example, there is no mention at all of either Bacon or Francis Hutcheson (1694–1746), and neither John Locke (1632–1704) nor David Hume (1711–1776) merit more than passing mention, although Hutcheson merits a brief comment in his authoritative *Cesare Beccaria and the Origins of Penal Reform* (1973, p. 21). Similarly, Chadwick (1981, op. cit., p. 96) writes regarding the Milanese Enlightenment that "Paris loomed much closer. The English and Scottish writers were less important." Venturi (1983, "Scottish Echoes in eighteenth-century Italy") has noticed several fortuitous "parallels" between Beccaria's text and Scottish authors, but he identifies Henry Home, Lord Kames, Ferguson, and Smith rather than Hutcheson.

This is not to suggest that it was only the Scottish philosphers who were concerned to develop a scientific account of society. Far from it. Beccaria's French colleague Jean d'Alembert, for example, typically believed that only his Baconian-inspired "geometry," or "science of man," could unravel intricate religious doctrine, and when he addressed issues of human rights and duties he did so with the rhetoric of *esprit géométrique* and the methods of the exact sciences; see, for example, d'Alembert (n.d.1), "De l'abus de la critique en matière de religion," pp. 571–72; and d'Alembert (n.d.2), "Explication détaillée du Système des Connaissances humaines," pp. 99–114. On one occasion, he even argued that "mathematics should be used to subvert the inquisition. Infiltrate enough geometers into the citizenry of a country oppressed by the Church, and Enlightenment would follow inevitably" (d'Alembert, quoted in Hankins, 1970, *Jean d'Alembert: Science and the Enlightenment,* p. 14).

53. Cited in Maestro (1942), op. cit., p. 53.

54. Gay (1966), *The Enlightenment: An Interpretation,* p. 12.

55. Landry (1910), *Cesare Beccaria: Scritti e lettere inediti,* p. 13–14.

56. Shackleton (1972), "The Greatest happiness of the greatest number: The history of Bentham's phrase", pp. 1470–71.

57. Robertson (1983), "The Scottish Enlightenment at the limits of the civic tradition."

58. Swingewood (1970), "Origins of Sociology: The Case of the Scottish Enlightenment"; Phillipson (1981), "The Scottish Enlightenment."

59. Beccaria (1762a), *Del disordine e de' rimedi delle monete nello stato di Milano nell'anno* 1762.

60. Schumpeter (1954), *History of Economic Analysis,* p. 298.

61. Beccaria (1762a), op. cit., p. 8.

62. Ibid. p. 8. " *'Nuove considerazioni'...*" was doubtless Locke's *Further Considerations Concerning Raising the Value of Money* of 1695; see also Hutcheson (1755), *A System of Moral Philosophy,* Book 2, chap. 12). Locke's book had been translated into Italian in 1749 by the Tuscan Abbés Pagnini and Tavanti, although its publication was delayed until 1751, probably because the translators feared that there must have been "some hidden mystery, as for instance that it might not be to the liking of certain important persons"; see further Venturi (1963), "Elementi e tentativi di riforme nella Stato Pontificio del Settecento," p. 783; and Venturi (1972), *Italy and the Enlightenment,* pp. 230–31.

63. Locke (1689), *Essay Concerning Human Understanding,* 1:97–122. See further Schumpeter (1954), op. cit., pp. 297–99; and especially Caffentzis (1989), *Clipped Coins, Abused Words, and Civil Government: John Locke's Philosophy of Money,* pp. 61–68.

64. See Beccaria (1762b), "Tentative analitico su i contrabbandi." According to Schumpeter (1954, op. cit., p. 179), it is possible that Beccaria's algebraic response to this question inaugurated the idea of indifference theory in modern economics; see also Beccaria (1804), *Elementi di economia pubblica,* pp. 551–62. For present purposes, it is fair to say that this idea anticipates Beccaria's attempt in *Dei delitti* to calculate the precise amount of pain needed to deter the pleasure gained from committing a crime. Thus, "the prison sentence of a tobacco smuggler should not be the same as that of a cutthroat or a thief, and the smuggler's labor, if confined to the work and service of the royal revenue administration that he had meant to defraud, will be the most suitable type of punishment" (Beccaria, 1764, op. cit., p. 64).

In 1765 Beccaria (1765b, "All'arciduca Ferdinando d'Austria, duca di Modena, governatore della Lombardia," p. 858) confessed to Archduke Ferdinand, the Austrian governor of Lombardy, that he had never enjoyed the study of law and that, rather than don the judicial robe, he wanted to serve his country by engaging in sciences more relevant to the economic regulation of a state. Indeed, from 1769 to 1773 he lectured on political economy at the Palatinate while occupying the new Chair of Political Economy and the Science of Police. At the same time he began a career in government administration in Lombardy, until his death in 1794. Further details of Beccaria's career can be found in Maestro (1973), op. cit., pp. 81–150; and Canetta (1985), "Beccaria economista e gli atti di governo."

65. Beccaria (1762b), op. cit., p. 164.

66. For example, see Jaucourt (1751), "Crime (faute, péché, délit, forfait)"; and Helvétius (1758), *De l'ésprit;* and see the commentary in Wood (1989), "The Natural History of Man in the Scottish Enlightenment."

67. Beccaria (1766), op. cit., p. 865.

68. Shackleton (1972), op. cit., pp. 1468–70.

69. Scott (1900), *Francis Hutcheson,* p. 273; and see Robbins (1968), *The Eighteenth-Century Commonwealthman,* p. 195.

70. Compare Beccaria (1765c, "Frammento sullo stile," p. 169) with Hutcheson (1725b, *An Inquiry Concerning, Beauty, Order, Harmony, Design,* pp. 48–51).

71. Beccaria (1764), op. cit., p. 3; and see Scott (1900), op. cit., pp. 273–74. In the introduction to *Dei delitti,* this exclamation comes on the heels of Beccaria's statement of belief in the utilitarian formula; see further Scott (1900), pp. 273–74.

72. Hutcheson (1725a), *An Inquiry into the Original of our Ideas of Beauty and Virtue, In Two Treatises,* p. vii.

73. In 1738 Hutcheson had circulated the manuscript of his *System of Moral Philosophy* in Scotland, Ireland, England, and Holland. It had therefore been known on the continent considerably before its actual date of publication in 1755; nowhere was it more popular than in Italy, especially in Lombardy.

74. Compare, respectively, Hutcheson (Book 2, chap. 6, pp. 319–22) with Beccaria (p. 7); Hutcheson (Book 2, chap. 15, pp. 86–87) with Beccaria (p. 17); Hutcheson (Book 2, chap. 15, pp. 101–2) with Beccaria (pp. 11–12); Hutcheson (Book 3, chap. 9, pp. 322–23) with Beccaria (pp. 12–13, 75); Hutcheson (Book 2, chap. 15, pp. 88–89) with Beccaria (p. 78); Hutcheson (Book 2, chap. 15, pp. 88–91) with Beccaria (pp. 39–40, but see pp. 34–35); Hutcheson (Book 2, chap. 15, pp. 87, 93–94; Book 3, chap. 9, p. 333) with Beccaria (pp. 23, 33, 47, 50, 74–75); Hutcheson (Book 3, chap. 9, pp. 331–38) with Beccaria (pp. 14–16, 23, 46–47, 55, 64); and Hutcheson (Book 2, chap. 15, p. 97; Book 3, chap. 9, pp. 337–38) with Beccaria (pp. 29–33, 70–72).

75. By the middle of the eighteenth century the term *esprit géométrique* had lost much of its original meaning as a mathematical antonym for "the philosophical spirit." Instead, it had become "a kind of ritual invocation of a whole cluster of virtues associated with science of all kinds, including the anti-mathematical science of the empirical tradition," (Knight, op. cit., pp. 18–19).

76. It is reasonable to suppose that Beccaria derived this—the foundation of *Dei delitti*—from the algebraic formulations in Hutcheson's *Inquiry into the Original of Our Ideas of Beauty and Virtue* (1725a). See also Scott, 1900, op. cit., pp. 273–74; Shackleton, 1972, op. cit., pp. 1466–72). In the first edition of his *Inquiry* Hutcheson had written, "That action is best, which procures the greatest happiness for the greatest numbers; and that worst, which in like manner, occasions misery" (1725a, op. cit., pp. 177–78). In the fourth and final edition, although much else in it had been considerably modified, Hutcheson argued that "the most perfectly virtuous actions" are those "as appear to have the most universal unlimited Tendency to the greatest and most extensive Happiness of all the rational agents, to whom an Influence can reach" (1738, p. 184).

I do not mean to suggest that the utilitarian principle originated in the work of Hutcheson. See, for example, the even earlier formulation by Locke: "The highest Perfection of intellectual Nature lies in a careful and constant Pursuit of true and solid Happiness" (1689, op. cit., 1: 112). Indeed, its roots can be discovered in the works of Cicero (wishing his friend "bonis affici quam maximis" in *De Finibus*) and in that of late Stoics such as Antoninus (see Scott, 1900, op. cit., pp. 275–77). Alternative contemporary candidates, albeit with far weaker claims than Hutcheson's, were Pietro Verri "[là] felicità pubblica o sia la maggior felicità possible divisa colla maggiore uguaglianza possibile" (1763, *Meditazioni sulla felicità*, p. 84) and Helvétius ("l'utilité du public, c'est-à-dire, du plus grand nombre d'hommes soumis à la même forme de gouvernement" (1758, op. cit., p. 175). See further the speculations about alternative candidates by Gianni Francioni in *Cesare Beccaria: Opere,* (1984, directed by Luigi Firpo, Milan: Mediobanca, 6 vols., 1: 23).

77. Beccaria (1764), op. cit., p. 3. Beccaria's wording of this utilitarian slogan differed slightly (*contra* Young's translation of it) both from Hutcheson's original statement and from the version of it later popularized by Bentham, a fact due to its frequent translation from one language to another—beginning in English (1725, Hutcheson), then to French (1749, Marc Antoine Eidous), to Italian (1764, Beccaria), to French (1765, Morellet), and finally back to English (1768, Priestly). See also Shackleton (1972), op. cit.

78. In Beccaria's discourse the content of the relationship between the state and its citizenry is never properly spelled out in words like *felicità*. To him "happiness" seems to have meant both the warm mental sensations associated with individualism—where the public good is the aggregate of individually pursued self-interest—and also such virtues as courage, liberty, justice, and honor.

79. Beccaria (1764), p. 9.

80. Ibid., p. 62

81. Ibid., p. 7.

82. Ibid., p. 5. Unfortunately, except for the crime of suicide, Beccaria was otherwise quite circumspect on this issue. About suicide he argued that "it is a crime which God punishes (since He alone can punish even after death)" (ibid., p. 63).

83. Ibid., pp. 14–15.

84. Ibid., p. 16.

85. Ibid., p. 3.

86. Ibid., p. 66.

87. Ibid., p. 62.

88. See also Zeman (1981), "Order, Crime and Punishment: The American Criminological Tradition," p. 20; and Wills (1978), op. cit., pp. 153–54.

89. Beccaria (1764), op. cit., p. 76.

90. Ibid., pp. 7, 34.

91. Ibid., p. 7.

92. Ibid., pp. 41–42, and ibid., p. 66.

93. Ibid., p. 49.

94. Ibid., p. 40.

95. Locke himself attached great importance to the roles of number, probability, and mathematics in the analysis of human affairs. "In all sorts of Reasoning," he argued, "every single Argument should be manag'd as a Mathematical Demonstration" (Locke, op. cit., 1689, 3: 397; and see I: 85, 308–9). It is tempting to suggest that Beccaria also drew inspiration from the writings of one of Hutcheson's mentors, the English statistician and physician Sir William Petty (1623–1687). Besides his noted contribution to the development of statistics, Petty was a staunch critic of physical punishments. In chapter 10 of his *Treatise of Taxes and Contributions,* he urged that pecuniary "mulcts" (i.e., fines), made over to the Commonwealth as 'reparations,' were far better than physical punishments, which benefit no one and actually deprive the state of useful labor. Thus, "Here we are to remember in consequence of our opinon [that 'Labour is the Father and active principle of Wealth, as Lands are the Mother'], that the State by killing, mutilating, or imprisoning their members, do withall punish themselves; wherefore such punishments ought (as much as possible) to be avoided and commuted for pecuniary mulcts, which will encrease labour and publick wealth" (Petty, 1662, p. 68; cf. Hutcheson, 1755, op. cit., 2: 318–19, 341).

96. Unlike that of the *philosophes,* Hutcheson's utilitarianism was explicitly formulated in mathematical and economic terms. Thus, when

Hutcheson wrote, "That action is best, which procures the greatest happiness *for the greatest numbers*" (emphasis added), he meant it literally and mathematically; when he attempted to calculate the precise incidence of "perfect virtue" and "moral evil," he did so strictly in terms of algebraic equations (1725a, op. cit., pp. 187–93). Indeed, the original title of Hutcheson's *Inquiry* contained the words *"with an attempt to introduce a mathematical calculation in subjects of morality."* This inclination was shared by Beccaria.

     97. Beccaria (1764), op. cit., p. 4.

     98. Ibid., p. 24.

     99. Ibid., p. 15.

     100. Ibid., p. 4.

     101. Ibid., pp. 74–75; and see p. 5.

     102. Ibid., p. 14.

     103. Ibid., p. 15.

     104. Ibid., p. 13.

     105. Ibid., p. 12.

     106. Ibid.

     107. Ibid., p. 56.

     108. Beccaria's arguments on torture were greatly influenced by the counsel of his friend Pietro Verri, whose book *Osservazioni sulla tortura* was only published posthumously in 1804. Whether Beccaria was correct in his assumption that judicial torture was still a widespread practice in mid-eighteenth-century Europe is an interesting question, but one which will not be addressed here. In his provocative book *Torture and the Law of Proof,* Langbein (1976; and see Hirst, 1986, op. cit., pp. 152–54) has fundamentally reinterpreted the history of the transformation of judicial torture in Europe. He claims that the conventional account of the demise of torture through the Enlightenment efforts of Beccaria and others is a fairy tale. His thesis is that there is an unmistakeable causal relationship between the abolition of judicial torture and a contemporaneous revolution in the law of proof. He suggests that a fundamental reason why historians have written hardly anything on the importance of changes in the law of proof is that they have uncritically accepted the critical explanations of the eighteenth-century abolitionist writers, who themselves knew very little about these changes or, if they did, did not understand their significance.

     109. Beccaria (1764), pp. 37, 40. Moreover, Beccaria urged that among the serious crimes, those such as infamy, which "are founded on pride, and [which] draw glory and nourishment from pain itself" (ibid. p. 41), did not warrant the use of painful corporal punishments.

110. Ibid., p. 23.

111. Ibid., p. 71.

112. Ibid., p. 31.

113. Ibid., p. 34.

114. Ibid., p. 24; and see Locke (1689), op. cit., I: 309. Elsewhere in *Dei delitti*, Beccaria extended to magistrates his idea of the relation between the number of concurring witnesses and the certainty of a verdict. Thus, he wrote about the "corps of those charged with executing the law that "the greater the number of men who constitute such a body, the less the danger of encroachments on the law will be" (Beccaria, 1764, op. cit., p. 78). It should be noted that Beccaria's observations on witnesses, juries, and magistrates were instrumental in the development of a *science sociale* by Condorcet (see, *infra*, n.157) and by Laplace (1814, *A Philosophical Essay on Probabilities*).

115. Beccaria (1764), op. cit., p. 24.

116. Ibid., pp. 24–25.

117. Ibid., p. 25.

118. Ibid., p. 54.

119. Ibid., p. 25.

120. Ibid., p. 58.

121. Ibid.

122. Ibid., p. 57.

123. Ibid., p. 27.

124. Ibid., p. 15.

125. Ibid., p. 36. The philosophical writings of Hume and Helvétius (both followers of Hutcheson) were among the "French books" to which Beccaria admitted "I myself owe everything" (1766, op. cit., p. 862; and see *supra*, p.21). About Hume's general influence on *Dei delitti* see, for example, his *Treatise of Human Nature* (1739, especially Book 1, parts 1 and 3); specifically, compare Beccaria (1764, op. cit., p. 19) with Hume (1739, op. cit., Book 1, part 1, sec. 4, p. 10); see also Beccaria (1762a, op. cit.) and Beccaria (1766, op. cit., p. 865). Helvétius contributed little that was original to the principle of associationism, although Beccaria's (1766, p. 862) generous comment about Helvétius' influence on *Dei delitti* probably refers to Helvétius' *De l'esprit* (1758, discourse 1, chap. 1–2; discourse 2, chap. 15).

126. Respectively, *ibid.* p. 33, 23 and 29, and 23. This is not to suggest that Beccaria's recommendations for penal strategies were based exclusively on an intended purpose of deterrence. At certain points in *Dei delitti*, his equation of crime with social harms also led Beccaria to a posture of retributivism toward criminals. However, given his overwhelming concern with deterrence, Beccar-

ia's retributivism was not and could not have been an important feature of his text (*pace* Young, 1983, op. cit.).

127. Beccaria (1764), op. cit., p. 81.

128. Ibid., p. 36.

129. Ibid., p. 37.

130. Ibid., pp. 46–47.

131. Ibid., p. 14; and see p. 15.

132. Ibid., p. 16. For this reason Beccaria therefore suggested that some punishments might even be considered as crimes (*ibid.*, p. 17); for example, "It appears absurd to me that the laws . . . commit murder themselves . . . [and] command public assassination" (*ibid.*, p. 51).

133. Ibid., p. 37.

134. Interestingly, appearing in a frontispiece engraving in a 1765 edition of *Dei delitti* is the figure of *Justice,* who is portrayed as combining law and wisdom in the features of Minerva. *Justice* herself recoils from the executioner's offering of three decapitated heads, and instead gazes approvingly at various instruments of labor, of measurement, and of detention. The engraving of *Justice* was incised for the third edition of *Dei delitti* (1765, Lausanne), and according to Venturi (1971, op. cit., p. 105), the sketch for the engraving was completed by Beccaria himself.

135. Only much later did Beccaria argue that the rights of an accused are violated by the death penalty because, once an execution had been carried out, there is no "possibility" of reversal even after proof of innocence (1792, "Voto per la riforma del sistema criminale nella Lombardia Austriaca riguardante la pena di morte," pp. 739–40).

136. Beccaria (1764), op. cit., p. 50.

137. Ibid., p. 50.

138. Ibid., p. 19; and see Halévy (1928), *The Growth of Philosophical Radicalism,* p. 57.

139. Beccaria (1764), op. cit., p. 19.

140. Beccaria (1770, *Ricerche intorno alla natura dello stile*), pp. 81–93; and see Beccaria (1766), op. cit., p. 866. Beccaria's unfinished book of 1770 was condemned in its French translation by Diderot who politely discounted it as "an obscure work based on a subtle metaphysic" (1771, "Des recherches sur le style par Beccaria," p. 60).

141. Locke (1689), op. cit., I: 95.

142. Condillac (1754), *A Treatise on the Sensations,* p. 338.

143. Beccaria (1764), op. cit., p. 25.

144. Ibid., p. 7.

145. Ibid., p. 31.
146. Ibid., p. 14.
147. Ibid., p. 64.
148. Ibid., p. 13.
149. Ibid., p. 81.
150. Ibid., p. 76.
151. Ibid., pp. 76–79.

152. When Duclos, the permanent secretary of the French Academy wrote, in his *Considérations sur les moeurs de ce siècle* of 1750 that "there is plenty of instruction among us and little education," he envisioned a system of general secular education that would create a patriotic and morally responsible citizenry (quoted in Baker, 1975, *Condorcet: From Natural Philosophy to Social Mathematics,* p. 286). Education, as opposed to "mere instruction," would produce moral individuals who understood the proper relation between individual advantage and the general good and who, as citizens, would feel a patriotic duty to obey the particular state that would defend the enjoyment of their natural rights. In the discourse of the *philosophes*, patriotic education was therefore a political weapon that looked backward to the future. It looked backward, wistfully, to a time when an educated citizenry was an essential part of the constitution of the Greek *polis*. It looked forward to the dawn of a new age when an educated citizenry would jettison the tyranny of the *ancien régime* and secure the existence of an enlightened republic.

153. Ibid.

154. Ibid., p. 79.

155. In his *Elementi di economia pubblica,* a series of lectures completed at the Palatine School in 1771, Beccaria displayed a keen interest in various aspects of the new statistics of populations that had become a key factor in the development of the science of man. These included statistical tables and comparative evidence on births, marriages, education, and life expectancy (1804, pp. 401–33). On the uncanny similarities between Beccaria's *Elementi* and the *Wealth of Nations* by Hutcheson's pupil, the Scotish political economist Adam Smith, see Schumpeter (1954), op. cit., pp. 179–83).

156. On Grimm and Ramsey, see *supra*, p. 14. Besides Beccaria, Melchior Grimm also attacked Beccaria's mentor Condillac for being "too geometrical"; see Knight (1968), op. cit., pp. 2–3, 235; and Becker (1932), op. cit., pp. 83–84.

157. Condorcet (1795a), *Tableau historique des progrès de l'esprit humain,* p. 178; see also Baker (1975), op. cit., p. 193. In France, Chancellor Maupeou's vain announcement of a new criminal code in 1771 stimulated the young

Condorcet to write letters to Beccaria and Turgot in which he condemned the injustices of existing criminal jurisprudence and he began to apply mathematics in the search for rationality in judicial decision-making. Recent analyses of Condorcet's contributions to the understanding of jury behavior are Baker (1975), pp. 231–32, and Hacking (1990), *The Taming of Chance*, pp. 87–90. Moreover, though it was perhaps first used in late 1791 by his friend Dominique-Joseph Garat, it was Condorcet who in 1795 popularized the term *science sociale* in his *Tableau historique des progrès de l'esprit humain* (and see Baker, 1975, p. 391). In the *Tableau*, Condorcet (1795a, pp. 177–78) referred to *l'art social* as one of the sciences.

158. Condorcet, cited in Baker (1975), op. cit., pp. 231–32.

159. Condorcet (1785), "Letter to King Frederick II of Prussia, 2 May 1785."

160. Blackstone (1769), *Commentaries on the Laws of England*, 4: 17.

161. See *supra*, p.22, p.29, pp. 31-32, pp.38-39.

162. Beccaria (1764), op. cit., p. 51.

163. Ibid., p. 39.

164. Ibid., pp. 58–59.

165. Ibid., p. 60.

166. Ibid., p. 60. *Dei delitti* provides no real clue as to Beccaria's understanding of the gendered position of women before law, although in the chapter on "The Spirit of the Family" Beccaria (*ibid.*, pp. 43–45) seems to oppose authoritarian (i.e., male-dominated) families ("little monarchies"). Nowhere in his text does Beccaria indulge in the antifeminism of those such as Rousseau and Buffon, although its publication date precludes his participation in the progressive ideas of feminist *philosophes* like Condorcet. On the periodicity of Enlightenment feminism, see generally Clinton (1975).

167. About the actual appearance of the term *dangerous classes*, see *infra*, p. 69.

168. Ibid., pp. 18, 47.

169. Ibid., pp. 39, 47, 77 and 7, respectively.

170. Ibid., pp. 22, 74. From Beccaria's vague references to social life in the "state of nature" it is very difficult to know whether he appropriated this term from Hobbes' *bellum omnium contra omnes*, from *philosophes* such as Montesquieu and Rousseau, or even from the Hutchesonian "mutual offices of good will," all of which are very different notions from the one that he proposed.

171. Ibid., p. 57.

172. Ibid., p. 22. In the following passage Beccaria even indicated a stark contrast between an embryonic dangerous class and the law-abiding citizenry:

Enslaved men are more sensual, more debauched, and more cruel than free men. The latter think about the sciences; they think about the interests of the nation; they see great examples, and they imitate them. The former, on the other hand, content with the present moment, seek a distraction for the emptiness of their lives in the tumult of debauchery. Accustomed to uncertain results in everything, the doubts they have about the outcome of their crimes strengthen the passions by which crimes are determined" (ibid., p. 75).

173. Ibid., p. 58.

Chapter 3

The Rise of Positivist Criminology: Adolphe Quetelet's "Social Mechanics of Crime"

> Society itself contains the germs of all the crimes committed. It is the social state, in some measure, which prepares these crimes, and the criminal is merely the instrument which executes them.
>
> —Adolphe Quetelet

During the formative period of social science Adolphe Quetelet was for half a century one of the most influential figures in Europe, though it is only in astronomy, statistics, and meteorology that his reputation as a pioneer and seminal thinker is secure. Quetelet's analysis of social organization was frequently pressed into service for a broad spectrum of political and ideological interests: about his two-volume book *Sur l'homme* ("On Man") of 1835, Karl Marx wrote in the *New York Daily Tribune* that it was "an excellent and learned work,"[1] and of the same book Emile Durkheim claimed in *Suicide* that its notion of the *homme moyen* ("average man") embodied "a theory, moreover, which has remained the only systematic explanation . . . [of] the remarkable regularity with which social phenomena repeat themselves during identical periods of time."[2] The historian of science George Sarton has recorded that *Sur l'homme* "was one of the greatest books of the nineteenth century" and that "a great injustice is made when Comte is called the founder of sociology, for Quetelet has better claims to this title than he."[3] However, this analysis has never gained the level of recognition it perhaps deserves.

My concern here is not, though, with Quetelet's largely unheralded role in the founding of sociology as such. That unfinished task is

larger and more ambitious than mine. In what follows, I restrict myself
to outlining Quetelet's contribution to the origins of positivist criminology. This contribution also has never properly been acknowledged. The principal biographies of Quetelet were written nearly a
hundred years ago, and none of them has his criminology as its explicit
focus.[4] None of Quetelet's writings on crime was translated for the
prestigious series of European works published between 1911 and 1918
under the auspices of the American Institute of Criminal Law and
Criminology.[5] Neither Quetelet nor any other member of the Franco-
Belgian school of criminology of the 1830s was represented in Hermann Mannheim's *Pioneers in Criminology*, an important biographical
collection of 1972 that contained essays on lesser figures, such as Alexander Maconochie and Arnould Bonneville de Marsangy. In most
recent histories of criminological theory, Quetelet's writings receive
either scanty attention or no mention at all.[6]

The sustained neglect of Quetelet's work on crime can in part be
explained, somewhat ironically, by the thrust of the cursory recognition accorded him by criminologists in the United States in the 1930s.
At that time two specific claims were made about his work. First, it
was claimed[7] that Quetelet rather than Lombroso had been responsible
for rescuing the study of crime from the mire of metaphysics and ele-
vating it to the status of an infant science and, somewhat paradoxically,
that the tradition established by Quetelet gave Lombroso's contemporaries both the standards and the evidence to criticize and reject atavistic
notions of the "born criminal."[8] Second, it was claimed that Quetelet
and Guerry were the founders, or at least the precursors, of the ecological school in crime.[9] Both claims have some merit. It is true, for example, that the most insightful critics of Lombrosianism, such as
Tarde, Topinard, Manouvrier and Lacassagne, marshalled their evidence against the notion of the born criminal with generalizations
about the effects of the social environment on criminality. In some respects, Quetelet and his contemporary André Michel Guerry anticipated the work of ecological theorists a century later.

However, both claims tended to ignore the historical context and
thus the originality of Quetelet's own analysis of crime. The effect of
the first claim was to characterize Quetelet's intervention in criminol-

ogy merely as pre-Lombrosian. The effect of the second claim was to make Quetelet's importance hinge on the success of the ecological movement that matured in Chicago in the 1930s, and of which, in fact, Guerry—rather than Quetelet—was usually identified as the precursor.[10] Both claims, therefore, tended to render Quetelet's specific analysis of crime invisible or, at best, derivative.

My intention in this second chapter, therefore, is chiefly to identify Quetelet's own particular contribution to the rise of positivist criminology. This I do by means of: (1) an outline of the historical context of the genesis of Quetelet's oeuvre, namely, the conjunction of the apparent failure of French penal strategies and the expansion in the scope of the statistical movement to include empirical social research; (2) a summary of Quetelet's method of inquiry and of the structure and content of his criminology; and (3) an indication of the controversial reception of his writings.

The Failure of the "Classical" Project

The emergence of positivist criminology should initially be understood as an important effect of the transformation in penal strategies that occurred in France, rapidly in some spheres and gradually in others, between the middle of the eighteenth and the beginning of the nineteenth centuries. On the far side of this transformation there were the amorphous penal strategies of the *ancien régime*. As we saw in the previous chapter, these strategies were officially dictated by a discourse couched in the rhetoric of the free legal subject, the transgressions of whom were rewarded with the infliction of brutal physical punishment.

The spectrum of the new penal strategies had at its center a network of carceral institutions inscribed with Enlightenment rationalism and the humanism of the *philosophes*. These institutions were devised as mechanisms of surveillance of comparable worth and were intended to act with the same monotonous precision on their individual subjects as the school, the barracks, and the monastery. In the Napoleonic era these strategies operated in concert with a new criminal code (with additional categories of delinquency), a professional gendarmerie, a system of passports and identity cards, and an extensive network of paid informers and spies directed by the notorious minister of police, Fouché.[11] Their growing inventory included hospitals, leprosariums, asylums, workhouses (*dépôts de mendicité*), reformatories, houses of correction, and prisons.[12] Their "delinquent" and "pathological" inmates comprised syphilitics, alcoholics, idiots, eccentrics, vagabonds, immigrants, libertines, prostitutes, and petty and professional criminals; their stated objective was moral rehabilitation through the deprivation of liberty. This project has been variously described as "the power of normalization," "the fabrication of a reliable person," and "the sequestration of unreason."[13]

Foucault has proposed, in uncharacteristic passages redolent of crude instrumentalism, that positivist criminology (of which Quetelet and Guerry were to be the leading figures) emerged in France in the 1820s as a calculated response to the need for an official and comprehensive discourse which could justify these new strategies of penality.[14] But this view assumes, a priori, an identity (or at least a complementarity) between the intentions of those, like Quetelet, who constructed this discourse and the conscious objectives of French penal policy. Even if ultimately true, such an assumption does little to illuminate for us either the specific content of such a discourse or the theoretical and conceptual maneuvers that were to characterize this period of its adolescence. While it emerged from the state and as a state practice, positivist criminology was not an unmediated expression of state or class interests.

Against Foucault, it can be said that positivist criminology really emerged from the intersection of two hitherto unrelated domains of state activity. From the domain of penality, criminology garnered an institutional position, a measure of financial support and considerable popular interest in its pronouncements. From the domain of the statistical movement, criminology acquired its intellectual orientation and recognition by the scientific community of its major discursive techniques. The many sites of each of these two domains were almost entirely separate until, during the Bourbon Restoration (1814–30), they coincided in a common issue—the apparent failure to normalize the conduct of the "dangerous classes."[15]

That the new penal strategies had significantly failed to normalize the conduct of the dangerous classes was apparent in three ways. First, it was implicit in the very existence of a large group of poor, semi-proletarian thieves (*les misérables*)—a separate nation within the French nation—whose continued presence among them represented a fearful affront to the sensibilities of the law-abiding citizenry. Frégier estimated that robbery was the sole means of support for at least 30,000 Parisians;[16] Balzac, who in his *Code pénal des honnêtes gens* was of the opinion that life is a perpetual struggle between the rich and the poor, recorded that there were 20,000 professional criminals and as many as 120,000 "rogues" in Restoration Paris.[17] To a certain extent the social visibility of the dangerous classes was an intractable effect of the new demographic composition of Restoration France. This was most obvious in urban areas such as Paris. Despite a doubling of its population in the half-century after 1800, Paris remained structurally intact. It is not difficult to imagine how quickly this immense population increase, in so relatively short a period, led to a far-reaching social deterioration, which was manifest in the incidence of infant mortality, sanitation and sewage, housing, food supplies, employment, public order, and crime. According to Chevalier, the sudden change in the population of Paris was such that the city's inability to adapt itself to its new composition relegated a large part of the working class "to the furthest confines of the economy, of society and almost of existence itself, in material, moral and, basically, biological circumstances conducive to crime, of which crime itself was a possible consequence."[18]

The new prominence of crime in the description of urban life in France can be attributed to the fear of the criminality of the so-called dangerous classes that endured, at all levels of French society, throughout the nineteenth century. Chevalier depicts Restoration Paris as a city in which the citizenry was engrossed in reports of crime as one of their normal daily worries; in certain winters of cold and destitution the fear of crime reached heights of panic and terror. Reports of crime were ubiquitously conveyed in newspapers and eagerly devoured by their readers; in some cases, such as in the sensational accounts of the police informer (and ex-thief) Vidocq and the poet-bandit Lacenaire, fear was transformed into morbid fascination. Occasionally, popular literature even celebrated those such as Cartouche and Mandrin who dared to defy the law.[19] Hugo's *Les Misérables* was a brilliant and typical literary example of the fearful attitude toward crime in general; other authors, like Balzac, portrayed the fear of specific forms of crime, such as theft by domestic servants. Popular melodramas about crime were regularly staged in the Boulevard du Temple. This widespread fear of crime was itself exacerbated by working-class insurrections. Between 1815 and1840 a real structural overlap existed between the dangerous class and the French working class, when there was no right to unionize and strikers were sent to prison. Michelle Perrot provides a glimpse of the class solidarity that derived from this overlap by recording that "in 1825, on the occasion of a union league meeting at Toulon, the workers laughed as they were marched off to prison and . . . there was constant communication between the prison and the town."[20] Indeed, as Robert Tombs has recorded, it quickly became an unquestioned tenet of middle-class thought that crime and revolution were symptoms of the same disease; this assumption, in turn, led to extreme harshness on the part of juries—whose composition in the nineteenth century was thoroughly bourgeois in origin—toward those accused of ordinary property crimes.[21]

In the public concern with crime the centrality of the dangerous classes was fixed by two further facts. First, in 1815 and for several years thereafter, a sudden increase was recorded in the rate of felony offences. This increase occurred primarily in the areas of theft and disturbances of public order;[22] between 1813 and 1820 alone the number of convictions in the criminal tribunals nearly doubled. In part, these recorded increases in crime can be explained by the turbulent transition to peace after Napoleon's final military defeat in 1815.[23] A second and even more decisive factor was the increasing rates of recidivism; these implied that the stated rehabilitative object of the carceral institutions had failed. It is difficult to know what degree of accuracy should be attributed to the figures of recidivism before 1835, but the publicity of them was rampant and they generated much indignation. Indeed, about the recidivism rate in the mid-1820s, the statistical organ of the Ministry of Justice later stressed that "[it was] without contradiction the most important part of the *Compte* because it reveals the inefficacy of repression and the inadequacy of punishment."[24] According to other contemporary accounts, the extent of recidivism between 1828 and 1834 ranged from 21 to 33 percent of those convicted of crimes during this time.[25] Before 1831, 38 percent of those who left the *maisons centrales* were convicted again, as were 33 percent of those sentenced to convict ships.[26] During the July Monarchy (1830–48), the recidivism rates were as high as 45 percent.[27]

That the carceral institutions had failed to normalize the dangerous classes was therefore confirmed, at least for a fearful and fascinated public, by the rising rates of crime and recidivism during the first years of the Restoration. This failure was an essential condition for the appearance of a vast corpus of studies, instigated by both state bureaux and private researchers, which sought to uncover the vital statistics of the dangerous classes.

The Statistical Movement and the *Compte Général*

> Statistics are the budget of things, and without a budget there is no salvation!
>
> —Napoleon Bonaparte

> There is a budget that has to be paid with frightening regularity: prisons, prison hulks, and the scaffold.
>
> —Quetelet

The failure of the carceral institutions to normalize the dangerous classes was an essential condition for the application of the techniques of the statistical movement to crime and penality. Important social events in the lives of the citizenry, such as baptisms, marriages, and deaths, had been recorded in the registers of parish churches in France since the sixteenth century. However, it was not until the middle of the eighteenth century that a variety of demographic and, especially, financial records were constructed as an aid to the pursuit of state policy.[28]

These records provided information, *inter alia,* for the planning of military expenditures, poor relief, and taxation. "As the state penetrated more deeply into traditional society to bring individuals within the direct purview of public authority as citizens," writes Keith Baker, "so it also felt the impulse to quantify them." [29]

The expansion in state control of the citizenry was not without cost. Before the Bourbon Restoration (1814–30), for example, the nascent statistical movement had been discredited because of its use as a naked instrument of political surveillance, especially between the Reign of Terror in 1793 and the end of the Empire in 1815. According to Chevalier, the census and similar state projects were commonly regarded as thinly veiled attempts by the police to identify suspects; the very announcement of a census unleashed a wave of denunciations, and the frequent reports by citizens tended to turn it into an inquisition. [30] During this time Paris became the "land of the documented city" and France the "gendarme state"; organized by Fouché, the notorious minister of police, convicted criminals were used by the police as spies and informers, and a nationwide system of surveillance was instituted that included hotel registers, passports, and identity cards. [31] After 1804 Napoleon "became more suspicious as he became more powerful, received domestic intelligence from many sources, and received, six nights a week, secret bulletins about innumerable items: desertions from the army, results of interrogations, news of crime, offenses by soldiers, fires, rebellion against the gendarmerie, agitation against the draft, suicides, prison epidemics, persons detained or under special surveillance." [32]

With the advent of a more relaxed atmosphere at the Restoration, in 1814, both the institutional and the technical aspects of the statistical movement began to flourish—as also did renewed interest in prison reform. Among the vital conditions of the population subject to regular state scrutiny were mortality, age, occupation, disease, and indigence. At the suggestion of the *administration préfectorale* of the Seine, supported by the Ministry of the Interior and administered by Fourier, the dissemination of these data was institutionalized in 1821 in the *Recherches statistiques de la ville de Paris.* [33] Although it had for a long time been understood that the exposure and surveillance of criminals could be served by enumeration, it was not until this precise juncture that the application of numerical analysis to penality achieved the status of an acceptable science whose object was the structured order of observable facts: "Facts, based upon direct observation and preferably expressed numerically, would decide all questions."[34]

Statistical inquiry into the dangerous classes began with the circumscribed population of subjects in the prisons.[35] Several quasi-governmental, philanthropic, and religious organizations began to investigate prison conditions with the intention of rejuvenating the moral health of the prisoners. In 1819, for example, the *Société royale pour l'amélioration des prisons* reported on such items as the quality of prison construction, diet, clothing, bedding, and infirmaries. The factual information provided by these organizations was supplemented by the inquiries of independent investigators from the movement in "public health" (*hygiène publique*), the leading figures of which included Benoiston de Châteauneuf, Parent-Duchâtelet and Villermé. By way of illustration, in 1820 Villermé's *Des prisons* pointed to the statistical links among gruesome prison conditions, moral degradation, and recidivism. In other words, incarceration itself was now thought to exacerbate the size of that section of the dangerous classes that was continually shuttled between civil society and prison.

In most of the inquiries into prison conditions, one question was invariably present: "Should (or could) the prisoners be returned to society and, if so, how?"[36] The resolution of this question could not be obtained, it was soon realized, with information derived exclusively from the facts about prison conditions. From a narrow focus on the prison population, then, the inquiry soon broadened to consider the larger population which passed through successive layers of the administration of justice. Within this broader inquiry the most important development occurred in 1825, the year that the Ministry of Justice initiated the first national statistical tables on crime, the annual *Compte général de l'administration de la justice criminelle en France*. The *Compte* was first published in 1827 under the efficient direction of two functionaries in the Ministry of Justice, Jacques Guerry de Champneuf (the director of Affaires criminelles from 1824 to 1830) and Jean Arondeau (responsible for the collection of judicial statistics).[37] Their publication immediately followed a winter in which the rates of crime and death increased in parallel and during which public fear and terror throughout Paris were the main themes of police reports and of newspaper articles.[38]

The *Compte* was drawn up from quarterly returns prepared by public prosecutors in every *département*. These were itemized on uniform printed forms and were checked for accuracy by the chief administrator of criminal prosecutors in Paris. The tables in the *Compte* were divided into four parts: the first included all prosecutions in the assize courts; the second, the verdicts of correctional tribunals; the third, the verdicts of the tribunals of the police courts; and the fourth, statistical information about the criminal process from other jurisdictions such as the royal courts. For each *département,* the *Compte* measured the annual number of known and prosecuted crimes against persons and property, whether the accused (if prosecuted) were acquitted or convicted, as well as the punishment accorded the latter. Additionally, it began to record the time of year at which these offenses were committed and the age, sex, occupation, and educational status of both accused and convicted. After 1828 the *Compte* recorded whether defendants were natives of the *département* in which they were arrested and, after 1830, whether they lived in urban or rural areas. Information about repeat offenders became more and more detailed with each successive year of publication, and new tables were constantly added on the correlations between the nature of the offences and the characteristics of the accused.[39]

The invention of the *Compte* was decisive in the development of positivist criminology. Both the Ministry of Justice and a group of "moral" or "social" statisticians believed that the factual data in the tables of the *Compte* could one day be used to perfect legislation in civil and moral matters.[40] In his introduction to the first volume of the *Compte* the minister of justice, Comte de Peyronnet, declared, "The exact knowledge of facts is one of the first needs of our form of government; it enlightens deliberations; it simplifies them; it gives them a solid foundation by substituting the positive vision and reliability of experience for the vagueness of theories."[41] About the *Compte,* Guerry wrote:

Never, in any nation, has a work of this kind been carried out in such a thorough manner. We owe it to M. Guerry de Champneuf, former Director of Criminal Affairs and Pardons, who has been constantly perfecting his work for the last five years. It is from there that we have drawn our information about all that relates to crime.[42]

The dissemination of the *Compte* was quickly followed by the labors of a somewhat amateur, loosely knit movement of moral statisticians which included the Parisian lawyer and social cartographer Guerry; the statisticians Louis René Villermé (1782–1863), Adolphe d'Angeville (1796–1856) and François d'Ivernois (1757–1842); the Italian geographer Adriano Balbi (1782–1848), an exile living in Paris; and the young Belgian astronomer Adolphe Quetelet. We now turn to Quetelet's immersion in the statistical movement and especially to his interpretation of the data in the *Compte*.

Quetelet's Social Mechanics of Crime

At the age of twenty-three, Lambert Adolphe Jacques Quetelet received a doctorate in science from the new University of Ghent. His dissertation of 1819, produced under the guidance of Jean Garnier, a noted professor of astronomy and higher mathematics, was an important and widely acclaimed contribution to the theory of conic sections; one of Garnier's colleagues went so far as to compare Quetelet's discovery of a new curve with Pascal's discovery of a cycloid.[43] Later in the same year, Quetelet was appointed to a chair in mathematics at the Brussels Athenaeum. In quick succession, he was elected to and at once revived the moribund Royal Academy of Sciences in Brussels in 1820, served as editor, with Garnier, of the influential *Correspondance mathématique et physique,* and helped to create the liberal (and soon-to-be suppressed) *Société Belge pour la Propagation de l'instruction et de la morale*. Quetelet's *Traité populaire d'astronomie,* falsely rumoured to have been placed on the Index Prohibitorum, contributed to the spread throughout Europe of popular education in astronomy.

Social Mechanics and the "Average Man"

These early achievements of the young Quetelet in astronomy and mathematics served as intellectual preparation for his pioneering contribution to the new discourse of "social mechanics" (*mécanique sociale*). The opportunity for this accomplishment was provided by the Belgian Royal Academy which, in 1823, sent him to Paris to study astronomical apparatuses for the vague, and often postponed, purpose of erecting an observatory in Brussels. This was a difficult period for émigré Belgian intellectuals, marked by the effective submission of Belgium to French and Dutch rule and by the cultural dominance of the French intelligentsia. Quetelet's interest in social mechanics was probably intensified by the Belgian nationalist movement, but there is no compelling evidence that he was active either in Belgian or French politics.[44]

On Quetelet's own admission, it was during his months in Paris that he was first introduced, by the astronomers Alexis Bouvard and Alexander Humboldt, to a variety of developments in the statistical movement.[45] From the German administrative *statistik,* from the English political "state-istics" of John Graunt and Sir William Petty, and from Condorcet's *mathématique sociale*[46] and his probabilistic analyses of the decisions of representative assemblies,[47] Quetelet learned of the general potential for the application of enumeration to "social matter" (*matière sociale*). From Thomas Malthus's *Essay on Population,* from Villermé's *Des prisons,* from Joseph Fourier's statistical research on Paris and its environs in the early 1820s and, above all, from the work of his friend and mentor Laplace on "celestial mechanics" (*mécanique celeste*), the principles of probabilistic theory, and the method of least squares,[48] Quetelet learned how to apply algebra and geometry to demographic tables.[49]

On his return to Belgium from Paris in 1824, Quetelet engaged in a variety of projects. His first statistical work utilized Belgian birth and mortality tables as the basis for the construction of insurance rates.[50] Soon thereafter, he published studies on physics, astronomy, and mathematics, and furnished a commentary on Dutch demographic policies; then, with the Belgian statistician Eduard Smits, he submitted plans in Belgium for a national census and the collection of crime statistics.

In these early works Quetelet attempted to reveal that the same law-like, mechanical regularity that had been determined to exist in the mechanics of the heavens and in the world of nature also existed in the world of "social facts" (*faits sociaux*). He reasoned that "in following attentively the regular march of nature in the development of plants and animals we are compelled to believe in the analogue that the influence of laws should be extended to the human species."[51] Quetelet believed that the identification of such laws in the social world was dependent upon statistical calculation: "We can assess how perfected a science has become by how much or how little it is based on calculation."[52] This ambitious project Quetelet termed social mechanics (later, in 1835, social physics), and he identified not inexactitude in method but insufficiency of empirical data as the chief obstacle to its realization. Human forces were notoriously susceptible to the influence of "secular perturbations"; only a very large number of empirical observations could reduce the perturbing effect of variation in a particular datum and, thereby, disclose the aggregate nature of social regularities.[53]

At first, Quetelet sought these regularities in relatively uncomplicated data that were subject to predictable variation and that could be observed directly: mortality rates, the heights of 100,000 French army conscripts, and the chest measurements of 5,738 Scottish soldiers. From his observations Quetelet calculated the average weight and height of his subjects, cross-tabulated these with sex, age, occupation, and geographical region, and then submitted these correlations to the perturbational influence of such factors as "the difficulties, toils and privations experienced in infancy, youth and infirmity."[54] The average value of any given scale was thought by Quetelet to be more accurate the greater the number of empirical observations. In combination, these average values produced an image of a fictitious, statistically derived creature whom Quetelet termed the "average man" (*homme moyen*). "If the *average* man were ascertained for one nation, he would present the type of that nation. If he could be ascertained according to the mass of men, he would present the type of the human species

altogether."[55] The average man therefore occupied a place among all
men that Quetelet envisaged as analogous to the center of gravity in
matter. His calculation of physical averages was undertaken as preparation for the extension of social mechanics to the vital phenomena of
"moral statistics," namely, to suicide, to marriage, and to crime.[56]

Quetelet's initial interest in crime was sporadic and somewhat
crude.[57] In 1827, in the course of a lengthy essay on moral statistics, he
constructed an "index of severity" (*indice de la sévérité*) which attempted to show the severity with which crimes and misdemeanors are
punished.[58] Toward this end he displayed in tabular form the average
prison sentences awarded for twenty crimes in Belgium in 1821, perhaps thinking thereby that this might provide the basis for an index of
criminality. His first statistical analysis of criminal behavior, and the
first time that he used the *Compte,* occurred in an address to the Royal
Academy of Brussels, delivered on 6 December 1828.[59] In this address
Quetelet used the *Compte* for 1825–27 to identify the annual incidence
of several categories found at different stages of the criminal justice system; these categories, presented in tabular form, included the number
of those accused of crimes against property and crimes against persons, of those convicted and acquitted, the ratio of males to females
convicted of crimes, and the distribution of convictions by age. But he
made no explicit reference to the obvious constancy either in the three-
year figures for France or in the remarkable similarity in the number of
crimes committed in France, England and Belgium, cautiously reasoning that "to pronounce with assurance it is necessary to have a longer
series of observations."[60] However, in regard to his tabulated findings
about the propensities (*degrés du penchant*) for crime at different ages,
Quetelet wrote in a footnote:

> We do not know if a table similar to the one which we have
> presented here has already been constructed. But it would be
> desirable to have a similar one for the principal countries, in
> order to report whether they follow a march as regular as the
> tables of mortality. Some will perhaps accuse me of seeing
> things too materialistically, and of believing in a sort of fatal-
> ism; we will reply that although we believe in the good idea of
> the perfectability of the human species, we think nevertheless

that there must be an order to those things which, when they are reproduced with astonishing constancy, and always in the same way, do not change quickly and without cause. For the moment we are adopting the role of an observer. In the study of human affairs we rely on the same principles used to study other natural events.[61]

The Constancy of Crime

Quetelet claimed that the enumeration of the vital phenomena of moral statistics was more complex than the measurement of nonvital, physical items. Vital phenomena were more complex not only in their individual identities and therefore in their comparability but also, and more important, because they emanated from "certain forces which [man] has at his command from his free will.[62] Because human action is volitional behavior, Quetelet suggested that it is reasonable to suppose that the volume of crime would vary from one year to another as widely as human caprice. This would especially seem to be true of unpremeditated crimes—murders, for example, committed during a quarrel or without motive or in fortuitous circumstances. However, Quetelet immediately warned that to argue that the human species is not subject to laws "would be more offensive to the divinity than the very research which we intend to do."[63]

This metaphysical wager was first elaborated by Quetelet in a *mémoire* presented to the Royal Academy of Brussels in July 1831, *Research on the Propensity for Crime at Different Ages*. While being careful to point out that social mechanics can never pretend to discover laws that can be verified for isolated individuals, he stated that—when observed indirectly on a great scale through the prism of statistical artifacts such as the *Compte*—the phenomena of crime nevertheless resemble the patterned behavior of physical phenomena.[64] To Quetelet's contemporaries, as we will see, this insight was to cause considerable discomfort. Indeed, Quetelet himself warned that

this way of looking at the social system has something positive about it which must, at first, frighten certain minds. Some will see in it a tendency to materialism. Others, in

interpreting my ideas badly, will find there an exaggerated pre-
tention to aggrandize the domain of the exact sciences and to
place the geometrician in an element which is not his own.
They will reproach me for becoming involved in absurd speculations while being occupied with things which are not susceptible to being measured.[65]

Quetelet's understanding of the limitations of the data in the
Compte reveals considerable sophistication for his era, although he was
following a path already trodden in Alphonse de Candolle's short
treatise on criminal statistics of 1830.[66] Quetelet argued that any scientific analysis of crime must assume *"a relationship pretty nearly invariable between offenses known and judged and the unknown sum total of
offenses committed."*[67] The size of this relationship, he suggested, would
depend on the seriousness of offences and on "the activity of justice in
reaching the guilty, on the care which these latter will take in hiding
themselves, and on the repugnance which wronged individuals will
feel in complaining, or on the ignorance in which they perhaps will be
concerning the wrong which has been done to them."[68] Quetelet argued that, if the causes that influence this relationship remain the
same, then their effects—or their representation in official statistics—
would remain constant; in a later study in Belgium, Quetelet found a
constant relationship between crimes known and crimes subject to judicial prosecution between 1833 and 1839.[69] That the ratio of unknown crimes to recorded crimes was, in practice, constant Quetelet
inferred from the astonishing regularity in the crime rates between
1826 and 1829 (Table 3–1).

In addition to the constancy in the annual number of accused and
convicted and in the ratios of accused to convicted, of accused to inhabitants, and of crime against persons to crimes against property,
Quetelet also points to regularities in the number of accused who
failed to appear in the tribunals, in the number of convictions in different types of tribunal, and in the number of convicts sentenced to
death, to confinement, or to forced labor for a term. Even the different
methods of murder were shown to be constant from one year to another. He therefore concludes that

Table 3–1. The Constancy of Crime, 1826–1829

Year	Accused (Tried)	Convicted	Inhabitants for One Accused	Convicted From 100 Accused	Accused of Crimes		Relationship Between the N of Types of Accused
					Against Persons	*Against Property*	
1826	6,988	4,348	4,557	62	1,907	5,081	2.7
1827	6,929	4,236	4,593	61	1,911	5,018	2.6
1828	7,396	4,551	4,307	61	1,844	5,552	3.0
1829	7,373	4,475	4,321	61	1,791	5,582	3.1
Totals	28,686	17,610	4,463	61	7,453	21,233	2.8

Adapted from Adolphe Quetelet (1831b), *Research on the Propensity for Crime at Different Ages*, p. 20.

one passes from one year to the other with the sad perspective of seeing the same crimes reproduced in the same order and bringing with them the same penalties in the same proportions. Sad condition of the human species! The share of prisons, chains, and the scaffold appears fixed with as much probability as the revenues of the state. We are able to enumerate in advance how many individuals will stain their hands with the blood of their fellow creatures, how many will be forgers, how many poisoners, pretty nearly as one can enumerate in advance the births and deaths which must take place.[70]

Criminal Propensities and the Causes of Crime

The apparent constancy of crime rates recorded in the *Compte* suggested to Quetelet that, whatever the idiosyncrasies of human agency, criminal behavior obeyed laws of the same order as those that regulate the motion of inanimate objects. He argued that there exists in all persons some possibility that they will develop an antipathy toward the law and indulge in some reprehensible and punishable act. For some persons this possibility approaches nil but for others it approaches a certainty, as Quetelet illustrated from his book *Physique sociale* (Figure 3–1). "At *point o*," Quetelet reasoned,

> the probability of crime is completely nothing. The probability increases as we move away from *point o* toward the right and it becomes a certainty at *point i*. The curved line *oai*, by the extent of its deviations from the straight line *oi*, shows the number of persons corresponding to each degree of probability. Thus, the greatest number, represented by the axis *ab*, has the probability *ob* of committing a crime.[71]

Quetelet was careful to assert that his concept of "the degree of possibility of crime" does not mean that the likelihood of any given person committing a crime remains constant. At any given moment an individual's propensity (*penchant*) to commit crime depends on "his

Figure 3–1.

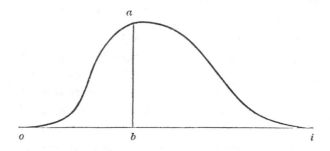

The Probability of Crime and the Number of Criminals
From Adolphe Quetelet (1869), *Physique sociale* p. 333.

constitution, his upbringing, and upon the efforts he has been able to make to better himself."[72] In this regard, the disproportionate and relentless presence of certain categories in the *Compte* between 1826 and 1829 indicated to Quetelet that young males, the poor, the less educated, and those without employment or in lowly occupations had a greater propensity than others to commit crimes and to be convicted of them.[73]

The data in the *Compte* seemed to enable Quetelet to take issue with several conventional accounts of the factors that precipitated crime. In particular, he adduced that neither the presence of poverty nor the absence of formal education warranted the monolithic causal importance commonly claimed for them. Against those who asserted the inevitable association of poverty with crime, Quetelet countered that some of the poorest areas in France (e.g., Creuse) and in the Low Countries (e.g., Luxembourg) had among the lowest crime rates; both areas also had among the highest rates of illiteracy.[74] Far more influential a factor than absolute poverty was the perturbing effect of inequality in wealth. Where great riches are amassed by a few, when an economy suddenly fluctuates, and when thousands of individuals pass rapidly from well-being to misery,

> these are the rough alternations from one state to another that
> give birth to crime, especially if those who suffer from them
> are surrounded by subjects of temptation and find themselves

irritated by the continual view of luxury and of an inequality
of fortune which disheartens them.[75]

Moreover, against those who argued that the growth of public education weakened criminal propensities, Quetelet disclosed that those
with higher "intellectual states" tended to commit crimes of a relatively more violent nature, such as rape and murder. It was thus an error to suppose that a country would have fewer crimes simply because
more children are sent to school there or because more of the population is literate; the departments with the lowest literacy rates, for example, tended to have only average crime rates. However, to those
who inferred from this that public education was potentially harmful
to society, Quetelet pointed out that, among the educated, the most
educated did not commit relatively more crimes. It was not, therefore,
education as such that altered the propensity to crime but the type of
education and the presence or absence of "moral instruction."[76]

For Quetelelet the data in the *Compte* implied that the two factors
most prominently associated with criminal propensities were age and
sex. As Table 3–2 shows, he tabulated crimes according to the ages of
their perpetrators and divided the number of crimes by the population
in the respective age groups. Results show the propensity for committing crime at various ages. This propensity is at its weakest at both
extremes of life—in infancy neither strength nor passion ("those two
powerful instruments of crime") are at all developed, and in old age
their intensity is restricted by the "dictates of reason." The propensity
for crime is at its highest between the ages of 21 and 25—when
strength and passions are most intense, and when reason is insuffi-
ciently developed to restrain their combined influence. Quetelet per-
ceives a cyclical pattern in his age-specific "steps in the career of
crime" between infancy and old age: physical immaturity allows only
for crimes such as indecent assault and rape in which the victim offers
little resistance; the age of dispassionate reflection seeks more "organized" crimes such as thefts on the public highways, murder by poisoning, and acts of rebellion; finally, using the little strength that nature
has left him, the elderly criminal uses a depraved treachery "to strike
his enemy in the shadow" through crimes such as forgery and child
molestation.

Table 3–2. Age and the Propensity for Crime, 1826–1829

Age	Crimes against Persons	Crimes against Property	Crimes against Property out of 100 Crimes	Population according to Ages	Degrees of the Propensity for Crime
Under 16	80	440	85	3,304	161
16–21	904	3,723	80	887	5,217
21–25	1,278	3,329	72	673	6,846
25–30	1,575	3,702	70	791	6,671
30–35	1,153	2,883	71	732	5,514
35–40	650	2,076	76	672	4,057
40–45	575	1,724	75	612	3,757
45–50	445	1,275	74	549	3,133
50–55	288	811	74	482	2,280
55–60	168	500	75	410	1,629
60–65	157	385	71	330	1,642
65–70	91	184	70	247	1,113
70–80	64	137	68	255	788
80 and over	5	14	74	55	345

Adapted from Adolphe Quetelet (1831b), *Research on the Propensity for Crime at Different Ages*, p. 56.

Table 3–3. Sex and the Propensity for Crime, 1826–1829

Year	Crimes Against Persons			Crimes Against Property		
	Men	Women	Relationship	Men	Women	Relationship
1826	1,639	268	.16	4,073	1,008	.25
1827	1,637	274	.17	4,020	998	.25
1828	1,576	270	.17	4,396	1,156	.26
1829	1,552	239	.15	4,379	1,203	.27
Average	1,601	263	.16	4,217	1,091	.26

From Adolphe Quetelet (1831b), *Research on the Propensity for Crime at Different Ages,* p. 47.

Quetelet noted that between 1826 and 1829 there were twenty-three women for every hundred men who appeared before criminal tribunals (Table 3–3). He suggests that one could therefore suppose that male criminal propensities were roughly four times greater than those of women. But these propensities do not inform us, Quetelet warns, about the differing seriousness of the crimes committed by each sex. Quetelet therefore notes that the ratio of women to men accused of property crimes was 26:100 but, for crimes against persons, it was only 16:100. Assuming the latter to be more serious than crimes against property, Quetelet concludes that French men were at least four times more "criminal" than French women. In trying to explain the difference in criminality between French men and French women, he argued that the commission of any crime requires the coincidence of a will (which depends on morality), an opportunity and the ability to act. The "will" of women Quetelet posited as more motivated than that of men by the sentiments of shame and modesty. Such an understanding of will would explain not only women's lower propensity for crime in general but also their higher indulgence in infanticide. "As to infanticide, not only does a women have more opportunities to commit it than a man, but she is in some ways often pushed into it by hardship and almost always by the desire to hide a mistake and escape the shame and contempt of society, which spares the man more in similar circumstances."[77] Moreover, women have less opportunity than men to commit crime because they lead more retiring, less passionate lives and are less often excited by alcohol; their lesser ability to act derives from their lesser strength in comparison with that of men and is reflected, for example, in their differential rate of parricide.[78]

In his first studies of crime, Quetelet was reluctant to draw specific causal inferences from the regularities manifest in the *Compte*. This was so, he lamented, because "the causes which influence crime are so enormous and so diverse, that it becomes almost impossible to assign to each its degree of importance.[79] But rather than adopt the unconscionable course of abandoning the search for causality altogether, Quetelet instead adopted a solution which, theoretically, allowed the insertion of an infinitude of possible causes. Thus, "the laws presiding over the development of man, and modifying his actions, are . . . the result of his organization, of his education and knowledge, means of wealth, institutions, local influences, and an endless variety of other causes."[80] Against those who employed hopelessly eclectic notions of causality, Quetelet suggested that the many causes of crime can be divided into three principal categories. First, there are accidental causes to which no probability can be assigned and which are manifested fortuitously and are indifferent as to their direction. Examples of these include wars, famines, and natural disasters. Their influence Quetelet understands within a teleological schema, and is confined to "the order of succession of events." Second, there are variable causes, such as free will and personality, which can oscillate within greater or smaller limits. These causes act in a continuous manner, although some variable causes such as climate and the seasons operate only periodically. The intensity and direction of variable causes change either as a result of determined laws or of the latter's absence. Finally, there are constant causes, such as age, sex, occupation, and religion. These causes have a fixed probability and act in a continuous manner with the same intensity and in the same direction; evidence for the predominance of this third causal category was adduced by Quetelet from the constancy of crime rates.[81]

Quetelet's insertion of criminal behavior into a formal structure of causality was a remarkable advance over the ad hoc and eclectic speculations of his contemporaries. Even more significant, within this formal structure, is the shift of his analysis to a different level, which allows him to claim that because crime is a constant, inevitable feature of social organization it was "society," "France," or the "nation" itself that caused crime. Thus, "Every social state presupposes, then, a certain number and a certain order of crimes, these being merely the necessary consequences of its organization.[82] Again, "The crimes which are annually committed seem to be a necessary result of our social organization . . . *society prepares crime, and the guilty are only the instruments by which it is executed*."[83] Logic aside and with the considerable advantages of hindsight, it can perhaps be argued that Quetelet's intuition that "society" caused crime marked a profound theoretical departure from the crude realism lodged in public opinion, in classical jurisprudence and in the criminal code, and flew in the face of the notion that criminals freely choose to engage in wickedness. But because Quetelet never developed his concept of the "social," his employment of the concept of social organization was based on the notion of society as an aggregate of individuals. His projections about the causal nexus between social organization and crime, therefore, and of the way in which propensities to crime are translated into criminal actions, remained thoroughly conventional—displacements in moral values, for example, somehow contributing to a relaxation in such qualities as moderation and thrift.[84]

To understand this aspect of Quetelet's work, we must return to his notion of the average man and to the way in which, especially during the 1840s, this concept infiltrated his discourse on criminality.

The "Average Man" and Social Regulation

In his work of the 1820s and early 1830s, as we have seen, Quetelet determined the average values of the human physique and correlated these with such variables as age and sex, with the result being a description of the bodily characteristics of the average man in a given population. In the early 1840s, especially after he became acquainted with the probabilistic error function in celestial mechanics, Quetelet insisted on the need to present not only the mean of a scale of given characteristics but also the upper and lower limits between which individuals oscillated. Minor or "natural" variation around the mean was then identified by Quetelet as deviation that should attract no unusual attention; extraordinary variation (e.g., the height of giants and dwarfs) he saw as "preternatural . . . monstrous."[85] In addition, Quetelet perceived that variation around the mean occurred not randomly but in a determinate order that approximated the principle of the normal distribution in celestial mechanics.[86] This principle, he now surmised, was also applicable to the distribution of all the non-physical qualities of man.

Quetelet's application of the principle of the normal distribution to crime presaged a fundamental redirection of his criminology and led directly to his erection of a rigid binary opposition between the statistical mean and "unusual" deviation. Although he inferred from the normal distribution that "every man, therefore, has a certain propensity to break the laws,"[87] it was also evident to him that the criminal propensities of the average man were rarely, if ever, translated into criminal actions. Accordingly, the dispositions of individuals with propensities at the mean were now imbued by Quetelet with the rhetoric of their conformity to law, physical and psychological health, and moral temperance. Quetelet's interpretation of the Aristotelian *differentia* of virtue in the *Nicomachean Ethics,* and of Victor Cousin's *juste milieu* in his *Cours de l'histoire de la philosophie* of 1829, persuaded him that the average man was one who regularly chose the mean course between the extremes of deficiency and excess. The virtues of the average man thus comprised "rational and temperate habits, more regulated passions . . . foresight, as manifested by investment in savings' banks, assurance societies and the different institutions which encourage foresight."[88]

Against the average man, who did not commit crimes, Quetelet frequently juxtaposed the criminality of vagabonds, vagrants, primitives, gypsies, the "inferior classes," certain races with "inferior moral stock," and "persons of low moral character." Against the virtues of the average man he juxtaposed the vices of those deviants who engaged in crime. This latter juxtaposition repeatedly infects his work of the 1840s and is found, for example, in his contrast between "an industrious and prudent people . . . [and] a depraved and indolent one."[89] The vices of

those who deviated from the average included "the passions for gam-
bling . . . failures . . . the frequenting of coffee-houses and low
haunts . . . drunkenness."[90]

During the 1840s, an abundance of quasi-medical metaphors appeared in Quetelet's writings, and he now openly resorted, even if in
rather a tentative fashion, to assigning to such factors as biological and
phrenological defects a causal role in the genesis of crime. In common
with a widespread emphasis on the biological basis of demographic and
social facts, Quetelet yielded to the notion that unhealthy morality was
manifest in biological defects and that those with such defects had high
criminal propensities.[91] Crime, he concluded, was "a pestilential
germ . . . contagious . . . (sometimes) hereditary";[92] elsewhere, he
immediately modified such a claim with the qualification that "these
tendencies develop themselves and are modified under the influences of
the milieu in which man finds himself."[93] In one of his final works, a
book of 1871 with the tantalizing title *Anthropométrie,* Quetelet explicitly juxtaposed crime rates and the proportions of the human body as
instances of complementary social facts. Both varied by age, sex, and
race, and obeyed the same law-like conditions. In this book Quetelet
places adjacent to each other his analysis of parts of the human body
with his analysis of crime. His analysis of the former concentrated especially on the human head (Figure 3–2). He also indicated that "the
head is the most expressive part of the human body; it is also to the
head that we especially turn in order to take the full measure of a
person."[94] Therein Quetelet reported that he had undertaken a variety
of anthropometric measurements, and he cited with approval the research on regularities of the human body, on pulsation, and of mental
illness undertaken by François Leuret and Jean-Etienne-Furmance Mitivié in France.[95] Some of Quetelet's measurements were popularized
five years later by none other than Lombroso himself.[96]

The practical outcome of Quetelet's criminology was the application of his binary opposition of normality and deviance to the domain
of penality. With an insistence that became more urgent with the approach of the 1848 revolution, Quetelet urged that governments identify the causes of crime in order to reduce or, if possible, eliminate the
frequency of crime. "Since the number (of crimes) cannot diminish

Figure 3–2.

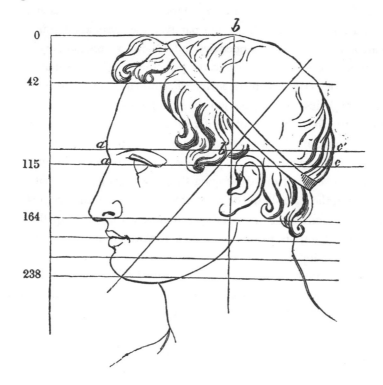

The Head, from Adolphe Quetelet (1871), *Anthropométrie*, p. 206.

without the causes which induce them undergoing previous modification, it is the province of legislators to ascertain these causes, and to remove them as far as possible."[97] Because it appeared on this theory that the same amount of crime was regularly produced by the same causes, Quetelet was optimistic that secular disturbances such as crime could be reduced simply by reducing the intensity of their causes. While legislators could not hope to prevent all crime there was, nevertheless, "an ensemble of laws, an enlightened administration and a social state (*état*) such that the number of crimes can be reduced as much as possible."[98]

According to Quetelet, because every government, like every physical body, is confronted by two types of force ("those that are attractive and those that are repulsive"), wise statecraft consists in the pursuit of two policies toward crime. First, the state should devise an appropriate reaction to combat and paralyze the recalcitrant minority with incorrigible criminal tendencies and, Quetelet suggested, this reaction should involve adherence to the principles of the criminal code, the constant detection and prosecution of criminals, a uniformity in the decisions of juries and judges, and the maintenance of an appropriate relation between the gravity of an offence and the punishment awarded it.[99] In addition, ameliorative reforms should be introduced so that "the elements of disorganization . . . those who provoke revolutions"[100] would be prevented from destroying the very basis of the social system. Second, the state should align itself with the inevitable progress of civilization by allowing the moral and intellectual qualities of the average man to flourish; to this end a government should enact and enforce laws to reduce the effect of secular disturbances and to encourage an equilibrium in the social system. The more do "deviations from the average disappear . . . the more, consequently, do we tend to approach that which is beautiful, that which is good."[101]

Quetelet and His Critics

According to the discursive standards of his era, Quetelet had demonstrated his mechanistic notions of the constancy of crime, its causes and its regulation, as well as it was then possible to do. His insistence that crime was an inevitable feature of social organization and, moreover, almost a necessary consequence of it, assured his texts a widespread notoriety. As Sarton has observed, no one could have carried scientific indiscretion further than by attempting, as did Quetelet, to analyze social transgressions as if they were physical accidents and to consider passions of the soul as if they were abnormalities of the weather.[102] Given public opinion, which identified the criminality of the "dangerous classes" with working-class failures and rebellion, Quetelet's notion that criminal propensities were distributed throughout the population was an affront to the moral sensibilities of the law-abiding citizenry. To a judiciary that couched legal responsibility and the application of punishment in the classical discourse of the free legal subject, Quetelet's notions about the causality of crime amounted to a deterministic heresy, for if crimes had social rather than individual causes, then perhaps criminals could not be held strictly accountable for their misdeeds.

In France Quetelet's criminology contributed to the growth of the empirical tradition represented by such important studies as Alexandre Parent-Duchâtelet's *De la Prostitution dans la ville de Paris* of 1836 and H.-A. Frégier's *Des classes dangereuses de la population dans les grandes villes* of 1840. The reception of his work outside Belgium and France was generally very favorable, especially in England. John Herschel, for example, reviewed the broad span of Quetelet's endeavors and argued strongly that, although Quetelet's social mechanics was evidence that statistical progress in the social sciences was less advanced than in the natural sciences, no one had better exerted himself in the scientific collection and analysis of political, social, and moral data. Quetelet's advice about how to repress "the violent and rapacious," Herschel continued, "deserved to be written in letters of gold."[103] Indeed, Quetelet's writings on crime continued to exert great influence on writings as diverse in content and as separated in time, as Henry Buckle's *History of Civilisation in England* and Charles Goring's celebrated *The English Convict*.[104]

However, in Quetelet's own lifetime the recognition of his criminology as such was largely preempted by controversy about the nature of his general contribution to statistical analysis. One facet of the controversy focused on the position that Quetelet was believed to have taken toward free will. In this debate there was no middle ground between the determinists and the spiritualists, between those who harnessed themselves to Quetelet's perceived social determinism and those who preferred to discern a faint promise of social equilibrium through individual moral improvement. To the spiritualists, determinism in any form represented an ungodly opposition to the soul, to Christianity and to free will.[105] To the determinists, spiritualism was a metaphysical doctrine with roots in the untenable philosophies of German romanticism and naturalism.[106] Moreover, it could not have escaped the attention of the spiritualists that the implicit determinism of *Sur l'homme* had a certain appeal in the 1840s to radical writers such as Marx and Engels, who saw in this book a demonstration of the fundamental links among modern bourgeois society, immiseration, and the amount and sorts of crime. Besides the writings of Quetelet and of those such as Marx and Engels, it was only in the workers' newspapers, such as *L'Humanitaire, La Fraternité* and *Almanach populaire de la France* that individualist descriptions of criminality were challenged by an alternative analysis which sought the origins of crime in the inegalitarian structure of society itself. Thus, *L'Humanitaire* of August 1841 decreed that "The man who kills you is not free not to kill you. It is society, or to be more precise, bad social organization that is responsible."[107]

Quetelet himself was clearly perplexed by the accusation that his moral statistics assumed human action to be totally devoid of choice and free will. Toward the end of *Research on the Propensity for Crime at Different Ages,* for example, he held out the following promise: "I am far from concluding . . . that man can do nothing for his amelioration. . . . He possesses a moral strength capable of modifying the laws which concern him."[108] The 1842 English translation of *Sur l'homme* contained a new preface in which Quetelet tried to defend himself against various charges of fatalism, atheism, and materialism. Moreover, at the beginning of this translation, he instructed the publisher to insert a notice to the effect that he was "no theorist or System-maker" and that he simply wished "to arrive at truth by the only legitimate way, namely, the examination of facts—the incontrovertible facts furnished by statistical data."[109] So sensitive was Quetelet to the charge that determinism necessarily embraced atheism that he frequently affirmed his belief in "the wise influence of divine power." In this way and in others, Quetelet consistently eschewed any explicit interpretation that others, for a wide variety of reasons, wished to foist on his facts.

In addition to the controversy surrounding Quetelet's position on free will, a second controversy stemmed from Quetelet's notion of the average man. To some theorists, this notion—which Quetelet implied was his pivotal concept[110]—was a source of acrimonious debate, scandal, and grief. Against Quetelet's belief that the statistical means of various physical traits could somehow be combined to form an average, paradigmatic human being, contemporary statisticians made three major objections. The first of these was made in 1843 by the rector of the Académie de Grenoble, the philosopher and mathematical economist Antoine-Augustin Cournot. Cournot argued that just as a right triangle cannot generally be formed from the average lengths of the three sides of many right triangles, so too the average man determined from the average physical measurements (of height, of feet, of strength, etc.,) of many men would simply be *"un homme impossible."*[111] Quetelet did not reply to this difficulty.

The attack against the average man was continued by Jacques Bertillon, professor of Demography at the *École d'Anthropologie,* who was a pioneer of statistical analysis of the rates of divorce, alcoholism, and suicide and who provided some of Durkheim's theoretical groundwork. Bertillon suggested that an average man, constructed from each of the human attributes, was not a scientific entity but an invention of the imagination. Far from being an ideal of human perfection, Quetelet's average man was the epitomy of mediocrity; he could only be a monster, a *type de la vulgarité.*[112] A third objection was made by Joseph Bertrand, who argued that Quetelet had defined human beings independently of particular persons considered at random. He reasoned that, because the average man must necessarily be average in all his attributes, therefore his features must simultaneously embody the averages of such antitheses as beauty and ugliness. The average man could therefore be neither ugly nor beautiful, neither foolish nor wise, neither virtuous nor criminal, neither strong nor weak, neither brave nor cowardly. Bertrand suggested, perhaps facetiously, that in the body of the average man Quetelet would place an average soul.[113]

To these three objections to Quetelet's notion of the average man a fourth should be added, namely, the objection provided by Emile Durkheim in *Suicide.* Having congratulated Quetelet for pointing to the existence of regularities in social phenomena, Durkheim went on to argue, however, that these cannot be explained by the concept of the average man. The description of social regularities, even if accurate and portrayed in great detail, does not explain them. In the particular case of suicide rates, Durkheim reasoned, this was so for two reasons.

Firstly, the fact that 15 out of 100,000 persons kill themselves each year "does not imply that the others are exposed in any degree."[114] Durkheim therefore reminds us that Quetelet's average man was constructed as the arithmetic mean of a quality that occurs in varying degrees in all individuals of a given type. But as with the vast majority of any given population that in practice has no propensity to suicide whatsoever, so also in Quetelet's terms could it be said that the average man does not kill himself. From this point on, Quetelet's notion of the average man, as a proper object of scientific inquiry, was not to be taken seriously.[115]

Quetelet never responded to specific criticisms of his work. Only at one point did he deign to recognize, and then unsuccessfully to dismiss, three charges directed against the broad enterprise of moral statistics: (1) the causes of social facts can never properly be observed because they are too numerous and too variable in their influence; (2) moral facts, unlike other statistical facts, are not comparable and one cannot therefore deduce an average from their aggregate; and (3) the study of moral facts must always be incomplete because one can never know everything about the actions—good or bad—of man. Quetelet's response to these difficulties was that, by recognizing their partial truth, he thereby delivered his own work from the criticism implied by these charges.[116]

Although his presociological discourse was soon to be transcended in fundamental ways by Marx and Weber and, especially, by Durkheim, it is perhaps fair to say that Quetelet and the Franco-Belgian school provided the positivist core for the dominance of a deterministic criminology subsequently manifest in the labors of Lombroso, Goring and Bonger, who emphasized, respectively, biologism, mental hereditarianism, and economism. Moreover, by identifying the existence of law-like regularities in recorded criminal behavior, by suggesting that crime was subject to causal laws of the order found in the natural sciences, and by implying that criminal behavior was as much a product of society as of volition—in all these ways Quetelet also opened up the possibility of a sociological analysis of crime. This great achievement was recognized by Durkheim and Paul Fauconnet when they traced to Quetelet the emergence of an autonomous sociology resolutely opposed to methodological individualism:

social phenomena could no longer be deemed the product of fortuitous combinations, arbitrary acts of the will, or local and chance circumstances. Their generality attests to their essential dependence on general causes which, everywhere that they are present, produce their effects. . . . Where for a long time there has been perceived only isolated actions, lacking any links, there was found to be a system of definite laws. This was already expressed in the title of the book in which Quetelet expounded the basic principles of the statistics of morality.[117]

Notes

1. Marx (1853), "Capital Punishment," p. 229. See also Colajanni (1884), *Il Socialismo: Socialismo e Sociologia Criminale,* pp. 13–14; and Lafargue (1890), "Die Kriminalität in Frankreich von 1840–1886", p. 12.

2. Durkheim, (1897), *Suicide: a Study in Sociology,* p. 300. Jack Douglas (1967) in *The Social Meanings of Suicide* has even suggested that Durkheim's *Suicide* of 1897 differed only in degree from the principles, methodology, and empirical findings of the moral statisticians, and that Quetelet's *Sur l'homme* was "the most influential moral-statistical work of all" (p. 11); and see Giddens (1965), "The Suicide Problem in French Sociology," pp. 3–4. A three-part review of Quetelet's *Sur l'homme* in the *Athenaeum* of August 1835 (pp. 593–95, 611–13, 658–61) concluded, "We consider the appearance of these volumes as forming an epoch in the literary history of civilization." According to Stigler, "recent Darwin scholarship argued that Darwin's reading of this review and subsequently of Quetelet and Malthus played an important role in his development of the theory of natural selection" (1986), *The History of Statistics: The Measurement of Uncertainty before 1900,* p. 170, n. 12).

3. Sarton (1935), "Preface to Volume XXII of Isis (Quetelet)," pp. 4, 14.

4. These biographies include Mailly (1875), "Essai sur la vie et les ouvrages de L.A.J. Quetelet"; Hankins (1908), "Adolphe Quetelet as Statistician"; and Lottin (1912), *Quetelet: Statisticien et sociologue.*

5. The Modern Criminal Science Series included works by Enrico Ferri, Bernaldo de Quiros, Hans Gross, Cesare Lombroso, Gustav Aschaffenburg, Raymond Saleilles, Gabriel Tarde, Willem Bonger, and Raffaele Garofalo.

6. Taylor, Walton, and Young's celebrated *The New Criminology* (1973, p. 37), for example, refers briefly to Quetelet, but then only in terms of the unsubstantiated assertion that Quetelet and his colleague A. M. Guerry largely

effected the transition in penology from free will to determinism. Similarly, see Radzinowicz (1966), *Ideology and Crime,* pp. 29–37.

7. See, for example, Lindesmith and Levin (1937), "The Lombrosian Myth in Criminology," pp. 654–55; and Sellin (1937), "The Lombrosian Myth in Criminology—Letter to the Editor," pp. 897–99.

8. The intellectual maturation of Lombroso's concept of the born criminal has been charted in great detail in Wolfgang (1972), "Cesare Lombroso"; see also an excellent account of the "medicalization of deviance" implicit in this concept and also of the various oppositional currents to it, especially in France, given in Nye (1984), *Crime, Madness, and Politics in Modern France,* pp. 97–131.

9. For example, Elmer (1933), "Century-old ecological studies in France"; see also Morris, *The Criminal Area* (1957), at pp. 37–52.

10. See Shaw and McKay (1942), *Juvenile Delinquency and Urban Areas,* p. 5.

11. See Foucault (1979), *Discipline and Punish: The Birth of the Prison,* p. 280; and Stead (1983), *The Police of France,* pp. 47–48.

12. The modern prison system was inaugurated by imperial decree in 1810. Although the socioeconomic characteristics of the prison population were not collected in any systematic way until the 1870s, it is safe to assume that, until at least the 1850s, 80 percent of prisoners were young unmarried males from the skilled or unskilled working class; see O'Brien (1982), *The Promise of Punishment: Prisons in Nineteenth-Century France,* pp. 54–61. Excluding military prisons (*bagnes*) and debtors' prisons, the Restoration established at least five categories of prison, each based on a complex classification of inmates; see further ibid. pp. 3–51, and Petit (1984), "The Birth and Reform of Prisons in France." Strategically, the prisons isolated delinquents from the law-abiding citizenry; the development of agricultural colonies, transportation, and the galleys carried this strategy to its logical extreme.

13. See, respectively, Foucault (1979), op. cit., p. 308; Treiber and Steinert (1980), *Die Fabrikation des zuverlässigen Menschen;* and Doerner (1981), *Madmen and the Bourgeoisie; A Social History of Insanity and Psychiatry,* pp. 14–17.

14. Foucault (1980), *Power/Knowledge: Selected Interviews and Other Writings 1972–1977,* pp. 47–49.

15. *Classes dangereuses* was a term that first appeared during the Restoration, although it was not popularized until H.-A. Frégier's classic study of urban criminality, *Des classes dangereuses de la population dans les grandes villes, et des moyens de les rendre meilleurs* (1840). A good account of the stock moral categories on which the term was constructed and of the ways in which it was

often invoked to justify military repression is provided by Tombs (1980), "Crime and the Security of the State: The 'Dangerous Classes' and Insurrection in Nineteenth-Century Paris."

16. Frégier (1840), op. cit., p. 45; see also Chevalier (1973), *Laboring Classes and Dangerous Classes in Paris During the First Half of the Nineteenth Century*, p 448. Frégier's book was a wide-ranging documentary study of social conditions in Paris during the Restoration. Its speculative conceptual focus is the interpenetration of the "dangerous classes," the working class, and the poor and the combined threat that these posed to *l'homme moral*.

17. Balzac (1829), *Code pénal des honnêtes gens*, pp. 394–96. On Balzac see Guyon (1969), *La pensée politique et sociale de Balzac*, especially pp. 202–15.

18. Chevalier (1973), op. cit., p. 258.

19. See further Perrot (1978), "Delinquency and the Penitentiary System in Nineteenth-Century France," p. 238.

20. Ibid. p. 238.

21. Tombs (1980), op. cit., pp. 214, 95–96. See further Donovan (1981), "Justice Unblind: The Juries and the Criminal Classes in France, 1825–1914."

22. Wright (1983), *Between the Guillotine and Liberty: Two Centuries of the Crime Problem in France*, pp. 48–50; and Duesterberg (1979), "Criminology and the Social Order in Nineteenth-Century France," pp. 29–31.

23. During the 1820s, the *Compte général* recorded a decrease in the crime rate, the official record of which has been generally supported by methodological analyses. See, for example, Lodhi and Tilly (1973), "Urbanization, Crime, and Collective Violence in Nineteenth-Century France"; and Tilly, Tilly, and Tilly (1975), *The Rebellious Century: 1830–1930*. However, a more persuasive argument is that the declining official rate was deceptive because of the increasing tendency for prosecutors not to follow through on reports of crime and for property crimes to be tried in lower courts as misdemeanors; see Zehr (1976), *Crime and the Development of Modern Society*. Combining data from correctional and assize courts, Zehr reveals a significant increase in all indices of property crime, except for arson (pp. 34–43, 146, n. 11). These trends had earlier been identified and condemned by Gabriel Tarde (1886) in his book *La criminalité comparée*, pp. 61–121.

24. *Compte général de l'administration de la justice criminelle en France* (1882), p. 83.

25. An estimate that one in every three convicts (*condamnés*) was a recidivist is given in Guerry (1833), *Essai sur la statistique morale de la France*, p. 17.

26. See Foucault (1979), op. cit., p. 265; and Duesterberg (1979), op. cit., p. 89.

27. Wright (1983), op. cit., p. 50.

28. See Westergaard (1932), *Contributions to the History of Statistics;* and especially, Perrot and Woolf (1984), *State and Statistics in France 1789–1815,* pp. 92–103.

29. Baker (1975), *Condorcet: From Natural Philosophy to Social Mathematics,* p. 262. The word *statistique* was probably first employed in France in 1789, by Brion de la Tour, the author of a number of works on geography; see further Guerry (1864), *Statistique morale de l'Angleterre comparée avec la statistique morale de la France,* p. 1.

30. Chevalier (1973), op. cit., p. 49.

31. See further Foucault (1979), op. cit., p. 280.

32. Stead (1983), op. cit., pp. 47–48.

33. On the professional and institutional setbacks of the statistical movement prior to the Restoration, see Westergaard (1932), op. cit., pp. 114–16; and Perrot and Woolf (1984), op. cit. On the insulation of the statistical movement from mathematical theory until the Restoration, see Porter (1985), "The Mathematics of Society: Variation and Error in Quetelet's Statistics." On the "opening-up" of the statistical movement during the Restoration see Fauré (1918), "The Development and Progress of Statistics in France"; Chevalier (1973), op. cit., pp. 29–69; Chassagne (1981), "Les bureaux centraux: le personnel et les mécanismes administratifs"; Bargeton (1981), "Les personnels et les moyens locaux de la statistique"; and Porter (1985), op. cit.

34. Coleman (1982), *Death is a Social Disease,* p. 123.

35. See, for example, Bérenger (1818), *De la justice criminelle en France;* Danjou (1821), *Des prisons, de leur régime et des moyens de l'améliorer;* Taillandier (1824), *Réflexions sur les lois pénales de France et d'Angleterre;* and Lucas (1827), *Du système pénal et du système répressif en général, de la peine de mort en particulier.*

36. Petit (1984), op. cit., p. 137.

37. A brief prehistory of the *Compte* appears in Perrot (1976), "Premières mesures des faits sociaux: les débuts de la statistique criminelle en France (1780–1830)," pp. 125–28.

38. Chevalier (1973), op. cit., p. 3.

39. The various deposits into and the infrequent withdrawals from the *Compte* between 1827 and the 1880s are chronicled in Perrot (1978), op. cit., pp. 218–19.

40. In 1827 the *Compte* was distributed only to peers, to members of parliament, and to several powerful state functionaries. Its restricted availability led one reviewer in the *Revue encyclopédique* to demand that the royal government should sell a limited quantity of the *Compte* to satisfy the desires of en-

lightened men for its statistical contents: Taillandier (1827), "Review of *Compte général de l'administration de la justice criminelle en France, pendant l'année 1825*," p. 361.

41. *Compte général* (1827), p. x.

42. Guerry (1833), op. cit., pp. 5–6. Prior to the appearance of the *Compte*, for example, Balbi's (1822, pp. 247–48) comprehensive statistical ethnography *Essai statistique sur le royaume de Portugal et Portugal et d'Algarve, comparé aux autres états de l'Europe* contained a descriptive entry on criminal justice but nothing on crime.

43. Hankins (1908), "Adolphe Quetelet as Statistician," p. 455.

44. However, Quetelet frequently commented on the professional hardships wrought by the 1830 revolution for himself and for his many protégés; see further Porter (1985), op. cit., p. 58.

45. See Quetelet (1871a), "Des lois concernant le développement de l'homme."

46. According to Baker, "Quetelet fulfilled his [i.e., Condorcet's] program for a social mathematics" (1975, op. cit., p. viii). Condorcet regarded social mathematics as the difference between ignorance and enlightenment. For Condorcet social mathematics would lead mankind to humanity, benevolence, and justice, and would show that "the origin and first cause of any vicious habit, any custom contrary to good faith, and any crime, [can be] found in the laws, in the institutions, and in the prejudices of the country wherein they are observed" (1795a, *Tableau historique des progrès de l'ésprit humain*, p. 180); and see Condorcet (n.d.), "Essai sur les probabilités en fait de Justice." On the relationship between Beccaria and Condorcet, see Baker (1975), op. cit., pp. 227–42; and Perrot (1976), op. cit., p. 128.

47. Much of Condorcet's (1743–94) intellectual and political life was devoted to discovering how the methods of the natural sciences could be harnessed to the understanding of human societies, a study that he termed, toward the end of his life, *science sociale*. Condorcet regarded as the object of social science the determination of rules with which to choose, from the infinite number of possible combinations, the precise system that would best secure the general principles of equality and natural rights. The most promising avenue for the emergence of such a science, he surmised, lay in the application of "the calculus of combinations and of probabilities" because only this could yield results with an almost mathematical certainty (Condorcet, 1795a, op. cit., p. 178). In his essay "Tableau général de la science," published in the *Journal d'instruction sociale* in 1795, Condorcet (1795b) hinted at the diverse social and economic objects to which calculation should be applied:

We know how much he [man considered as an individual] is affected by the temperature of the climate, the composition of the soil,
diet, the everyday customs of life, curative practices, and social institutions. And one can investigate how these diverse causes influence
the life span, the relative number of individuals of each sex (either at
birth or at different ages), how they affect the relationship of the
number of births, marriages and deaths to the number of people still
living; how they affect the relationship of the number of single, mar-
ried and widowed persons (of each sex or both) to this same total
number.

Then we will see how these factors influence the mortality produced by the different sorts of illnesses.

Finally, we will see to what degree we can discern their influence
on strength, on size, on the figure of individual persons, or indeed, on
moral qualities.

We may either consider separately the effect of each of these factors, or the effect of several of them jointly; and we must at the same
time investigate whether, in the latter case, two or three of these factors conjoined will have an isolated effect or if, actually combined,
they temper or increase the effects which each one of them would
have been able to produce" (p. 552).

Condorcet's work on the calculus of combinations and of probabilities
concerned the decisions of representative assemblies, tribunals, and juries: see
especially his obscure *Essai sur l'application de l'analyse à la probabilité des décisions rendues à la pluralité des voix* of 1785; and his *Tableau général de la science*
(Condorcet, 1795b). For commentay on Condorcet's *Essai*, see Todhunter
(1865), *History of the Theory of Probability*, pp. 352ff; and Baker (1975), op. cit.,
pp. 228–34, who does an excellent job of making it intelligible to nonmath-
ematicians. These two essays by Condorcet formed an important link between
Beccaria's *Dei delitti* and the rise of moral statistical analyses of crime in the
1820s; in them Condorcet devised a tediously complicated mathematical system
for determining the probability that public bodies will arrive at correct decisions based on the popular will. Condorcet's response to this problem need
not concern us here, but it should be noted that he pinpointed the importance
of scientific and rational decision-making in the modern bureaucratic state of
Turgot's France; on this, see Baker (1975), op. cit., pp. 237ff.

48. In 1795, at the request of the National Convention, the Marquis de
Laplace (1749–1827) delivered a lecture to the École normale de Paris, where he

was professor of mathematics and which was published in 1814 as his *Essai philosophique sur les probabilités*. In this essay, which was widely read by the moral statisticians, Laplace (1814) moved toward a thoroughgoing determinism, arguing that "all events, even those which on account of their insignificance do not seem to follow the great laws of nature, are a result of it just as necessarily as the revolutions of the sun" (p. 3). Also subject to determinate laws, argued Laplace, were the objects of the political and moral sciences; his analyses of the probability of testimony in representative assemblies can be found in Laplace (1814), pp. 109–39, 175. On the intellectual links between Laplace and the moral statisticians, especially Quetelet, see further Lottin (1912), op. cit., pp. 200–204, 352–53; and Stigler (1986), op. cit., p. 162.

49. It is possible that Quetelet had gleaned the general direction for social-scientific analysis from writers such as Henri Saint-Simon and the young Auguste Comte, but no reference to either appeared in any of his early works. The absence of Comte is especially puzzling, and though Lottin (1912, op. cit., pp. 356–67) correctly points to the fundamental differences between them, it is difficult to believe that Quetelet had not been influenced by works such as Comte's (1822) *Plan des travaux scientifiques nécessaires pour réorganiser la société*. Possibly under Fourier's guidance, Quetelet adopted Comte's term *physique sociale* as the subtitle of his book *Sur l'homme* of 1835. Later, in his *Cours de philosophie positive,* Comte protested the usurpation of the discipline of social physics by "a Belgian scholar who has adopted it, in recent years, as the title of a work whose concern is merely simple statistics" (1838, bk. 4, p. 15). Thus did Quetelet force Comte to invent the neologism *sociology.*

50. Quetelet (1826), "Mémoire sur les lois des naissance et de la mortalité à Bruxelles."

51. Ibid. p. 495.

52. Quetelet (1828), *Instructions populaires sur le calcul des probabilités,* p. 230.

53. At first, during the 1820s when he began to use census materials in order to calculate crime rates, Quetelet was attracted to Laplace's (1814, op. cit., pp. 66–67) method of nonrandom sampling suggested in his *Essai philosophique sur les probabilités*. But he was persuaded by de Keverberg that Laplace's method was impractical. Even if reliable ratio estimates could be made for births and deaths, Quetelet realized that there was no sure way to estimate the population loss produced by emigration; see, for example, Quetelet (1829b), "Du nombre des crimes et des délits dans les provinces du Brabant méridional, des deux Flandres, du Hainaut et d'Anvers, pendant les années 1826, 1827 et 1828," pp. 178–79. Henceforth, Quetelet decided to use only a complete

census in his calculations. The intellectual difficulties raised by de Keverberg against Quetelet's reliance on Laplace's method have been fully described by Stigler (1986), op. cit., especially pp. 163–69.

54. Quetelet (1829a), "Recherches statistiques sur le royaume des Pays-Bas." See also Quetelet (1831b), *Research on the Propensity for Crime at Different Ages,* pp. 3–11 passim; and Quetelet (1842), *A Treatise on Man,* pp. 57–72.

55. Quetelet (1831b), op. cit., p. 3. There is some evidence that, during Quetelet's visit to Weimar, several conversations with Goethe helped him to form his concept of the average man. See further John (1898), *Quetelet bei Goethe,* p. 314. An interesting summary of the relationship between Quetelet and the aged Goethe is provided in Collard, "Goethe et Quetelet."

56. The founding of moral statistics is commonly attributed to Johann Peter Süssmilch in his book *Die Göttliche Ordnung in den Veränderungen des menschlichen Geschlechts, aus der Geburt,dem Tode und der Fortpflanzung desselben erwiesen* (1742, 3 vols.). See, for example, Durkheim (1897), *Suicide: A Study in Sociology,* p. 300, n. 1; and Funkhauser (1937), *Historical Development of the Graphical Representation of Statistical Data,* p. 279. Among the Franco-Belgian statisticians, it was most likely Guerry who first applied the term to the phenomena of crime. *Contra* Lottin (1912, op. cit., p. 37), Quetelet first explicitly applied it to his own work in 1842; see Quetelet (1842), *Treatise on Man,* pp. 79–80), where he urged that moral statistics be expanded to include witchcraft practices, torture, and execution for religious reasons, as well as political and religious fanaticism of various sorts. To these items Quetelet later added intellectual faculties, mental illness (*aliénation*), alcoholism, dueling, and accidental death (1869, *Physique sociale, ou Essai sur le développement des facultés,* pp. 232–368).

57. These early works included Quetelet (1829b), op. cit.; Quetelet (1830a), "Sur la constance qu'on observe dans le nombre des crimes qui se commettent"; and Quetelet (1830b), "Relevé des crimes et délits commis dans les provinces du Brabant méridional, des deux Flandres, du Hainaut et d'Anvers, pendant l'année 1829." In my account here of Quetelet's criminology, little reference is made to any of his writings after 1848, including his widely acclaimed book *Physique sociale* of 1869. Despite Quetelet's continued propensity to publish, his work after 1848 contains no departures from his earlier analyses of crime; indeed, as Quetelet (1869, op. cit.) himself later recorded, "in publishing the first edition of my *Physique sociale,* in 1834 and 1835, I believed it necessary to give a special place to criminal statistics. I have found, to a striking degree, the most conspicuous proof of the confirmation of my ideas about the size and the constancy of social regularities. . . . Today I do not

think that I have to change any of my conclusions" (p. 269). Hankins has noted that after Quetelet suffered a stroke in 1855, his writings "needed the most thorough revision . . . his books published after 1855, insofar as [they are] new in composition, are full of ambiguous or unintelligible phrases, ill-managed and very repetitious" (1908, op. cit., pp. 473–74).

Actually, repetitiousness had set in well before the date marked by Hankins. For example, except for the addition of some paragraphs on suicides and dueling, Quetelet's *Treatise on Man* (1842) merely repeats the content of his *Research on the Propensity for Crime at Different Ages* (1831b). Moreover, the sections on crime in *Physique sociale* (1869) only reiterate his work published three decades earlier (1831b) and (1835). The title of *Physique sociale* was but a reversal of the title and subtitle of *Sur l'homme,* and even the introduction to *Physique sociale,* written by the English astronomer Sir John Herschel, had previously appeared in the *Edinburgh Review* of 1850.

58. Quetelet (1827), "Recherches sur la population, les naissances, les décès, les prisons, les dépots de mendicité, etc., dans le royaume des Pays-Bas," p. 155.

59. Quetelet (1829a), op. cit.

60. Ibid. p. 29.

61. Ibid. pp. 32–33.

62. Quetelet (1831b), op. cit., p. 3.

63. Ibid. p. 5.

64. Quetelet was the first moral statistician to suggest this resemblance, although this was disputed by Guerry. Considerable personal animosity existed between Quetelet and Guerry, an example of which occurs at the end of the third book of *A Treatise on Man,* which was directed against Guerry's *Essai sur la statistique morale de la France* of 1833. Here, Quetelet (1842) writes about his discovery of the constancy of crime: "As this idea has continually presented itself to me in all my researches on man, and as I have exactly expressed it in the same terms as those of the text, in my conclusions on the *Recherches sur le penchant au crime,* a work which appeared a year before that of A. M. Guerry, I have thought it necessary to mention the point here, to prevent misunderstanding" (p. 96). See also Quetelet's (ibid. p. 79) unnecessary comment that Guerry paid insufficient attention to his documentary sources.

65. Quetelet (1831b), op. cit., p. 4.

66. De Candolle was probably the first moral statistician to acknowledge the problem of the dark figure of crime; see de Candolle (1830), "Considérations sur la statistique des délits." According to de Candolle, because knowledge of the actual number of crimes is complicated by such factors as the

activities of the police, "Statistics can only give us such facts as: *a certain number of crimes known and tried [jugés] from an unknown sum total of crimes committed*" (ibid. p.177). Moreover, "the ratio between crimes known and crimes committed is entirely unknown; it varies prodigiously from one country to another and from one type of crime to another. . . . It is purely specious to believe that the ratio of known to unknown crimes is constant" (ibid. p. 176).

67. Quetelet (1831b), op. cit., p. 7.

68. Ibid., p. 18. Michelle Perrot (1978) unduly exaggerates in lamenting that, to the moral statisticians, "the data of the *Compte* were absolute values, and as a result they used the statistics of the defendants charged with crimes and offenses not only for studying crimes and offenses, which might possibly be considered legitimate, but also for studying criminals and delinquents. The distinction between alleged (defendants), legal (convicted prisoners), and real criminality, usually taken for granted today, had not yet become part of their thinking" (p. 219). In fact, although they did not incorporate it into their analysis as such, de Candolle and Guerry were each somewhat aware of this problem in the early 1830s; see, for example, de Candolle (1830, op. cit.) and Guerry (1833, op. cit., pp. 6–8). Quetelet himself did not tend to indulge in the sort of distinctions referred to by Perrot; see, for example, Quetelet (1831b), op. cit., pp. 16–19.

69. Quetelet (1848a), "Sur la statistique morale et les principes qui doivent en former la base," pp. 19–20. See also Houchon (1976), "Lacunes, Faiblesses et Emplois des Statistiques Criminelles," p. 25.

70. Quetelet (1831b), op. cit., p. 69.

71. Quetelet (1869), op. cit., bk. 4, p. 333.

72. Somewhat different versions of this graph and accompanying text can be found in Quetelet (1831b, op. cit., plate 3) and Quetelet (1848a, op. cit., p. 21). "The degree of possibility," Quetelet elaborated in the latter, "does not always stay the same; now it is stronger—now less so. And if one were able to measure its exact value, amidst all of the extrinsic factors which exert an influence, it would happen that in designating the possibility as 'o' when it becomes nil and its measurable values as intervals along the axis 'oi' . . . we would obtain a line such as 'oai'. This line would show by its deviations the number of times that the individual in question finds himself in one state or the other consistent with his moral constitution. The determining points and the form of the curve will vary with each different man."

73. It is important to note that Quetelet's inferences about criminal propensities were drawn exclusively from the data in the *Compte* or, as criminologists only from Charles Goring onward would say, from a single-cell design.

While Quetelet was aware of the need to compare the social characteristics of the population in the *Compte* with those of the general population, it was a comparison he never made. Examples of Quetelet's awareness of the need to make this comparison can be found in Quetelet (1831b), op. cit., p. 53 and p. 58. However, his representation of the obstacles to such a comparison—and of its significance could it be made—was consistently confined to a methodological rather than a theoretical realm.

74. Quetelet (1831b), op. cit., pp. 37–38; and Quetelet (1842), op. cit., p. 89.

75. Quetelet (1831b), op. cit., p. 38.

76. Ibid. p. 37; and see Porter (1985), p. 55.

77. *Ibid*. p. 49.

78. Women's lack of visibility in the *Compte* was a reflection of the lenient attitude offered them by the courts throughout the nineteenth century; women were more often successfully able to plead mitigating circumstances and were rarely sentenced to death. On the difficult explanatory problems that such leniency raises, see Perrot (1978), op. cit.

79. Quetelet (1831b), op. cit., p. 37. About the problem of measuring the different causative weights of different factors, Quetelet later wrote, "It is not sufficient to perceive that an effect depends on several causes; it is extremely important that we be able to assign the proper degree of influence of each of these causes" (1842, op. cit., p. 103). This he proceeded unsuccessfully to do (ibid. pp. 103–8).

80. Quetelet (1842), op. cit., p. 7.

81. Quetelet (1846), *Lettres à S.A.R. Le Duc Régnant de Saxe-Coburg et Gotha sur la Théorie des Probabilités*, pp. 157–256.

82. Quetelet (1842), op. cit., p. 6.

83. Ibid. p. 108.

84. This tendency is found, for example, in Quetelet's (1831b, op. cit.) discussion of the effects of the intellect and of climate on the propensity for crime. Quetelet's focus here was the description of crime rates in different parts of France, Italy, and Germany. Rather then explain these difference in terms of uneven economic development, as Guerry had tried to do (see *infra*, pp. 119–123), Quetelet instead referred to the different moral qualities of different races: Corsicans, Sicilians, and mixed races havng the weakest morals, and Celts the strongest (*ibid.*, pp. 24–43).

85. *Ibid*. p. x.

86. Quetelet (1846), op. cit., p. 114; and Quetelet (1848b), *Du système social et des lois qui le régissent*, p. ix.

87. Ibid. p. 94.

88. Quetelet (1842), op. cit., p. 78.

89. Ibid. p. 41.

90. Ibid. p. 78.

91. Quetelet (1842), op. cit., pp. vi–vii; and see Chevalier (1973), op. cit., pp. 437–41. The word *biology* was originally intended to describe the real hierarchical chains of life that exist in the world of nature. It was first used in 1802, when it appeared in both Monet de Lamarck's *Hydrogéologie* (1802) and in Gottfried Reinhold Treviranus's (1802). *Biologie, oder Philosophie der lebenden Natur für Naturforscher und Aertze.*

92. Quetelet (1848b), op. cit., pp. 214–15. This conclusion should be compared with Quetelet's seemingly innocuous phrase, voiced earlier, that "man carries at birth the germs of all the qualities which develop successively and in greater or lesser proportions" (1831b, op. cit., p. 14). This phrase betrays the unmistakable influence on Quetelet of the discourse of phrenology promulgated by Franz Joseph Gall (1806), *On the Origin of the Moral Qualities and Intellectual Faculties of Man, and the Conditions of their Manifestation;* and by J. G. Spurzheim (n.d.), *Observations on the Deranged Manifestation of the Mind, or Insanity.*

Gall had been a resident of Paris since 1807, and it is fairly safe to assume that, perhaps through a common network of friends, he and Quetelet either knew each other or moved in the same intellectual circles. It must also be mentioned that Comte himself was one of the earliest members of the *Société phrénologique,* and that it was in Gall's phrenology that he hoped to find a mediating principle for his sociology and biology. Such a biological reading of Quetelet is supported by Durkheim's (1897, op. cit., pp. 301–2) discussion in *Suicide* of the concept of the average man.

93. Quetelet (1846), op. cit., p. 318.

94. Quetelet (1871b), *Anthropométrie, ou mesure des différentes facultés de l'homme,* p. 207; and see, in general, Quetelet's discussion in ibid., pp. 205–9.

95. Ibid., pp. 370–74.

96. It is tempting to suggest that the criminal anthropology in Lombroso's (1876) *L'Uomo delinquente* had been directly influenced by the measurements undertaken by Quetelet in his *Anthropométrie.* While Lombroso himself made no explicit reference to this particular book, he certainly knew of Quetelet's work and actually acknowledged its importance. See, for example, Lombroso (1899), *Crime: Its Causes and Remedies,* pp. 179, 182, 185.

97. Quetelet (1842), op. cit., p. 108.

98. Quetelet (1846), op. cit., pp. 357–58.

99. Ibid., pp. 356–57. More than a decade after Quetelet's death, French criminologists and anthropologists tended to adopt the neo-Lamarckian "degeneracy" model of criminality, rather than the Lombrosian "born criminal" type because this position allowed belief in voluntarism and rehabilitation. See further Nye (1984), *Crime, Madness, and Politics in Modern France*, pp. 101–2, 119–21.

100. Quetelet (1848b), op. cit., p. 295.

101. Quetelet (1848b), op. cit., p. 108.

102. Sarton (1935), "Preface to Volume XXII of Isis (Quetelet)," p. 4.

103. Herschel (1850), "Review," pp. 17, 37. Following Quetelet, Herschel wrote that "to render the consequences of our actions certain and calculable as far as the conditions of humanity will allow, and narrow the domain of chance, as well in practice as in knowledge, is so thoroughly involved in the conception of law and order as to make it a primary object in every attempt at the improvement of social arrangements" (p. 17).

104. Quetelet's influence even extended to the great Victorian nurse Florence Nightingale, known in popular imagination as "the lady of the lamp," although among some members of the scientific community she was hailed as "the passionate statistician." To her, Quetelet was "the hero as scientist, and the presentation copy of his *Physique Sociale* is annotated by her on every page" (Pearson, 1924, *The Life, Letters and Labours of Francis Galton*, 1: 414).

105. The criminology of the dominant group of French and Belgian criminal law jurists known as the spiritualists has been described by Van Kan (1903), *Les causes économiques de la criminalité. Étude historique et critique d'étiologie criminelle*, pp. 332–72.

106. These competing positions resulted in a rather fruitless debate that continued until the end of the century. See Lottin (1912), op. cit., pp. 413–58.

107. Quoted in Foucault (1979), op. cit., p. 287. By the middle of the century the relative solidarity that existed between the "dangerous classes" and the French working class had all but evaporated. Perrot explains that "the continued impact of stringent repressive measures, but also the powerful influence of the opinion-making system that had been elaborated over the preceding decades, and whose mainstays were the school system and the large-circulation press, began to show results; the lower classes assumed a moralistic attitude and gradually turned their backs on the denizens of the prisons, who lost what little glory had remained to them and sank deeper into the dreary and lackluster anonymity of petty delinquency" (1978, op. cit., p. 239).

108. Quetelet (1831b), op. cit., p. 69. See also Constant (1961), "A propos de l'école Franco-Belge du milieu social au XIXième siècle"; and Dupréel (1942), *Adolphe Quetelet: Pages choisies et commentées*, p. 31 and passim.

109. Quetelet (1842), op. cit., p. iv.

110. Quetelet (1848b), op. cit., p. vii.

111. Cournot (1843), *Exposition de la théorie des chances et des probabilités*, p. 210.

112. Bertillon (1876), "La théorie des moyennes en statistique," p. 311.

113. Bertrand (1889), *Calcul de probabilités*, p. xliii.

114. Durkheim (1897), op. cit., p. 304.

115. Attempts have occasionally been made to resurrect Quetelet's concept of the average man, most recently by the French mathematician Maurice Fréchet. Fréchet has suggested that Quetelet's *homme moyen* can be rescued by the more precise concept *homme typique*. The latter has two basic qualities: "(1) the typical man of a population will be the *one* individual of this population who excludes all possibility of incompatibility among the different characteristics of this typical man; (2) the typical man ought to be typical in relation to the ensemble of his characteristics without being necessarily typical relative to each of them" (1955, "Réhabilitation de la notion statistique de l'homme moyen," p. 327.

116. Quetelet (1848a), op. cit., pp. 13–20.

117. Durkheim and Fauconnet (1903), "Sociology and the Social Sciences," pp. 201–2.

Chapter 4

The Social Cartography of Crime:
A. M. Guerry's *Statistique Morale* (1833)

❖ ❖

As we saw in the previous chapter, concept formation in positivist criminology was closely tied to the movements in public health, in prison reform and in statistics. This chapter considers the influence on concept formation in criminology of the movement in social cartography. Its focus is the contribution of the French lawyer and moral statistician André-Michel Guerry (1802–66), whose eclectic interests included folklore, music, and meteorology.[1] One of Guerry's many accomplishments was the invention of the *ordonnateur statistique,* a machine designed to abridge statistical calculations by hastening the classification of numerical elements. In criminology Guerry's most important contribution was originally delivered as a lecture to the Academy of Sciences in July 1832, and then published the next year as *Essai sur la statistique morale de la France* (hereinafter *Statistique morale*). It is to this book, which exerted great influence in France and especially Britain, that this chapter principally attends.

The Movement in Cartography

Like the movements in public health, in prison reform and in statistics, the development of cartography in France was closely linked with the vastly expanded sphere of state activities.[2] Since the second half of the seventeenth century, from the moment of Colbert's ambitious collaboration with the Cassini family on a national map project, French cartographers enjoyed a relative technical and conceptual ascendancy in Enlightenment Europe. During this period a variety of mathematical concepts was refined, including trigonometrical ratios, logarithims,

111

and decimal fractions. The refinement of these concepts was matched by the invention of scientific instruments that were capable of executing precise measurements. That these developments were seized on in France rather than in other countries was due to a variety of factors. The most important of these was the fervent desire of the French state to centralize cartographic activities, a process that increased with both the demise of the *ancien régime* and also the creation of new administrative units during the 1790s, and then intensified with the rise of Bonapartism. An additional factor in the ascendancy of French cartography was the good fortune that the French happened to have a greater intellectual interest in developing cartography than did their European counterparts, including even those in Italy and England.

The many troughs and peaks in the fitful history of the cartographic movement were marked by a number of factors. These included bureaucratic struggles for power between the centralizing tendencies of the French state and the erstwhile autonomy of some local authorities, a serious lack of public funding (a crucial problem for large projects as costly as a national survey), competition between different ministries and state agencies for scarce resources and authority (especially between the army and the diplomatic corps and between the army and the Departments of Foreign Affairs and Public Works), and the fickle secondary pursuits of those interested in cartography, including public officials, military personnel, explorers, engineers, scientists, and philanthropic amateurs.

From the 1660s to the 1790s a great quantity of maps was produced in France. These examined and measured the spatial distribution of natural phenomena like the heavens, the seas, the mountains, and the landforms of international boundaries. Sections of the frontiers were mapped by the army's topographical engineers, and after 1715 its fortifications engineers were mapping its defenses. In 1720 the French navy created a separate hydrographic office. Toward the end of the eighteenth century the state began to invest heavily in the mapping of numerous public works and transportation projects that required precise knowledge of canals, roads and highways, rivers, and harbors. These maps concentrated on variations in one category or "theme," and they were originally termed *cartes figuratives* by their makers, and then *cartes thématiques* ("thematic maps"). Other prominent examples of thematic mapping included epidemiological maps concerned with the spread of diseases like yellow fever and cholera; fiscal atlases; economic maps charting information about agriculture, commerce, and urbanization; and maps of crime and criminality.

The early maps of criminality produced by the French moral statisticians drew their inspiration from the labors of several early pioneers.[3] Among these, in particular, was the Englishman William Playfair (1759–1823), the younger brother of the famous mathematician and geologist John Playfair. In his teens Playfair had been apprenticed to Andrew Meikle, the inventor of the threshing machine, later serving as a draftsman with James Watt. In his *Commercial and Political Atlas* of 1786, Playfair used stained copper-plate charts to illustrate "the progress of the commerce, revenues, expenditures, and debts of England" from the middle of the sixteenth century to the last quarter of the nineteenth century. The first edition of the atlas included forty-four charts, which were well-executed copper-plate engravings colored by hand in three and four shades, and it contained many fine examples of the line graph, bar graph, circle graph, and pie diagram. Playfair's atlas was translated into French in 1789 and at once the *Académie des Sciences* testified its approbation of his "attempt to apply geometry to accounts."[4] Guerry cited with resounding approval of Playfair's view:

> The giving form and shape to what otherwise would only have been an abstract idea has often rendered easy and accurate a conception that was in itself imperfect and acquired with difficulty. . . . Men of great rank or active business, can only pay attention to general outlines; nor is the attention to particulars of use any farther than as they give a general information. And it is hoped, that with the assistance of these charts, such information will be got without the fatigue and trouble of studying the particulars of which it is composed.[5]

Similar views about the importance of social cartography were held by the great naturalist Baron Alexander von Humboldt (1769–1859). In his four volume *Political Essay on the Kingdom of New Spain* of 1811, Humboldt wrote about his graphical method:

Natural philosophers have long indicated by similar figures the
state of the barometer and mean temperature of months. It
would be ridiculous to endeavour to express by curves, moral
ideas, the prosperity of nations, or decay of their literature; but
whatever relates to extent and quantity may be represented by
geometrical figures; and statistical projections which speak to
the senses without fatiguing the mind, possess the advantage
of fixing the attention on a great number of important facts.[6]

The first maps of moral statistics were produced and annotated by
Baron Charles Dupin (1784–1873). According to the cartographic historian H. G. Funkhouser, in 1819 Dupin published a map showing by
gradual shadings from black to white the distribution and intensity of
illiteracy in France, although there is no reliable evidence that Dupin
actually produced such a map in that year.[7] In November 1826, Dupin
addressed a meeting of the Conservatoire des Arts et Métiers (at which
he was a part-time professor) on "popular education and it relation to
France's prosperity." During the meeting Dupin exhibited a choropleth
map which, he claimed, inaugurated the cartographic portrayal of
moral statistics—a term encompassing "a wide array of characteristics
of populations."[8] Dupin's map showed "by shading the number of
persons per male child in school in each *département,* in order to show
how one part of France differed from another."[9] Then, at a meeting of
the *Académie des Sciences* in December 1826, Dupin presented a work
on the geographical distribution of education and prosperity in France.
In a forum at the end of the meeting Dupin suggested that he was pres-
ently studying the condition of morality in France, and that he would
demonstrate that immorality increased in proportion to "ignorance"
and poverty.[10]

The first example of the use of shaded maps to portray crime rates
was produced jointly in Paris in 1829 by Guerry and his colleague the
Venetian geographer Adriano Balbi.[11] Guerry and Balbi's one-page
Statistique comparée del'état de l'instruction et du nombre des crimes was
based on the *Compte général* for the years 1825 to 1827 and on the census
of 1822, and it contained three shaded maps of crime. These latter displayed clearly the rates of crime against the person (the number of in-

habitants for each crime), crimes against property, and rates of illiteracy (based on the number of male schoolchildren in educational districts). In the brief accompanying text, the authors suggested: (1) in general, the *départements* with the high rates of personal crimes had low rates of property crime, and vice versa; (2) an area northeast of a line between Orléans and Lyons had both the highest levels of education and also the highest rates of property crime in the whole of France; and (3) urban areas, especially Paris; tended to have the highest rates both of property crime and of crimes against the person. On each of these three claims Guerry elaborated in his book *Statistique morale,* and to it we now turn.[12]

Crime, Development, and Education in *Statistique Morale*

> We might perhaps be reproached for overturning long-held theories which have been consecrated by the most respectable authorities. We reply that we are not making a point of doctrine. We expose simply what is, without explaining it.
>
> —Guerry, *Statistique morale,* p. 50.

Epistemologically akin to Quetelet's "social mechanics of crime," Guerry's cartography of crime was erected on the positivist belief that "the observation and study of facts are the basis of our knowledge."[13] The empirical contents of *Statistique morale* derived from the statistical data in the *Compte,* and they were remarkably similar in origin and in content to those displayed at about the same time by Quetelet. They included the type and the number of crimes (against persons and against property) committed annually in France between 1825 and 1830, with variations in their commission associated with sex, age, and season; the underlying motives behind capital crimes such as poisoning, murder, and assassination; and the geographical distribution of personal and property crimes, and of education, illegitimacy, and charitable donations, and suicides. Guerry himself expressed his belief in the facticity of the data in the *Compte* in the following terms:

If we now consider the infinite number of circumstances which can lead to a crime, including both the exterior and the purely personal influences which determine its character, we could not possible imagine how constant are the results; indeed, acts of free will develop in a fixed order and they are confined to very narrow limits. We are compelled to recognize that the facts of the moral order, like those of the physical order, are subject to invariable laws. In several respects, judicial statistics offer a perfect example of this certainty. Moreover, despite their frequent misuse, and the criticisms of those whose theories they contradict, judicial statistics have given a new direction to the study of criminal law and public morality.[14]

In at least two important respects Guerry's labors differed from Quetelet's. The first lay in Guerry's more extensive reliance on maps in support of his arguments about crime rates.[15] Guerry's collaboration in 1829 with Adriano Balbi had resulted in a one-page sheet of three maps, and accompanying text, that allowed the reader to see some elementary relationships among property crimes and personal crimes. This set the tone for Guerry's graphical method of depicting crime rates through the use of shaded maps in *Statistique morale*. However, the arguments of *Statistique morale* were illustrated by six *cartes figuratives*—respectively, crimes against persons, crimes against property, "education" (*instruction*), illegitimate births, charitable donations to the poor, and suicides. The *cartes figuratives* appeared in graded tints from dark brown to white, and are the first examples of colored maps of crime. In a short appendix Guerry provided the reader with nine colored *collones* ("histograms," or columns) representing both the monthly and the annual volumes of crimes against persons and against property (subdivided by age and by sex), of capital crimes, of education, and of suicide (by pistol and by hanging). Guerry himself explained:

In order to make our results more striking, we have resorted to the use of graphical illustrations. Without excluding the enumerations which the reader can make if he so chooses, these illustrations have genuine advantages. The shades of color of our maps provide instant geographical images which tend to be lost in a long series of numbers; relative quantities can be expressed with precision through contours which leave a visible and lasting impression on the eye.[16]

Moreover, in the course of *Statistique morale* Guerry addressed three methodological problems of the moral statistics of crime in a more explicit fashion than had Quetelet. The first problem referred to by Guerry was whether the total number of crimes is better indicated by the number of indictments or by the number of convictions. About this problem Guerry argued that he preferred to use the number of "indictments" (*accusés*) as the basis of his calculations rather than the number of those "convicted" (*condamnés*). This he chose to do even though he realized that a person charged with a crime is not necessarily guilty and even though the number of crimes cannot be deduced from the number of indictments. Guerry suggested that, though both bases are liable to error, the number of indictments is open to less serious errors than the number of convictions. This is so because the indictments reflect the activities of public prosecutors, whereas the convictions depend on the whims of juries. Indictments depend on the activities of public prosecutors who, except in the case of political crimes, exercise their duties with a measured uniformity; convictions depend on the verdicts of juries, which vary according to the severity of punishment facing the accused, to the nature of the crime, and to the location of the trial.[17]

A second methodological problem addressed by Guerry concerned how much the geographical distribution of crime is confounded by the changing composition of strangers and natives in any given area. In this respect Guerry asked whether it is correct to attribute to the inhabitants of a *département* the crimes that occur there. This question was formerly quite impossible to answer, but suggestive data are contained in the *Compte* of 1828, which showed that 72 percent of those accused of crimes were either born in the *département* where their crimes were committed or else lived there. Moreover, only 3 percent of those accused of crimes in France were foreigners.[18]

Guerry also questioned whether, and if so how, the crime rate after 1825 (the year to which data in the *Compte* first applied) was higher than in previous years. About this third problem Guerry pointed out that until one knows accurately what sorts of crimes have diminished, and whether criminal laws have changed since 1825, there is in fact no adequate means with which the pre- and post-1825 crime rates can actually be compared. Thus, he opposed as devoid of proof the widespread opinion that violent crimes had been increasing dramatically. Indeed, prior to 1825, criminal proceedings were held in secret, and only rarely were their details known publicly. Guerry also opposed those publicists who claimed speciously that the approximate number of crimes committed in France could be assessed simply by examining the official records of those condemned to forced labor by the assize courts. To those others who supposed that prison expenditures always correspond exactly with the number of prisoners, and that the number of prisoners indicates the number of crimes committed, Guerry replied that although prison costs had fallen, it was wrong to conclude that the reduction in expenses was caused by a proportionate reduction in the number of crimes rather than by better prison administration or by the introduction of productive work: "One sees that in statistical arguments the facts must be verified, as much as possible, and that the most legitimate hypothesis cannot replace direct observation."[19]

However, in a preliminary and polemical way Guerry suggested that after 1825 the number of property crimes had increased. This trend he attributed to the failure of prison reform and to the rising number of juvenile recidivists.[20] The *Compte* also revealed that the number of crimes against the person had actually fallen since 1825.[21] This reduction was hidden from most commentators, Guerry surmised, because of the exaggerated way in which the press conveys to the public every gruesome detail of a violent crime as soon as it is committed; the most heinous circumstances are reproduced during the trial itself and at every stage of the proceedings. Often they are again recalled during an appeal to the high court, after a recommendation of mercy, and at the time of execution. This publicity, which otherwise is not without advantage, inevitably results in making the number of crimes seem greater than it actually is.

Having completed these opening methodological forays in *Statistique morale,* Guerry then turned to a substantive analysis of the causes of crime. Much of this analysis covered the same terrain as Quetelet— although in a somewhat original way, Guerry also examined two areas of contention which Quetelet had left relatively unexplored. These concerned the influence on crime of variations, respectively, in economic development and in education.

Economic Development and Crime Rates

Among the moral statisticians it had been not Quetelet but the Belgian author Edouard Ducpétiaux who had suggested that variations in levels of wealth and education might be the "motive" for variations in crime rates. Ducpétiaux had claimed in his 1827 book *De la justice* that poverty and "ignorance" were the source of nearly all crime; this claim he attempted to support with comparative data from France, Spain, Italy, England, and the United States. To Ducpétiaux the evidence suggested that in a variety of geographical settings crime rates were always associated with the number of "beggars" (*indigents*).

In *Statistique morale,* Guerry's response to claims about the negative relationship between wealth and crime was to complicate the issue by subsuming it within the wider rubric of "economic development." To Guerry, regional variations in the level of economic development are visible in regional variations in factors such as "the development of commerce and industry," "population density," and "wealth." Guerry provided his audience with vivid graphical representations of regional variations, respectively, in rates of crimes against persons (see Figure 4–1) and crimes against property.(see Figure 4–2). These two maps allowed him to demonstrate that, even though from one year to another the overall crime rate was constant, considerable variation existed in the types and quantity of crimes committed in different regions of France.

On the map of crimes against persons (Figure 4–1), Guerry marked a line from the middle of Ariège running to Isère, which

Figure 4–1.

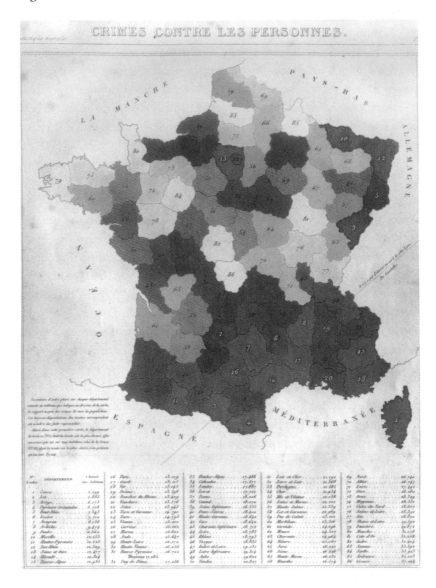

Crimes Against Persons, 1825–1830. From A. M. Guerry (1833), *Essai sur la statistique morale de la France,* facing p. 38.

showed that all olive cultivation was to the south of the line; so also, by and large, were the highest rates of crimes against the person. Guerry's precise thinking in imposing this line on the map is not known, but the strong implication is that he believed the social changes brought about by differential economical development to be somehow associated with the relative distribution of crimes against the person and property crimes. Indeed, to explain geographical variations in rates of crimes against the person, he wrote that "it is the difference in acquired or original organization which, despite the regularity or our new administrative divisions, still allow us to discern several distinct nations in the kingdom, each with its own language, mores, habits, and traditional prejudices."[22]

If southern France was dominated by crimes against the person, then northern and northeastern France were characterized by high rates of property crime (Figure 4–2). Why was this so? In response to this question Guerry took issue with two conventional accounts of crimes against property—that such crimes are monotonously associated with high population density and with poverty. In Guerry's time it was widely believed, first, that high population density is a chief cause of property crimes precisely because such crimes are usually more common in the densely populated towns than in areas where the inhabitants are less numerous. But according to the *Compte,* Guerry pointed out, relatively less property crime occurred in the *départements* with the large cities of Nantes, Bordeaux, Nîmes, Toulouse, Montpellier, and Marseille than in the northern *départements* containing the towns of Troyes, Châlons, Arras, Evreux, and Chartres, and which were less populated. The generalization associating crime and population density was therefore "premature," a mistake that "derives from attributing to population density diverse facts which, although they frequently accompany it, are not necessarily caused by it. Because they occur simultaneously, it is difficult to discern, within the common outcome, the precise causal nature of each one."[23]

A second cause commonly attributed to crime, and which Guerry also disputed, was poverty. Given that the poorest *départements* have the fewest property crimes, it would not be illogical to hold that poverty is not the chief cause of these crimes. Provocatively, he countered

Figure 4–2.

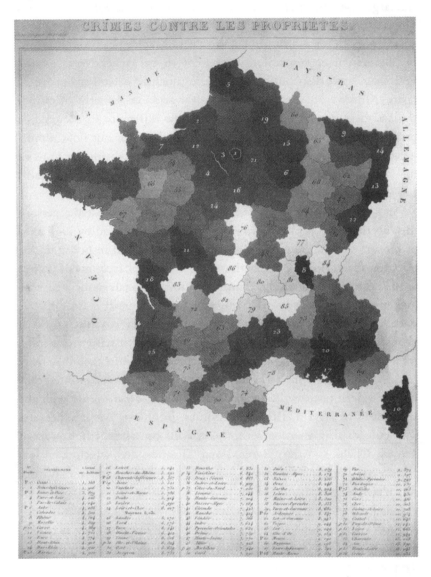

Crimes Against Property, 1825–1830. Note: (1) "P" = a *département* with a large number of patents; (2) "p" = a *département* with a small number of patents. From A. M. Guerry (1833), *Essai sur la statistique morale de la France,* facing p. 42.

that wealth—as it is manifest in variations in a combination of taxes on persons and property—rather than poverty (or a high population density) is far more often associated with property crimes. This is shown both by the data n the *Compte* and by Guerry's representation of them in his map of crimes against property. Suppose we accept, Guerry surmised, that the northern *départements* actually do have both the greatest wealth and the greatest number of property crimes and that the central and southern *départements* have the least wealth and the smallest number of property crimes. Does this mean that wealth causes crime? Not necessarily, he replied. Indeed, why is it, he asked, if the average level of wealth in the south (in Charente, Guyenne, Languedoc, and Provence) is roughly the same as in the north, that the property crime rates of these regions are not similar? Could it be, perhaps that wealth is only an "indirect" cause of crime, and that the wealthiest *départements* are those where the poverty of some inhabitants is the most dire?

Such thorny questions led Guerry to realize that the relationships among wealth, poverty, crime, and mortality are more complex than they at first seem. What is needed, he concluded, was a more sensitive index of "economic development." One avenue which should be explored as an index of regional economic position, he recommended, is the proportionate number of indigents and beggars in each department. Additionally, variations in the number of patents issued in each *département* might be a good index of regional variation in the development of commerce and industry. Thus, on his map of crimes against property Guerry transcribed a capital *P* next to *départements* with a large number of patents and a lowercase *p* next to those with a small number of patents. Those *départements* with the most patents nearly always had greater than average rates of property crime while, with the exception of Corsica, those with the fewest patents tended to have lower than average rates. Guerry allowed that there were some interesting exceptions to this generalization. For example, in coastal Bretagne there was little industry but theft was nevertheless very common. Moreover, in the Ardennes, the Meuse, and the Côte-d'Or very intense industry was accompanied by few property crimes. Guerry wisely reasoned, therefore, that the apparent link between property crime and the level of regional economic development merits further study.[24]

Education and Crime Rates

> Education, however limited it may be, offers to society some pro-
> tection, and to individuals a safeguard, against the propensity to
> crime."
>
> —*Compte général* (1830), p. 7.

It should be noted that in his brief remarks on economic development
and crime rates, Guerry never actually claimed that crime is "caused"
by material factors such as the complex of poverty and wealth. Rather,
his thesis is that certain social problems encourage "immorality" and
demoralization, which then lead directly to crime. For Guerry the list
of social problems that have an indirect causal relationship with crime
rates is in principle a very long and varied one, and for him it included not only poverty and differential economic development but
also "race" and "physiological character."[25] Indeed, at the same time he
was assembling *Statistique morale,* Guerry was also doing research with
Jean Esquirol and François Leuret on "the statistics of lunatics." In a
letter to Quetelet, Guerry reported that

> I am now occupied, with Doctor Esquirol and Doctor Leuret,
> in the statistics of lunatics. We are measuring in every way the
> heads of people confined to Charenton, Bicêtre, and Saltpêt-
> rière. We are also measuring the brain and cerebellum of those
> among them who die. I have been led thus to undertake the
> *Histoire du développement de la tête humaine moyenne.* I have been
> resolved in it entirely by the reading of your excellent *Mémoire*
> on the height of man. For two weeks, we have been noting at
> Saltpêtrière the state of the pulse of ninety furious lunatics, at
> five o'clock in the morning until seven and while they are still
> fasting. We find already in the number of pulsations certain
> periodic regularities. These observations will be continued
> until the end of the month. If it were possible to make a match
> of it for Brussels, precisely at the same hour, it would be in-
> teresting to compare the results obtained for the two cities.

I hope to be able to measure the angles of the head sufficiently exactly to have the proportions and the shape of an average maniac, hallucinatory, idiot, imbecile, epileptic head,
etc. Who knows what we will encounter?[26]

However, only on the relationship between education and crime
rates did Guerry offer any sustained comments, and to his controversial observations in this respect we now turn.

Guerry disdainfully rejected as baseless what public opinion and
bodies such as Parlement and the Société Royale des Prisons had
adopted as an "unquestioned fact" (verité vulgaire), namely, that ignorance (i.e., lack of instruction or education) is the chief cause of crime.
More education (instruction), so these bodies mistakenly alleged, would
be enough to improve morality and increase happiness. For Guerry this
mistake derived from the widely-held view that the départements with
the least education had the highest crime rates. But he insisted that this
association had not been proved: to examine it properly one would
need precise data about the distribution of education and crime
throughout France during a certain number of years. Fortunately for
Guerry, those data had just become available because the Ministry of
War had been recording, for the three years since 1827, the reading and
writing abilities of all young men liable for military conscription.
These data, published first in 1828 and then annually in the Compte de
l'administration de la justice militaire, allowed Guerry confidently to represent both in graphic and in tabular forms ("for all social classes and
for all France") the contrast between what he termed la France obscure
and la France éclairée.

Guerry's rank-ordered data showed that the most "enlightened" départements, on the one hand, were in northeastern France—Meuse,
Doubs, Jura, Haute-Marne, and Haut-Rhin, where nearly 75 percent
of young men could read and write. In the western and central départements of Berry, Limousin, and Bretagne, on the only hand, only 7.2
percent had such skills. There were, needless to say, some exceptions.
For example, some départements in the West (e.g., Deux-Sèvres,
Charente-Inférieure, Charente, Gironde, and Basses-Pyrénées) had
higher than average levels of education; and in supposedly backward
Corsica 50 percent of all youngsters were able to read and write.

Table 4-1. The Distribution of Education in France, 1827–1829

| | A. Young Male Conscripts | | | B. Those Accused of Crimes | | | C. Schoolboys |
| | The number of those out of every hundred who know how to read and write | | | | | | Number of inhabitants for each schoolboy |
	1827	1828	1829	1828	1829	1830	1829
East	51	56	58	52	52	53	14
North	48	53	55	49	47	47	16
South	32	33	34	31	28	30	43
West	26	27	27	29	25	24	45
Center	24	25	25	25	23	23	48

Source: A. M. Guerry, *Essai sur la Statistique morale de la France* (1833), p. 47.

Guerry delved into the association between educational levels and crime rates, and the results were sensational! He showed that areas with the highest educational levels (e.g., Corsica) had the highest rates of crimes against the person (and the highest rates of property crime as well); conversely, areas with the lowest rates of crimes against the person had the lowest levels of education.[27] Moreover, he found that those prosecuted for crimes against the person tended to have higher than average levels of education; in general, the more depraved and perverse the crime, the higher tended to be the educational level of the accused.[28]

It is not difficult to imagine how Guerry's data exacerbated contemporary fears about crime, and how they added to the confusion surrounding debates about the amelioration of French society through education. As we will soon see, however, his findings exerted even greater effects in Britain. But no one seemed especially attentive when Guerry himself, in a few brief and hurried passages in *Statistique morale,* suggested that there is a world of difference between, and in the respective social effects of, the imparting of the ability to read and write ("instruction"), on the one hand, and the inculcation of sound morals in the healthy citizen ("education") on the other. The process of demoralization which leads to crime could not, Guerry insisted, be retarded by mere instruction. It would be facile to conclude from the associations in his data that one should therefore oppose "education":

> One would perhaps be tempted to conclude from the preceding that the cultivation of the mind, far from weakening the propensity for crime, rather tends to strengthen it. That would be a new error. Instruction is an instrument of which good or bad use can be made. That [instruction] which one obtains in our elementary schools, and which consists only of learning, in a rather haphazard manner, to read, write, and calculate, does not make up for the lack of education and does not appear to perform the duty of exerting a great influence on morality. We think it makes the student neither better nor more depraved.[29]

Crime and Education: *Statistique Morale* and British Empirical Research

Among the Franco-Belgian moral statisticians it was in the realm of social cartography that Guerry's influence was most pronounced. This was especially visible in the presentation of the empirical claims of the two most important pieces of research to emerge from this tradition. One was Adolphe d'Angeville's *Essai sur la statistique de la population française, considérée sous quelques-uns de ses rapports physiques et moraux,* a major work of 1836 organized around social thematic maps. Its sixteen maps and lengthy accompanying text described many aspects of the development of French modernity, including crime;[30] its focus was undoubtedly the cartographic representation of moral facts, and in this it followed Guerry's method of portrayal very closely.[31] Another major work influenced by Guerry was Alexandre Parent-Duchâtelet's *De la Prostitution dans la ville de Paris* of 1836, the most widely read work on prostitution in the nineteenth century. This book was a history of prostitution in Paris from the mid-sixteenth century, and it followed Guerry in using shaded maps to show the distribution of prostitution in France and in the 48 quarters of the city.[32] It included detailed information about prostitutes: their ages, religious sentiments, and physical health; their social backgrounds; their experiences in prison (with and without their children); and their relations with the police and public health authorities.[33]

However, it was in Britain rather than in France or in Belgium that Guerry's analysis of crime exerted its greatest effects. During the 1830s, the respective national paths of British and French social reformers were propelled by similar ideologies of enlightened and charitable amelioration. In both societies the reformers concentrated their energies on issues of public health and education, and in these two areas the success of their French colleagues was an inspiration to the paternalistic, if well-intentioned, interventionism of the British moral statisticians. To this end the latter's test was facilitated by new institutional settings such as the meetings of the quasi-governmental Statistical Society of London.[34] In the three decades between the publication of *Statistique morale* and its author's death in 1866, Guerry's labors held considerable sway over the development of empirical social research in Britain. Indeed, Guerry took care to cultivate the personal contacts that would nourish his intellectual influence. In this vein we find him, at different ends of his career, responding in May 1834 to an enquiry from the public health reformer Edwin Chadwick about French prison diets,[35] and then participating, as an honorary member of the Statistical Society of London, in the Congress of the British Association, held in Bath in September 1864.

British moral statisticians were mesmerized by the empirical findings of *Statistique morale*. Its findings about crime and education, in particular, seemed diametrically opposed to respectable British opinion about the positive value of education, especially as this was championed by bodies such as the Central Society of Education. Its suitably British aura of nonspeculative facticity was enhanced by its sophisticated use of social maps (*cartes figuratives*), no examples of which appeared in the *Journal of the Statistical Society of London* until 1847.[36] Guerry's book was immediately greeted, both for and against, with intense controversy. In the *Westminster Review,* for example, an anonymous critic wrote glowingly that *Statistique morale* was "of substantial interest and importance" and that it was "on the whole eminently calculated to lie on the tables of members of parliament and others, who to the possession of competence unite a taste for legislative inquiries."[37] But Guerry's findings, as far as they could be discerned, were at once bitterly attacked by members of the new statistical societies in London and Manchester. At stake in this debate—which occurred in the intensely politicized era of the 1830s and 1840s—was resolution of the apparent paradox that in England and Wales an increase in the official crime rate had been coterminous with a great extension in public education. Did education not repress crime, as the social reformers claimed that it did? From this question the British focus soon widened to questions of the relationship between crime and numerous other 'social' factors, such as industrialization, alcoholism, pauperism, and demoralization.[38]

The first salvo in this brooding feud was fired in 1835 by the laissez-faire industrialist William Rathbone Greg, one of the founders of the Manchester Statistical Society and a man who was committed to moral improvement through education. In his essay *Social Statistics of the Netherlands,* Greg juxtaposed the "curious and novel information contained in the elaborate and profound work of M. Guerry" with the comparative evidence provided by Quetelet's research on Belgium, the Netherlands, and France. To Guerry's "startling speculations" Greg replied that Guerry could not assert with confidence that education has no effect on crime because it is impossible to measure education reliably. "That education *has* its effect in diminishing crime," Greg lamely observed, "few, we should imagine, can really doubt."[39] Indeed, he continued, it is likely that the wealthy and those persons with good education "naturally" commit relatively less property crimes because they are less tempted to steal.

In 1837 George Richardson Porter took up the battle against Guerry because "the subject is one of such vital importance to the well-being and moral progress of society that it would be wrong to pass by an opportunity for subjecting it to a further examination."[40] Porter remarked that it would not be too surprising to find, as Guerry had, that more offenses against the person are committed in "dark" portions of France than in "enlightened" areas because such acts of barbarism tend to be concentrated among the ignorant. However, Porter pointed out, first, that Guerry had failed to remember what he had accused others of forgetting, namely, that trends in crime rates cannot be gleaned from the use of the returns for a single year. Yet, according to Porter, Guerry had "correlated" the level of instruction and the amount of crime of French *départements* only for the year 1831. Yet this very year, according to Porter's re-analysis of the data, was the only one in which the *départements* with the highest levels of instruction had the highest amounts of crime, a "bad effect" which disappeared over a longer series of observations for the years 1829–33. Second, Porter charged that, in comparing the average instructional levels of a given department with the number of crimes per inhabitant therein, Guerry had failed to distinguish the average instructional levels of offenders from that of the general population. According to Porter, offenders had significantly lower levels of instruction than the general population.

Finally, Porter complained that in dividing the population simply into those who had received instruction and those who had not,

Guerry had failed to identify the different levels and types of instruction received by individuals. Good instruction consists not only in learning how to read and write but even more so in the imparting of "that degree of careful culture which alone is deserving of the name of education, and which teaches men to respect the rights of others by imbuing them with sound moral and religious principles."[41] A careful examination of the backgrounds of offenders would reveal, Porter concluded, that education exercises a restraining power upon evil passions and criminal propensities.

In 1840 Rawson W. Rawson, secretary to the Statistical Society of London, delivered to the Society an important paper on education and crime in which he argued that in discussions of education and crime there had been an unfortunate tendency to confuse "mere instruction in the elementary arts of reading and writing" with education, and that the good or evil effects of the former had wrongly been used to support or to attack the latter.[42] For Rawson neither the "mere intellectual training" that comprises instruction nor the "moral and intellectual training" of education could possibly repress crime. "Criminal passions . . . are not the result of any action of the mind," he pontificated, "but spring from the secret impulses of the heart."[43] Nevertheless, and somewhat disingenuously, Rawson continued that proper education does tend to lead to a higher state of morality and that an approximate indicator of this could be found in convicts' degrees of instruction that had been published annually in the Criminal Tables since 1835.[44] Blatantly disregarding some counterfactual evidence for the year 1836, as had Porter for 1831, Rawson inferred from the Criminal Tables for the three years 1837–39 that, for every 100 offenders in England and Wales, 35.4 could neither read nor write, 54.2 could only read and write imperfectly, 10.0 could read and write well, and 0.4 had received "a superior degree of instruction."[45] From these data he concluded that the claim that education fails to repress crime is decisively refuted. Apart from extolling the virtues of moral education, Rawson then leaped to the surprising conclusion that, if the crime rate actually had risen at the same time as education had been extended to the masses, then "the causes must be looked for elsewhere . . . in circumstances connected with the social, rather than with the moral, condition of communities.[46]

In 1843 the fray was entered by Joseph Fletcher, a barrister and during the 1840s the most prolific British writer on questions of education and crime. Fletcher began at the very point where Rawson had ended, and he warned that in making sense of the educational statistics one must realize that a positive excess of the ignorant over the instructed means neither that a lack of education causes crime nor that an extension of education would decrease it. "No proof whatever is afforded by these data of the greater association of crime with ignorance than with instruction, unless it be shown that the ignorance which prevails among those committed to prison is greater than that which prevails throughout society generally."[47] Finding an "excess of ignorance" among those incarcerated, Fletcher suggested,

> only proves that the greater number of them are derived
> from the poorer classes of society, upon whom, as such, are
> acting a thousand deteriorating influences, in the places of their
> abode, their pursuits, their companionship, their want of do-
> mestic discipline, and their neglected social position, sufficient
> to produce far more evil than is usually laid to their want of
> schooling.[48]

Finally, mention should be made of Thomas Plint's book *Crime in England* of 1851, perhaps the best, and certainly the most polemical, work to come out of this genre at midcentury. In this book Plint intended "to show the real progress and character of crime, since 1805; and its significance as a test of the moral condition of the people at large—its connexion, or not with new industrial organizations; and directly to combat the prevailing theory, that ignorance and immorality are greatly on the increase."[49] From the official crime returns Plint demonstrated that between 1801 and 1845 the crime rate continued to increase, but at a rapidly diminishing rate, largely as a result of the growing volume of larcenies. Throughout his book Plint was adamant that the changing crime rate could not be explained by what earlier commentators had identified as education (or lack of it), namely, the ability to read and write. Because this sort of education had been constant during this period, it could have had no direct bearing on the issue, and other factors must therefore have been at work. His explanation of this increase pointed firmly away from monocausal factors such as lack of education, and toward Quetelet's notion of multicausal factors in the domain of the social.[50] For Plint relevant social conditions included the price of bread, the social institutions that fostered the continued existence of the "dangerous classes," and the debilitating effects of urban slum life—although precisely how each of these conditions influenced crime he refrained from comment.

Notes

1. Guerry, a native of Tours, completed his legal studies at the University of Poitiers and then went to Paris to practice law. His career as an *avocat* at the royal court was disrupted in 1827 by his great fascination with the *Compte*. Guerry then deserted the bar altogether to study statistics. After the 1830 Revolution he was appointed director of Criminal Statistics in the Ministry of Justice. He was a member of the French Academy of Sciences and an honorary member of the London Statistical Society. The Academy applauded his *Essai sur la statistique morale de la France* of 1833 and awarded him its statistical prize for the seventeen plates of *cartes figuratives* in his later folio book *Statistique Morale de l'Angleterre comparée avec la Statistique Morale de la France* of 1864. Further biographical details about Guerry can be found in Anon. (1866a), "Guerry (André-Michel)"; and in a funeral oration delivered by Alfred Maury (1867), *Guerry (André-Michel)*.

2. The term *cartography* was not coined until 1839. Writing in Paris in that year, Manuel Francisco de Barros y Souza used *cartographie* in a letter, and the word was first printed in the *Bulletin* of the Société de Géographie de Paris (Konvitz, 1985, *Cartography in France, 1660–1848: Science, Engineering and Statecraft*, p. xix); it first appeared in English in 1843: see Skelton (1972), *Maps: A Historical Survey of their Study and Collecting*, pp. 76–78. Good surveys of the development of cartography in France are provided by Robinson (1982), *Early Thematic Mapping in the History of Cartography;* and by Konvitz (1987), op. cit.

3. See, for example, Guerry's praise of Playfair and Humboldt in *Statistique morale* (1833, p. 3), and his explicit identification of Playfair, Humboldt, and Dupin as his mentors in Guerry (1864), *Statistique Morale de l'Angleterre comparée avec la Statistique Morale de la France*, p. 56.

4. See Funkhouser (1937), "Historical Development of the Graphical Representation of Statistical Data," p. 292; and Funkhouser and Walker (1935), "Playfair and His Charts, pp. 103, 107. According to Funkhouser (1937, op. cit., p. 292), Playfair's *Atlas* went unrecognized in England for such a long time with the result that no reference to it by an English statistician or economist can be found until 1879, when Jevons remarked on its importance to the London Statistical Society.

5. Guerry (1833), op. cit., p. 3, n. 1, citing Playfair (1786), *The Commercial and Political Atlas*. Additionally, Guerry (1833, op. cit., p. 50) referred to the importance of *"Statistical Illustrations,"* which was almost certainly the volume of more than 200 pages that appeared in 1827 and which was commissioned by the London Statistical Society to popularize data on population, finances, commerce, and so on: *Statistical Illustrations of the Territorial Extent and Population, Rental, Taxation, Finances, . . . of the British Empire. Compiled for and Published by Order of the London Statistical Society* (1827, London, 3d ed.). See further Funkhouser (1937), op. cit., pp. 293–94.

6. Von Humboldt (1811), *Mémoire sur les lignes isothermes*, vol. 1, pp. cxxxii–cxxxiii; and see Guerry (1833), op. cit., p. 3, n. 1. In his lengthy essay of 1817 about isothermal lines, read to the Académie des Sciences, Humboldt used isotherms ("curves drawn through those points on the globe which contain equal quantities of heat") to show the distribution of climatological relationships around the globe. The cartographic importance of Humboldt's essay in the history of climatology has been discussed in Robinson and Wallis (1967), "Humboldt's Map of Isothermal Lines: A Milestone in Thematic Cartography"; and in Robinson (1982), op. cit., pp. 70–71.

7. Funkhouser (1937), op. cit., p. 300; see further Robinson (1982), op. cit., pp. 156–58, 232, n. 276. About the importance of Dupin's influence Guerry himself wrote that "of all the works whose object was the propagation of elementary education none created such excitement as did Dupin's, and none contributed so much to increasing the number of schools" (1864, op. cit., p. 56, n. 5).

8. Dupin (1872b), *Carte figurative de l'instruction populaire de la France*. See further Robinson (1982), op. cit., pp. 62–63, 157.

9. Robinson (1982), op. cit., p. 62.

10. Dupin's presentation to the academy was reported in the *Globe* (7 December 1826); it has been outlined by van Kan (1903), *Les causes économiques de la criminalité. Étude historique et critique d'étiologie criminelle*, p. 375.

11. Balbi (1782–1848) was born in Venice of a noble family and as a young man studied successively mathematics, geography, and physics. In 1808 he

published his first work on geography. After 1815 he worked in the employ of the Italian customs, producing his *Compendium of Universal Geography* and other comparative studies of monarchy and philology. In 1832 he moved to Paris. He was identified simply as a *savant géographie vénetien* by Guerry (1833, op. cit., p. 45), and he is described as a producer of general maps—except for his map of crime with Guerry—by cartographic historians. Further biographical details about Balbi can be found in the entry on him in the *Grand dictionnaire universel* (Anon. 1866b, "Balbi [Adrien]," p. 91).

12. At least two parts of this book Guerry had already published earlier. "Motives in Capital Crimes" (pp. 31–37) had appeared as Guerry (1832a), "Motifs des crimes capitaux, d'après le compte de l'administration de la justice criminelle"; and "Education and Crime" (pp. 45–51) as Guerry (1832b), "La statistique comparée de l'état de l'instruction et du nombre des crimes."

13. Guerry (1833), op. cit., p. 1. The first time that Guerry made utterances about the "constancy of crime" was September 1831, although Quetelet (1829a, pp. 33, n.) had done so as early as December 1828 in his essay "Recherches statistiques sur le royaume de Pays-Bas." On the alleged decisiveness of this point, see further Lottin (1912), *Quetelet: Statisticien et sociologue*, pp. 137–38; and van Kan (1903, op. cit., pp. 374–76), who expands the list to include the Belgian moral statistician Edouard Ducpétiaux.

On the potentially stormy intellectual and emotional relationship between Guerry and Quetelet, see Chapter 3 *supra,* p. 105, n.64; see Lottin (1912), op. cit., pp. 136–37; and Knapp (1872), "A. Quetelet als Theoretiker," pp. 99–103. Guerry's first public reference to Quetelet's work appears in his *Statistique morale* (op. cit., p. 24, n. 1), where he praises the analysis of age and crime in the latter's *Recherches sur le penchant au crime aux différents âges.* However, in his great opus *Statistique morale de l'Angleterre comparée avec la statistique morale de la France* (1864, op. cit., p. vi), Guerry makes only one reference to Quetelet.

14. Guerry (1833), op. cit., pp. 11–12.

15. Quetelet's (1831b) *Research on the Propensity for Crime at Different Ages* contains two *cartes figuratives* and a curve showing the propensity for committing crime at different ages. Quetelet's maps differ from the choropleth examples in both Dupin (1827) and Balbi and Guerry (1829) in that his covered a larger area (France, the Low Countries and the lower Rhine) and also abandoned the boundaries marked by *départements* to show "a smoothed, continuous distribution with tones proportioned according to the principle that the darker the greater (ratio of crimes)" (Robinson, 1982, op. cit.,p. 160; and see Konvitz, 1987, op. cit., p. 148).

16. Guerry (1833), op. cit., p. 3.

17. Ibid., pp. 6–7.

18. Ibid., pp. 7–8. Doubt was cast on Guerry's findings in this regard by Adolphe d'Angeville's important book of 1836, *Essai sur la statistique de la population française, considérée sous quelques-uns des ses rapports physiques et moraux.* Against Guerry's dismissal of the influence of non-natives in the overall crime rate of France, d'Angeville demonstrated, in an ominous section on *émigrations et des immigrations des criminels,* that in the *département* of the Seine, for example, 58 percent of the accused came from other departments (ibid., p. 94).

19. Ibid., pp. 16–17.

20. Guerry complained that "every third convict is a recidivist and, incredibly, in our *maisons centrales* where philanthropy has almost exclusively occupied itself with prison conditions, the number of recidivists is today *larger than in the galleys*" (ibid., p. 17).

21. Ibid., p. 17. Citing the *Compte* of 1831, Guerry emphasized that in 1825 the number of accused brought before the assize courts for crimes against the person was 2,069; by 1830 this number had fallen to 1,666. However, in the same period crimes against property rose from 5,018 to 5,552.

22. Ibid., p. 40. This implication is also drawn by Perrot (1978), "Delinquency and the Penitentiary System in Nineteenth-Century France." pp. 226–27. As further evidence of it, Perrot argues that the importance of uneven economic development was fully understood in works by contemporary economists, a specific instantiation of which was Dupin's "pre-Marxist" book of 1827, *Des forces productives et commerciales de la France.*

23. Guerry (1833) op. cit., p. 42.

24. Guerry noted, finally, that in Paris and its environs, in great manufacturing towns and in seaports, a large proportion of crimes is committed by 30,000 to 40,000 professional thieves (*voleurs de profession*) of both sexes (1833, op. cit., pp. 43–44). This observation also applied very well to London, "where thieves, more numerous and more entrenched than in France, comprise a sort of corporation, a well-organized society" (ibid., p. 44 n. 1); and see the similar remarks made by Balzac (1829) in his *Code pénal des honnêtes gens.* Guerry complained that among these professional thieves were many young persons "whose apprenticeship in their infamous profession" is routinely served in the *maisons de correction*. Moreover, after their sentences have been served, "released convicts (*forçats*) rarely commit the violent (*atroces*) crimes most feared by society, as is commonly supposed. By then they understand criminal law only too well, and accordingly they avoid crimes which can lead to capital punishment. Their actions are directed not against persons but against property, and they become thieves and forgers" (ibid.).

25. Guerry's remarks on the respective effects of "race" and "physiological character" can be found in ibid., p. 40; although with typical caution he pointed out that more data collected over a long period of time would be needed to arrive at positive results here.

26. Guerry (1831), "Letter to Quetelet, September 11th," p. 75. An advertisement on the back cover of *Statistique morale* announced the forthcoming publication of a book by Leuret, Mitivié, and Guerry entitled *Recherches statistiques sur les dimensions du crâne de l'homme sain, de l'aliéné et du criminel, d'après les observations faites dans les hospices de Charenton, de Bicêtre, etc.* Interestingly enough, it is not clear that such a jointly authored book was ever published; a book bearing the same title was published in Paris by Crochard in 1845, but with Guerry as sole author.

27. Trying to ward off possible objections to the nature of his data, Guerry (ibid., p. 47) warned, "From the three parts of the table (A, B, C) [i.e., Table 4–1 above], it is clear that any errors in reporting peculiar to one of them are entirely independent of those which might affect each of the two others. The results of each part are checked separately. Therefore, whether we are considering the relationship of students to population, that of accused criminals who have received instruction with total number of accused or, the preferable method, the relationship of the number of young people knowing how to read and write with that on the census lists, we always find the same distribution of education in the five regions of the kingdom."

28. On the original of Guerry's (1831, op. cit.) letter to Quetelet the latter had made marginal notations to the effect that high levels of education could not prevent crime. Quetelet instead saw "a correlation between well-developed transportation routes and high educational levels and emphasized ethnic and cultural variations to account for the statistical patterns of criminality" (reported in Konvitz, 1982, op. cit., p. 148).

29. Ibid., p. 51. Guerry then approvingly quoted a discourse of 1817 to the effect that "without education, instruction would be only an instrument of ruin. . . . Morals are born of education, education alone creates and furthers them, because it alone truly teaches duty by reducing it to practical terms" (ibid., p. 51, n.). "It is not our intention," he continued, "to look for possible means of uniting moral education and instruction. We will state, however, without exaggerating the influence of books, that it would be necessary to encourage, by a system of national subsidy, the composition of good works for popular instruction and, above all, of works that are useful for morals."

30. D'Angeville (1836), op. cit., pp. 93–107 and map no. 13. An excellent introduction to the reprint edition of d'Angeville's book is provided by Le

Roy Ladurie (1969), who also points to the influence of Dupin, especially Dupin (1827a, op. cit.) and Dupin (1827b, op. cit.).

31. Compare, for example, the great similarities in design and in social categorization of d'Angeville's map no. 13 "Crimes" (*Combiens d'habitans pour fournir un accusé de crimes pendant les années 1828, 1829, 1830, 1831, 1832*) and Guerry's (1833, op. cit. facing p. 38) map *"Crimes contre les personnes."*

32. Parent-Duchâtelet (1836), *De la Prostitution dans la ville de Paris,* pp. 44–45, 574–75.

33. Parent-Duchâtelet's book, in turn, influenced the catalogues of prostitutes' physiognomy and physiology developed in Russia by Pauline Tarnowsky (1888), *Étude anthropométrique sur les prostituées et les voleuses;* and in Italy by Lombroso and Ferrero (1893), *La donna delinquente.* See further the devastating exposé of Parent-Duchâtelet in Gilman (1985), *Difference and Pathology: Stereotypes of Sexuality, Race, and Madness.*

34. British social thought was dominated by statistical empiricism at least until World War I, and well after it had been in part exorcised in France. The massive growth of the British statistical movement after the 1830s has been ably documented and explained by Philip Abrams (1968), *The Origins of British Sociology: 1834–1914,* pp. 13–52. The ideological contours of the British movement of this period have been chartered by Cole (1972), "Continuity and Institutionalization in Science: A Case Study of Failure," pp. 97–105; and by Cullen (1975), op. cit., pp. 135–49.

35. Guerry (1834), "Letter to Edwin Chadwick, May 14th, 1834."

36. See Fletcher (1847), "Moral and Educational Statistics of England and Wales," facing p. 192. Fletcher's map ("Map of England, Educational, Moral, &c.") showed the distribution of education in the counties of England and Wales, and was quite rudimentary in comparison with Guerry's of fourteen years earlier.

37. Anon. (1833), "Guerry on the Statistics of Crime in France," pp. 365–66. The English Member of Parliament Sir Henry Bulwer (1834, *France, Social, Literary, Political,* 1: 169–210) very much agreed with Guerry's refusal to identify lack of education as a necessary cause of crime, but he also suggested that it would have been even wiser had Guerry explored the influence of other variables such as weather, climate, age, and sex.

38. Among the most important tracts in this widening focus were William Rathbone Greg, *An Enquiry into the State of the Manufacturing Population, and the Causes and Cures of the Evils therein Existing* (1831, London); G. R. Porter, "Results of an Enquiry into the Condition of the Labouring Classes in the Five Parishes in the County of Norfolk," *Third Publication of the Central Society of*

Education, 1839; Joseph Bentley, *State of Education, Crime, etc., etc.; and proposed National Training Schools for all England and Wales* (1842, London: Longman); Joseph Fletcher (1847), op. cit.; Rev. Russell Whitworth, "Abstract of the 'Statistics of Crime in England and Wales, from 1839 to 1843,' " *Journal of the Statistical Society of London,* 10: 36–61, 1847; Jelinger C. Symons, *Tactics for the Times: As Regards the Condition and Treatment of the Dangerous Classes* (1849, London: John Olliver); Mary Carpenter, *Juvenile Delinquents* (1853, London: Bennett); Rev. John Clay, "On the Effect of Good or Bad Times on Committals to Prison," *Journal of the Royal Statistical Society,* 20: 378–88, 1857; R. H. Walsh, "A Deduction from the Statistics of Crime for the Last Ten Years," *Journal of the Royal Statistical Society,* 20: 77–78, 1857.

Discussion of the contemporary debate on crime in England and Wales during the 1830s and 1840s can be found in Morris (1957, *The Criminal Area,* pp. 53–61) and Cullen (1975, *The Statistical Movement in Early Victorian Britain,* pp. 139–45). Both Morris and Cullen focus on the British response to Guerry, the former in the context of the rise of an ecological school of crime, the latter in the context of the growth of the British statistical movement as a whole; Radzinowicz (1966, *Ideology and Crime,* pp. 32–37); and Radzinowicz and Hood (1986, *The Emergence of Penal Policy,* pp. 52–68), which contains a useful bibliography of the period.

39. Greg (1835), *Social Statistics of the Netherlands,* p. 24.

40. Porter (1837), "On the connexion between Crime and Ignorance, as exhibited in Criminal Calendars," p. 100.

41. Ibid., p. 102. After having read Quetelet's (1848a) essay "Sur la statistique morale et les principles qui doivent en former la base," Porter sent Quetelet official criminal justice data for Britain for the years 1846–49. In a letter of reply to Porter, Quetelet indicated that it was impossible to describe with any confidence the possible relationship between the level of education and crime, although "the British statistics furnish new proof of the precision of our assertions about the relationship between crime and age" (1851, "Sur la statistique criminelle du Royaume-Uni de la Grande Bretagne, Lettre à M. Porter à Londres," pp. 117–18).

42. Rawson W. Rawson (1841), "An Enquiry into the Condition of Criminal Offenders in England and Wales, with respect to Education; or, Statistics of Education among the Criminal and General Population of England and other Countries," p. 331. A year earlier, in 1839, Rawson had addressed the Statistical Section of the British Association on the subject of crime statistics in England and Wales. In his address—"An Inquiry into the Statistics of Crime in England and Wales"—Rawson set himself the task of applying to

English counties Guerry's uncontroversial findings on the influence of age and sex on crime rates. Interestingly, Rawson complained, as had Quetelet (see *supra*, p. 93–94), about the net cast by antideterminist views: "undeserved ridicule has been cast upon some attempts which have been made to show that moral phenomena are subject to established and general laws." (ibid., p. 344).

43. Ibid., p. 331.

44. About the origin of the returns for indictable offenses see Gatrell and Hadden (1972), "Criminal statistics and their interpretation," pp. 341–42; see also Radzinowicz and Hood (1986), op. cit., pp. 91–100.

45. Ibid., p. 336. Interestingly, the nonmovement statistician Joseph Bentley was roundly catigated by Lord Sandon (ex-president of the Statistical Society of London) for overemphasizing the very sort of data that Rawson had disregarded; see Cullen (1975), op. cit., pp. 139–40.

46. Ibid., p. 352.

47. Fletcher (1843), "Progress of Crime in the United Kingdom," p. 232. Elsewhere, Fletcher wrote that although Guerry's findings of 1833 might have been properly applicable to France, "how he can have arrived at the same conclusion in regard to England, as it is said he has, except through very rude and imperfect processes, I cannot conceive" (1849, "Moral and Educational Statistics of England and Wales," p. 154).

48. Ibid., p. 233. And see the methodological criticism of Fletcher's argument advanced by Cole (1972, op. cit., p. 125, n. 51). Fletcher's loss of faith in the power of education to reduce crime was short-lived, and is recorded in Fletcher (1847), "Moral and Educational Statistics of England and Wales," p. 211. According to Cullen (1975, op. cit., p. 143), Fletcher "became an inspector of schools shortly afterwards and this seems to have restored it [i.e., his faith in education]."

49. Plint (1851), *Crime in England,* p. ii. Methodological appraisals of Plint's book, and of the lofty position that it occupied in relation to other works of English criminology at midcentury, can be found in Cole (1972), op. cit., pp. 90–95; and in Kent (1981), *A History of British Empirical Sociology,* pp. 27–28.

50. Plint (1851), op. cit., p. 147. Pointing in a similar direction was Herbert Spencer's book *Social Statics* of 1850. Spencer argued that there was no evidence whatsoever that education acted to prevent crimes. He rightly pointed out that the studies which examined the educational levels among convicts and which compared the educational levels of convicts and nonconvicts were useless unless allowance was made for the variable influence of social origins and occupational position. Moreover, he surmised, "ignorance and crime

are not cause and effect; they are concomitant results of the same cause" (ibid., p. 171). Conscious of the ideological issues at stake in this debate, Spencer additionally attacked those who suggested that crime could only be corrected by the introduction of a particular style of educational system ("State-education, or the silent system, or the separate system, or any other system" (ibid., p. 175). To argue that education eliminated crime, he concluded, is merely a utopian belief held by those who pride themselves on being practical.

Chapter 5

Between God and Statistics: Gabriel Tarde and Neoclassical Criminology

❖ ❖

Jean-Gabriel Tarde was born in March 1843, in the small town of Sarlat in the Périgord region of the Dordogne in southern France. He belonged to an old family of minor aristocrats which for eight hundred years had staffed the municipal bureaucracy of Sarlat. His father, an examining magistrate, died when he was seven, and he was raised by his mother, a remarkable woman who combined an erudite and sensitive disposition with a deeply religious Catholic background. His first studies were held at the local Jesuit college, at which he received a broad classical education that was instilled by the famed discipline of that order. At this school young Tarde displayed an excellence in rhetoric that was to serve him well in future years, and he was a popular student although one regarded as too independent by his superiors.[1] He gained his baccalaurate in Toulouse, and then in 1869, having moved with his solicitous mother to Paris, he received his licence for the magistrature. Tarde at once returned to the environs of Sarlat, where he remained until the early 1890s. Here he held a variety of legal posts, among them that of examining magistrate. However, this employment was not too onerous for the energetic young Tarde, and he was able not only to cultivate his talents as artist, poet, and playwright but also to read extensively in the areas of social philosophy, psychology, and criminology.

Tarde's criminology was in part contained within, and in some respects ran in parallel to, two major intellectual projects that he began while practicing as a *juge d'instruction* ("examining magistrate") in the provincial town of Sarlat. The object of both projects was the construction of a program that would encourage national unity in a France that he, in common with other liberal intellectuals, saw as engulfed

143

with a rising tide of social and demographic problems. In the first project, lodged in his writings on philosophy and politics and also intermittently in his sociology, Tarde attempted to forge the sociopsychological dimensions of authority and obedience into a general theory of political obligation. Strongly opposed to the rise of Marxism, anarchism, and nihilism and deeply troubled by the evident decay of Christian morality, Tarde consistently applauded the growth of political democracy as a necessary condition of national reunification. However, the great value of democracy for Tarde lay not in its cultivation of a liberal political ethos; on the contrary, and somewhat disingenuously, he seems to have esteemed democratic forms merely as mechanisms whereby responsible members of the intelligentsia could safeguard the national interest. This paternalistic subscription to democratic forms bereft of principled content infiltrated his pivotal discourse in the compromised domain of neoclassical penality.

Tarde's second project was intended to construct a system of social theory based on the regular repetition, opposition, and adaptation that he perceived in all social action. Social action, or "intermental" activity, Tarde understood to be a complex interplay between the imitation of custom and the imitation of fashion, between tradition and invention, and between social morality and unbridled desire. The conceptual pivot of this project was the notion of imitation, which operated in his social theory as a counterpart to the notion of obedience in his philosophy and politics. In this second project, especially relevant to his criminology, Tarde attempted to mediate the sterile dichotomy into which the respective legal subjects of the doctrines of voluntarism and determinism had fallen among French social theorists in the second half of the nineteenth century. It was elements in Tarde's second project that chiefly earned him the reputation as the foremost criminologist in the France of his day. This reputation he established with two books: the short and rather polemical collection of 1886 *La criminalité comparée* and the massive tome *Philosophie pénale* of 1890. In addition, Tarde published numerous essays on crime and reviews of criminology in scholarly journals such as Lacassagne's *Archives de l'anthropologie criminelle* (of which in 1893 he was appointed coeditor responsible for the legal and sociological sections), the *Revue philosophique,* and the *Revue d' économie politique.*

However, Tarde's criminology is not approached without difficulty.[2] In any of Tarde's writings the reader should be prepared to discover a diversity of objects that are attacked with different modes of reasoning and which are supported by contradictory discursive techniques. His literary style was frequently convoluted and, although sometimes quite elegant, was more often than not irritatingly polemical and even obscure; it habitually indulged in a mass of embroideries, arabesques, and prolix secondary ideas.

What follows is not a comprehensive treatment of Tarde's criminology. The boundaries of this chapter are largely dictated by the intersection of Tarde's own concerns with some major themes of European criminology in the 1880s and 1890s. Because there is no coherent structure into which the unfolding content of his criminology can be inserted, I have chosen instead to focus on three persistent lines of enquiry in his work: (1) his virulent opposition to biological positivism, particularly as manifest in Cesare Lombroso's discourse about the "born criminal"; (2) his attempt to transcend the crude scientism of the Franco-Belgian moral statisticians; and (3) his debate with Emile Durkheim about the "normality" of crime. However, my intentions in this chapter are not solely expository. Each of the three major elements in Tarde's criminology embodied a dispute whose outcome would have intense practical significance for the domain of penality. In what follows I wish additionally to establish that Tarde's criminology represented the most coherent neoclassical attempt to repair the rupture of the classical legal subject inaugurated by the positivist revolution in criminology. It turns out, paradoxically, that in failing to conform with the dominant criminological terrain of his era, Tarde's criminology concealed the enduring success of neoclassical penality.

Classical Penality and the Positivist Revolution

The point of entry into Tarde's multifaceted criminology is very broadly provided by the fundamental transformation in state penal practices that had occurred, as we have seen in the previous chapters, between the middle of the eighteenth and the beginning of the nineteenth centuries. One index of failure in the stated reformative object of the new carceral institutions lay in rising rates of recidivism. These routinely confronted Tarde in his classical duties as *juge d'instruction* on the criminal bench.[3] Indeed, Tarde's experiential impressions about the growth of recidivism were annually confirmed, from 1827 onward, in the *Compte général de l'administration de la justice criminelle en France*.[4]

In the late 1820s the *Compte* had calculated the rate of recidivism to be 2 percent, but in 1832 new methods of identification revised this figure to 38 percent of all those released from prison.[5] Alexis de Tocqueville reported to Parliament in 1840 that 40 percent of inmates of the *maisons centrales* had prior prison records, and in 1844 the Minister of the Interior, Duchatelin, raised this figure to 45 percent.[6] After a temporary disruption of this trend in the 1860s, the number of recidivists convicted in the assize courts reached record proportions between 1873 and 1875.[7] The Prison Commission informed the National Assembly about the considerable presence of recidivists among the Parisian communards (of 1871) brought before the tribunals.[8] In the correctional courts 57,118 recidivists were convicted in 1872, and this increased to 74,009 in 1880 and then even further throughout the 1880s and 1890s. As Nye writes:

> Recidivism could be made to seem even more of a danger when the percentages of recidivists accused (*accusé*) of all offences over the century were reviewed. Thus, 28 of every 100 individuals charged with a crime in the 1820's had previously been convicted. By 1881 this figure had climbed to 51 out of each 100 previously convicted.[9]

As the authors of the *Compte* themselves argued, the rate of recidivism is "without contradiction, the most important part of the *Compte* because it reveals the inefficacy of repression and the inadequacy of punishment."[10] Between 1826 and 1880 the French population increased by roughly 20 percent, from 31 million to 37 million, but the number of recidivists more than doubled. To Gabriel Tarde these figures suggested that recidivism was "one of the most serious facts of our present times,"[11] a fact itself aggravated by the statistical revelation that recidivists, habitual criminals, and professional criminals more often engaged in serious crimes rather than misdemeanors.[12]

In France the most widespread explanation of recidivism, and of crime as a whole, derived from a biomedical amalgam of native Lamarckian heredity theory and the notion of a degenerative organism. This amalgam owed its existence to the creation of a strict medical rupture between the "normal" and the "pathological," a mid-nineteenth-century couplet that had successfully displaced the health-sickness couplet of eighteenth-century medicine.[13] Normal states of existence tended to be defined, following the lead of Quetelet and other moral statisticians, in terms of statistical averages; pathological states were statistical deviations from the norm that were invested with a moral vocabulary of condemnation. Henceforth, a complex array of pathologies were now measurable, quantitatively, with new gadgets such as the sphygmograph, the dynamometer, and the aestheseometer. Particular pathologies (alcoholism, suicide, recidivism, etc.) were seen as both cause and effect of moral or physical degeneracy. This medical rupture was expressed, in a bewildering variety of ways, in moral statistics (Quetelet, Guerry) in phrenology (Gall, Spurzheim), psychiatry (Pinel, Esquirol), mental pathology (Lucas, Morel, de Saulle, Ribot) and criminal anthropology. The common object of this new knowledge was the structured order of observable facts.

The Critique of Lombroso's "Criminal Man"

Irrespective of what they actually measured and why, the publicized increases in the recorded rate of recidivism helped to foster a widespread, popular belief in the existence of habitual "born criminals," collectively comprising a *classe dangereuse,* a group of poor, semiproletarian, professional thieves—Hugo's *les misérables*—who were committed to a way of life dependent on the proceeds of crime.

It was into this receptive atmosphere that the notion of the born criminal was first inserted, in 1876, in Lombroso's book *l'Uomo delinquente* ("criminal man").[14] The main sources for the claims in *l'Uomo delinquente* derived from a diverse positivist landscape containing the systematizing potential of Comtean sociology, the theory-free claims for their work by von Oëttengen and the Franco-Belgian moral

statisticians, and Darwinian evolutionism. To these positivist influences must be added Lombroso's lifelong hatred of idealism,[15] his ve-
hement opposition to which was especially evident in his objections
both to the neo-Hegelianism which then dominated Italian Marxism
and also to the spiritualism encountered in much bourgeois social
theory. Finally, brief mention should be made of the heated debates in
Italy about the causes and manifestations of the "Southern Question":
why was southern Italy so economically and culturally stagnant? One
answer to this question was provided by the Turin Communist Party,
which asserted that the real problem was not the backwardness of the
south but, rather, the racist myths circulated about the southern peas-
antry by the bourgeois press and bourgeois traditions. According to
Antonio Gramsci, these myths were seen to be embedded in a discourse that "the Southerners are inferior beings . . . lazy, incapable,
criminal and barbaric."[16] Key segments of this discourse were subscribed to by prominent members of the Italian Socialist Party, the
most reactionary tendencies of which were later espoused by Enrico
Ferri, Guiseppe Sergi, and Lombroso himself.

The arguments of *l'Uomo delinquente* stemmed from the "scientific" data largely outlined in its first two chapters. In the first chapter
Lombroso reported on his autopsies of sixty-six male "delinquents"
obtained from anatomical and anthropological museums in Italy. He
examined several aspects of the cephalic indices of these corpses in great
detail: capacity, facial angle, sutures, occipital depression, brain, and extent of microcephaly. Lombroso found that these men had a "significant" number of deviations that were compounded by other regressive
elements (falling away of the forehead, encasement of the ethmoids in
the orbital vaults, etc.). These anatomical features, he continued, were
similar to insane persons examined in his clinic, to the American black,
to the Mongolian races, and above all, to prehistoric man. In the second
chapter Lombroso engaged in an anthropometrical analysis of the
physiognomy of 832 living Italian criminals. This analysis he undertook because he thought that "to many it will have seemed a reckless,
vain task on my part to draw any conclusions from the few measurements carried out on corpses regarding the cranial forms of criminal
man." This second group of criminals included both males and fe-

males, and was selected from "among the most notorious and depraved." Of this group 390 members were then compared with 868
Italian soldiers and 90 "lunatics" along an even greater range of anatomical deviations. Lombroso's infamous conclusions from the analysis of these data were as follows:

> Many of the characteristics found in savages, and among the
> colored races, are also to be found in habitual delinquents.
> They have in common, for example, thinning hair, lack of
> strength and weight, low cranial capacity, receding foreheads,
> highly developed frontal sinuses, a high frequency of medio-
> frontal sutures, precocious synosteosis, especially frontal,
> protrusion of the curved line of the temporal, simplicity of the
> sutures . . . darker skin, thicker, curly hair, large or handle-
> shaped ears, a greater analogy between the two sexes . . . in-
> dolence . . . facile superstition . . . and finally the relative
> concept of the divinity and morals.[17]

In the second (1878), third (1884), and fourth (1889) Italian editions
of *l'Uomo delinquente* Lombroso refined his notion of the born criminal
and added to it several other types: the insane, the passionate, the female, and the occasional criminal. This classificatory system established Lombroso as the founder of the new science of criminal
anthropology, the *scuola positiva*. With the founding in 1880 of its own
journal *Archivo di Psichiatria i Antropologia Criminale,* and the publication of key supporting texts by Enrico Ferri[18] and Raffaele Garofalo,[19]
the *scuola positiva* can be said to have formed a coherent program. Its
reputation quickly extended beyond Italian circles, and its many sup-
porters believed that it would rescue the study of crime from the mire
of metaphysics and the bog of superstition. Its findings were tested in
France in the late 1870s and early 1880s and were received favorably by
a number of influential converts, including Bordier, Lebon, Taine,
Laurent, and indeed, Lacassagne himself.[20]

French enthusiasm for the Lombrosian program was not shared
by Tarde. With the publication, in 1884, of a French translation of the
third edition of *l'Uomo delinquente,* Tarde (in company with members of both the Paris Anthropological Society and the law faculty

Figure 5-1.

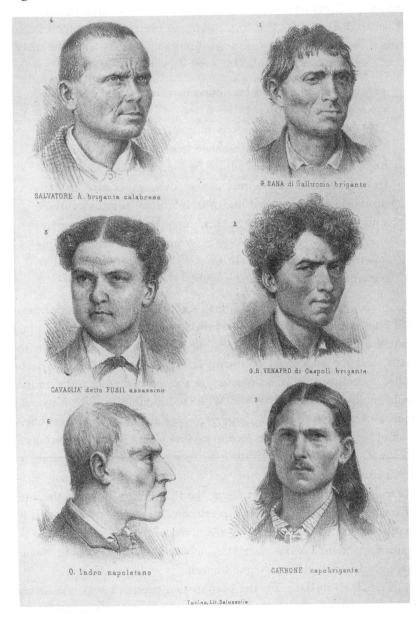

Heads of Criminals, from Cesare Lombroso (1876), *L'Uomo delinquente*. Reproduced with permission from the Lilly Library, Indiana University, Bloomington, Indiana.

Figure 5–2.

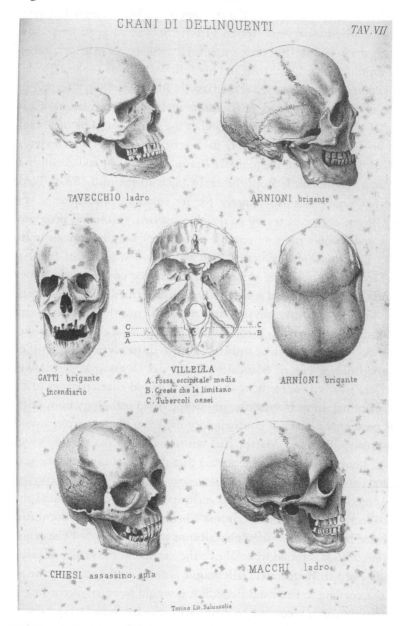

Skulls of Criminals, from Cesare Lombroso (1876), *L'Uomo delinquente*. Reproduced with permission from the Lilly Library, Indiana University, Bloomington, Indiana.

of Lyons, such as Topinard, Manouvrier, and by now, Lacassagne)
launched an offensive against the concept of the born criminal. Tarde's
attack occurred on several fronts. Firstly, he was an organizer, active
participant in and skillful orator at several conferences that were otherwise dominated by Lombroso and his followers. In this sphere Tarde's
main contributions occurred at the first (in Rome in 1885),[21] second (in
Paris in 1889),[22] and third (in Brussels in 1892)[23] International Congress of Criminal Anthropology and at the third Congress of Sociology (in Paris in 1894).[24] Next, in a series of articles and reviews,
published especially in the journals *Revue philosophique* and *Archives de
l'anthropologie criminelle* from the early 1880s to the mid-1890s, Tarde
criticized Lombrosianism largely for its empirical inadequacies. Finally, in the course of trying to develop his own theoretical program,
Tarde undertook a more systematic criticism of Lombrosianism in his
books *La criminalité comparée* of 1886 and *Penal Philosophy* of 1890.

Tarde's first objection to Lombroso occurred on Lombroso's own
terrain. This was directed against what Tarde termed "this famous and
very detailed anatomy, physical and moral, of murderers, rogues and
odious insane satyrs."[25] Tarde's wide-ranging attack here borrowed
from the work of criminal anthropologists themselves. In relying on
Marro, Bordier, Heger, Maudsley, Ferri, and Lacassagne, he showed
that there was little agreement about the imputed characteristics of the
born criminal. In their anatomy, physiology, and pathology born criminals presented a mass of contradictory evidence. For example, one of
Lombroso's disciples, Marro, had compared 456 "malefactors" with
1,765 "honest" persons and reported that the cranial capacity, the stature and the weight of delinquents was sometimes greater than average,
and sometimes less.[26] Again, the anthropologist Topinard found that
the collection of pictures of criminals brought together by Lombroso
reminded him of the photographic albums of his friends.[27] "The cranial
volume, which is found to be above the normal in the skulls of assassins by Bordier, Heger, and Dallemagne would, on the contrary, be inferior according to Ferri and Benedikt; it would be equal, according to
Manouvrier; and, according to Topinard, who happened to agree with
Lombroso on this point, it would be at one and the same time inferior
and greater."[28] And so on. Thus, the tremendous variety of conflicting

anatomical characteristics imputed to the born criminal led Tarde to suggest that there were as many different criminal types as there were anthropologists.

Another characteristic commonly imputed to the born criminal was moral atavism (variously embracing lunacy, degeneracy, and epilepsy), and to dispute it Tarde relied on data collected by the socialist Napoleone Colajanni. Following Colajanni's *Criminal Sociology* of 1889, Tarde argued that, on the one hand, the Italian provinces registering the highest rates of bodily illnesses and deformities characteristic of degeneracy were precisely the most moral ones—in northern Italy. On the other hand, the provinces with the highest rates of criminality—in southern Italy—were distinguished by the fine health of their inhabitants. "Does this mean," Tarde facetiously asked, "that degeneracy constitutes the best condition for the increase of morality?"[29] Above all, he continued, it is important to verify whether the Spencerian notion of "primitive man in general" accords with the particular primitives who weaved the beginnings of our own civilization. For this verification we must delve into such factors as their language, religion, law, and art.[30] Elsewhere, Tarde asserted that even if criminals are actually characterized by moral insensibility, as Lombroso had suggested, this defect might not be the cause of their criminality but the gradual effect of a long criminal involvement.[31]

Yet another aspect of Tarde's confrontation with Lombrosianism was his attempt to shift the empirical terrain from one field to another. He suggested, for example, that variations in crime rates among different French *départements* were caused not by different concentrations of born or habitual criminals, but by local variations in the incidence of such factors as poverty and alcoholism.[32] Another example of this eclectic tactic, among many others, was Tarde's attempt to displace the finding that born criminals very often indulged in the practice of tatooing. He explained this practice as:

> traditional among certain barbarous tribes coming into contact with our civilised people, sailors or soldiers, [and] communicated as a fashion to the latter, and then to the prisoners, as a result of the habitual isolation and the long periods of

idleness favorable to its propagation. . . . Thus prisons sometimes become, they are almost bound to, true studies of
tattooing.[33]

It should be noted that in this, the first of his three major debates
about crime, Tarde projected no alternative conceptual or theoretical
objects to Lombrosianism. Indeed, as we shall see in the context of his
third debate, Tarde believed, like Durkheim did especially in his work
of the 1890s,[34] that individual criminals were sometimes abnormal, inferior, and degenerate beings. Only rarely did Tarde and his contemporaries draw between biological and sociological categories the rigid
distinctions that we nowadays do. While accepting the notion that
some criminals had inherited their criminality, Tarde therefore needed
only to engage Lombrosianism on an empirical, counterfactual level to
refute the claim that *all* criminals were born to their misdeeds. Tarde's
efforts, in alliance with his admirers and colleagues in the juristic and
anthropological communities,[35] resulted if not in complete defeat of
Lombrosianism in France then in a very serious decline in its intellectual and political influence as early as the Paris Congress of 1889. In
turn, the attempt to rescue the causal purity of the notion of the born
criminal increasingly led Lombroso to a thoroughly eclectic notion of
causality in which an infinite number of factors, beginning with the environmental counterfactuals first supplied by Tarde, could predispose
a person to criminality. For example, in one of his last major pronouncements Lombroso admitted, "Every crime has its origin in a
multiplicity of causes, often intertwined and confused, each of which
we must . . . investigate singly."[36] It should be pointed out that Tarde
seemed also to have realized that empirical criticisms of the notion of
the born criminal tended to leave a pressing vacuum in penal policy. If
there were seen to exist among criminals neither a pathological relation
established through degeneracy or mental alienation, nor a physiological relation transmitted through some savage ancestry, then perhaps it
was impossible to ascertain some characteristics through which criminals could be classified. If criminals could not systematically be classified, then was it at all possible to construct a coherent theory of

punishment and responsibility? I will return, in a different context identified by Tarde himself, to his response to these difficulties.

From Moral Statistics to a Social Psychology of Crime

We have seen that magistrate Tarde understood, like public opinion, that the rising rate of recidivism was the most serious aspect of criminality in France. However, unlike public opinion, Tarde believed that recidivism could not adequately be explained in biological terms. In his *Penal Philosophy* Tarde specifically indicated that a major dimension of the crisis of French morality was the putative link, popularized in public imagination by the Lombrosians, between the incorrigible character of the born criminal and rates of recidivism.[37] In attempting to develop a social theory of crime that would represent a conceptual advance on his empirical confrontation with Lombrosianism, Tarde began with the presociological discourse of the moral statisticians. To a brief description of their discourse we must now turn.

The appearance of the *Compte* had been quickly followed by the labors of a loosely knit group of moral statisticians, prominent members of which included Quetelet, Guerry, d'Angeville, and d'Ivernois. The guiding theme of moral statistics was scientism, namely, a method predicated on the belief that there is a basic harmony between the methods of the natural and social sciences and which views its observational categories as theory-independent.[38] The discourse of the moral statisticians was most prominently represented in Adolphe Quetelet's seminal *Research on the Propensity for Crime at Different Ages*. Quetelet's many claims about crime can be reduced to five main propositions:

1. Human action is based on free will, but the aggregate of individual actions in a given population or category is a constant, law-like volume. Crime rates are therefore regular phenomena in all societies.

2. The statistical average for a given population produces an invariable propensity (*penchant*) for that population as a whole.

Propensities for crime vary with age, sex, race, occupation, and geographical location.

3. Crime rates are predictable. The greater the number of empirical observations (the law of great numbers), the more accurate the prediction.

4. Society is the cause of crime: "Society prepares crime, and the guilty are only the instruments by which it is executed" (Quetelet, 1842, p. 108).

5. Crime can be ameliorated by state legislation aimed at individual moral betterment.

Until the 1880s these propositions within moral statistics represented the dominant, almost the only, tendency toward a sociological analysis of crime.[39] Although Tarde generally praised the labors of the moral statisticians,[40] he also regarded their scientism as a great barrier to an adequate analysis of crime.[41] Tarde's mission was to develop sociology by bringing it down from the spectacular heights of grand but vague causes to the precise, real, and sociopsychological level of individual agents. For this endeavor his eclectic authorities included Spencer, Darwin, Hegel, and especially J. S. Mill and Augustin Cournot. From Cournot, Tarde learned about the ubiquity of imitation in the development of social phenomena and about the importance of social statistics in the resolution of what appeared to be empirical arguments.[42] From Mill (who, at the end of his *Logic* represented the study of social groups as a form of applied psychology), Tarde learned that everything in the social universe could marvelously well be explained by doctrines and dogma, except for the material of which they were composed and the point at which their operation was held to begin. Indeed, Tarde reasoned, even if such doctrines could be shown to be true—or, if not necessarily true, then at least more plausible than any of their competitors—nevertheless, they themselves would then be in need of an adequate explanation; lacking explanatory power, doctrines were capable merely of producing an assembly of problematic and irrational data.

Against the scientism of the moral statisticians Tarde made three principal objections. Firstly, he castigated as specious the view that free decisions, insofar as they are peculiar and accidental, are analogous to astronomical disturbances which eventually neutralize each other and culminate in a constant, predictable "average." A far better explanation of statistical regularity, Tarde asserted, is the power of imitation through custom.[43] Moreover, rather than assume some inexplicable innateness in the totality of items from which an average figure was produced, it is necessary to refer to these items and to the causes of their actions. Tarde therefore argued that Quetelet's law of great numbers served no purpose: the more the number of observations is increased, far from becoming less, the greater would become the inconsistency of the numerical average, and the less meaning would it have. Retrospectively, even if in a given year all the marriages, all the economic transactions and all the crimes were considered to have emanated from the independent choice of individuals, it would still be necessary to show how a meaningful average could be deduced therefrom; prospectively, statisticians could not predict the future because they could properly foresee neither invention nor the emergence of great men.[44]

Tarde was provided with more ammunition against the moral statisticians by the vicissitudes of birth, death, and marriage rates, all of which had shown great oscillation in the decade after Quetelet had first proposed the regularity of social phenomena. In common with most other European countries in the second half of the nineteenth century, France experienced a considerable upsurge in recorded crime that, Tarde bemoaned, resembled the slopes of the Alps or the Pyrénées rather than Quetelet's plateau.[45] In the half century after the introduction of the *Compte* the number of crimes trebled and the number of misdemeanors doubled, with only a small relapse between 1855 and 1865 that was probably caused by intensified police repression.[46] Toward the end of the nineteenth century France appeared to be in the throes of a pathological crisis the extent of which was the most profound in Europe. According to the official records, the exact dimensions of the crisis were visible in the rapidly accelerating rates of divorce, alcoholism, juvenile delinquency, assault, murder, suicide, and admissions to insane asylums.[47] Remarkably, these pathologies were increasing at a time when French population growth was very small—which became yet another index of the overall crisis. According to

Tarde it was the fluctuations in empirical reality described by successive editions of the *Compte* that imparted the most decisive blow to Quetelet's notion of the constancy of crime.[48]

A third difficulty with moral statistics, suggested Tarde, was its lack of proper conception of the causes of crime:

> If it was true, as Quetelet would have it, that the volume of crime was very nearly invariable and predetermined; if, in a word, crime and misdemeanors were things as inevitable as lightning and rain, but even more regular, it would be necessary to say that criminality can only be contained by the use of good lightning conductors against the criminal storm, i.e., through the perfection of locks, safes, revolvers, and other defensive weapons.[49]

In *Penal Philosophy* Tarde dismissed several of what were then generally regarded as causes of crime. For example, and in unwitting agreement with some of the moral statisticians,[50] he discounted education—or rather, lack of it—as an a priori influence on crime. In some places, and in some periods, criminals have been more "educated" than noncriminals.[51] Education without a moral or religious dimension could actually increase opportunities for crime. Tarde asserted that it had been "abundantly proved that as far as the world of potential small-time miscreants is concerned, schools have been neither a moral brake, since they do not prevent recidivism, nor a moral *spur,* since everyone agrees on delinquents' cowardice and weakness of character."[52] Likewise, he dismissed poverty as a general cause of crime. One end of the social structure, for example, is occupied by the peasant who typically "participates in [the] moderation of desires, and grows rich through his sobriety, his stoicism, his economy, and through his patch of ground the ownership of which he finally acquires";[53] at the other end is "the millionaire, the feverish financier, or the politician, who is compelled because of his very millions to use them as the material for his unsafe speculations, his swindles and extortion on a large scale."[54] The moral statisticians had signally failed to produce an explanation either of rising crime rates or, indeed, of crime at all. However, in trying to develop a coherent explanation of crime himself, Tarde realized that his negative conclusions against the moral statisticians, and so too against Lombrosianism, were theoretically inadequate: "we have now to show along what lines the laws of crime are to be sought. We shall find them in a special application of the general laws which appear to us to govern social science."[55]

Imitation and Crime

Tarde constructs his explanation of the "laws of crime" around the concept of imitation, namely, "a species of somnambulism"[56] and "the powerful, generally unconscious, always partly mysterious, action by means of which we account for all the phenomena of society."[57] For Tarde crime is a social phenomenon like any other, and is operated on by the process of imitation like any other.[58] Imitation occurs at the cerebral level, applies to the different psychological states and beliefs of individual actors, and always operates in a social context. Tarde viewed the individual as locked in a process of unceasing struggle and always placed at a crossroads of apparent choice: between theft and honest labor, arson and fire insurance policies, and vice and virtue. An actor travels one road rather than another for both logical reasons, such as those connected with utilitarianism, and extra-logical reasons, such as the imitation of a superior by an inferior; a particular road may be chosen consciously or unconsciously, voluntarily or through "coercion."[59]

Imitation has its source in the metropolis, in the nobility and in the rich (the masses are typically tied through imitative bondage to the conceptions and fancies of their superiors); it typically travels outward and downward, to rural areas, serfs, and the poor. One consequence of this intermental process is thus the stimulation of ardor and cupidity. However, according to Tarde the process of imitation does not operate exclusively at the level of the individual. On the contrary, it is also present socially and historically in urbanism and in the growth of cities, in national institutions and even in international warfare. It traverses all social, racial, and religious boundaries. It permeates all aspects of social life, from art to architecture and from music to militarism. It propagates both good and evil.[60] It encourages crime. In some detail Tarde tried to show that most crime originates in the "higher ranks" and descended to the "lowest ranks."[61] Drunkenness, smoking, moral offences, political assassination, arson, and even vagabondage (an activity of "the noble pilgrims and the noble minstrels of the Middle Ages,"[62] for example, are crimes that originated with the feudal nobility and are transmitted to the masses through imitation.

How then does socialization into criminality occur? Why, despite a common exposure to the same set of imitative processes, are some actors infected with criminality and others not? Tarde addressed these questions incompletely and with little obvious satisfaction. His diverse responses to them clearly reveals the difficulty of trying to combine a theory of motivation based on intermental imitation with a theory of sociality based on the associational interests of occupational solidarity. Tarde identified a number of stages in the commission of crime. To begin with, he reiterates his adamancy that actors are never born into criminality but "socialized" into it: "Perhaps one is born vicious, but it is quite certain that one becomes a criminal."[63] However, some people are born with psychological qualities that predispose them to crime. Those born with vicious dispositions are more likely to become violent than those with passive natures, and those born with avaricious natures are more likely to become thieves than those with pious or nonacquisitive natures. Thus, "allow pride, vanity, envy, and hatred to grow in you out of all proportion . . . become irascible and vengeful, and you will be very lucky if you do not kill anybody during the course of your life."[64] To the presence of these predisposing qualities Tarde added the necessary existence of "a special kind of fever"[65] which must be understood socially rather than psychologically. This he referred to variously as a "fermentation," an "agitation," and a "disturbance." Having accomplished his act, the criminal "feels himself at one and the same time strangely freed and lost, plunged into a new world which has opened up before him."[66] Tarde then suggested that subsequent criminality, or recidivism, is variously due to: (1) the psychological nature of crime itself: "crime is the one [action] which must be repeated the most in imagination, because it is the most energetic. . . . The pro-

pensity which drives a man to the repetition of a crime is thus a fatal
one";[67] (2) "the fault [of] society";[68] (3) a criminal's self-concept: "the
more a man feels or thinks himself to be separated from his fellow men
because of a fall . . . the more dangerous he is";[69] and (4) the reaction
of the "external world": "when prosecution against [the criminal] has
taken place, and when he has been condemned, the gulf within him becomes singularly widened and deepened by being revealed to the outside world."[70]

At the same time Tarde allowed that the plastic clay of our natural
innate qualities is only a material whose form is constructed by the
"social" world. It is therefore to the social world that we must look for
an explanation of why some people turn to crime but why others with
similar qualities and defects do not. Having admitted the distinction
between "criminals because of habit and criminals because of opportunity," he at once rejects the "social point of view" which focuses on
factors such as differential opportunity. "What criminal is not a criminal because of opportunity, and what crime that takes place acciden-
tally has not ordinarily a tendency to become repeated because of
habit, if there be no opposition offered to it?"[71] However, this "social"
avenue Tarde then self-consciously closes, and he proceeds to offer a
psychological classification of criminality that, it transpires, was in
part based on the legalistic categories of the French penal code.

The most basic classification of criminality stems from the rights
that criminals have breached, namely, the inviolability of the person
and the sanctity of property. Within this schema, approved of by
Durkheim,[72] Tarde continues, criminals should be classified according to the social categories or occupations which they held before the
commission of their criminal act.[73] The trade of crime, like every
other, must be understood in terms of its patterns of socialization and
professional formation.[74] But at this point Tarde again demurs, and
resolves his hesitation by subdividing the notion of occupational categories and impaling it on the advance of modernity (or "civilization"). On the far side of modernity there are agricultural occupations
and rural populations. These categories are faithful to custom and tradition, submissive to the example of their domestic or patriotic an-
cestors, and violent in their coarseness. The nature of their crimes

Tarde termed *imitation-coûtume*. With modernity is found the expanding presence of industrial and mercantile professions and urban populations. These categories are susceptible to infatuation and novelties, influenced by strangers, and 'depraved' in their refinements. The nature of their crimes he termed *imitation-mode*. This latter form of imitation Tarde held to be the dominant cause of crime in modern societies and perhaps the greatest source of political instability.[75]

Despite his principled opposition to any mechanistic notion of law-like regularity in the causes of crime, Tarde consistently identified two factors which in practice assumed causal status in his criminology. With a much greater intensity than any of his contemporaries, he isolated the modern city as the greatest repository of the imitative propagation of crime and also its greatest source.[76] It is the city which has the highest rate of homicide motivated by greed, where murderer and victim are apt to be utter strangers, and where recidivism is most pronounced. It is the city that for Tarde most displays the voluptuousness and the increasing dissolution of French customs: the formation of political sects; increasing rates of assassination, murder, and suicide; alcoholism; adultery; crimes against children and crimes by children; rape; and vandalism. The city encourages the substitution for traditional morality of the mercantile worship of gold. It is the modern city in which transformations in psychological state and in criminal intent are most evident: "The prolonged effect of large cities upon criminality is manifested, it seems to us, in the slow substitution, not exactly of guile for violence, but of greedy, crafty, and voluptuous violence for vindictive and brutal violence."[77]

An additional cause of crime, that itself is both an example of the processes of imitation and also closely associated with the impersonal social relations of modern urban life, Tarde identified as the violence fostered by mass collective behavior.[78] Indeed, most of Tarde's analysis of collective behavior entailed a frantic aversion to any body of people larger than a small and orderly gathering. In a speech of 1892 to the Brussels Congress of Criminal Anthropology, for example, he suggested, "The crowd, even among the most civilized populations, is always a savage or a faun, still worse, an impulsive and maniacal beast, a plaything of its instincts and unconscious habits, occasionally an animal of a lower order."[79] On another occasion:

> A mob is a strange phenomenon. It is a gathering of heterogeneous elements, unknown to one another; but as soon as a spark of passion, having flashed out from one of these elements, electrifies this confused mass, there takes place a sort of sudden organization, a spontaneous generation. This incoherence becomes cohesion, this noise becomes a voice, and these thousands of men crowded together soon form but a single animal, a wild beast without a name, which marches to its goal with irresistible finality.[80]

Concepts such as somnambulism, paroxysm, and mental contagion Tarde frequently invoked to explain the abnormality and dangerousness of crowds and mobs during the Third Republic. While it is perhaps inaccurate to suggest that he explicitly equated the violence of these groups with the organized activities of the French working class, this tendency was nevertheless usually implicit in the exemplification of his arguments about collective behavior. "The conduct of a crowd," Tarde argued, "largely depends on the social origin of its members, on their profession, class or caste."[81] Urban crowds are those whose contagion achieves the highest degree of speed and intensity. . . and "their members are drawn from those detached from family and tradition."[81] Appalled by events such as a strike by mill workers in his native region of Périgord, the 1871 Paris Commune, and the anarchist ("the light cavalry of socialism") bombings of mid-1892, Tarde asserted that the emotional turbulence of crowd behavior was most vociferously expressed in the deluded actions of striking workers, rioters, and revolutionary political movements ("the honest man is a conformist and the rogue a dissident").[83] These actions he characterized as proletarian, anarchic, irrational, and feminine.[84]

Some of these characterizations Tarde shared with Emile Durkheim, and it is to their prolonged and bitter debate that I now turn.

The "Normality" of Crime: Tarde's Debate with Durkheim

During the 1890s Tarde and Durkheim engaged in a series of ex-
changes that were relished by the former and, although doubtless seen
as a necessary part of his messianic quest to develop an autonomous
sociology, distasteful to the latter. Tarde's first published criticism of
Durkheim occurred in his review of Durkheim's *Division of Labor*. In
this somewhat respectful review of Durkheim's work, Tarde recommended Durkheim's description of penality to criminologists as "an
excellent critique" of Lombroso.[85] Wherein this excellence lay, he did
not elaborate. However, against Durkheim he asserted, first, that
Durkheim's account of social change ignored factors between nations
such as wars, massacres, and brutal annexations and also paid insufficient attention to the influence of the accidental, the irrational, and
the role of genius. Second, Tarde suggested that violent change was
itself caused by psychological factors such as ambition, cupidity, the
love of glory, and proselytizing fanaticism. Third, Tarde complained
that social life was derived neither from a similitude of consciences
nor from increasing social density and social volume, as Durkheim
had suggested, but by three other factors: (1) wars, the abuse of
power, murder, and spoliation; (2) inventiveness, imitative contagion,
and assimilation between individuals, then between groups, cities,
and nations; and (3) especially in countries with declining populations, such as France, by the famous *lutte pour la vie* ("struggle for
existence").[86] Finally, Tarde disagreed with Durkheim's opposition
between the two forms of social solidarity (mechanical and organic)
as the basis for transformations in the division of labor. Rather, he
suggested, the division of labor was, among other factors, the daughter of genius:

> The division of labor acts neither as a socialising nor a mor-
> alising agent. . . . Its habitual result is to develop and fortify,
> under new forms, the intellectual and moral community, by
> multiplying the objects of [this] common fund [*richesse*] and
> by singularly facilitating their diffusion.[87]

The "Normality of Crime: Durkheim

> Contrary to current ideas, the criminal no longer appears as an ut-
> terly unsociable creature, a sort of parasitic element, a foreign, un-
> assimilable body introduced into the bosom of society. He plays a
> normal role in social life. For its part, crime must no longer be con-
> ceived of as an evil.

> —Emile Durkheim[88]

Much of the first two chapters of Durkheim's (1894) *Rules of Sociological Method* was a polemical attack, both direct and indirect, on Tarde's
notion of the ontological and epistemological primacy of the individual
in social life. Durkheim's chief intention here was the rationalist
project of distinguishing sociology from other sciences, such as biology, politics, and psychology, by demarcating its object of study as the
"social fact." A social fact Durkheim identified as "any way of acting,
whether fixed or not, capable of exerting over the individual an external constraint"[89] or which "is general over the whole of a given society
whilst having an existence of its own, independent of its individual
manifestations."[90] Social facts are therefore obligatory, and they are general not because they are held by many people but because they are held
collectively. Because social facts are constituted collectively, they must
not be confused with organic or psychical phenomena which exist only
in and through individual consciousness. Durkheim reasoned that we
are often victims of the illusion that we ourselves have acted of our
own volition; in reality, that action was imposed on us externally. "Social phenomena," writes Durkheim, should thus "be considered in
themselves, detached from the conscious beings who form their own
mental representations of them."[91]

Durkheim provocatively admitted that his insertion of constraint
into all social facts was "in danger of infuriating those who zealously
uphold out-and-out individualism."[92] In a lengthy footnote he remarked, specifically, how far removed his own definition of the social
fact was from that which was the basis for the "ingenious" system of
Tarde. Nowhere, Durkheim asserted, did his research corroborate the

preponderant influence that Tarde attributed to imitation in the genesis of collective facts. Individual states that affect others are individual nevertheless, and if they are imitated it is precisely because their origin is social and coercive. Even in a crowd, when there is a spontaneous participation in a common emotion, individual experience is never so much generated as it is undergone. "Moreover," Durkheim continued, "one may speculate whether the term 'imitation' is indeed appropriate to designate a proliferation which occurs through some coercive influence. In such a single term very different phenomena, which need to be distinguished, are confused."[93]

The most acrimonious exchange between Durkheim and Tarde occurred over the former's view about the normality of crime in the third chapter ("Rules for the Distinction of the Normal from the Pathological") of the *Rules*. In this chapter Durkheim had attempted to restructure "the fundamental facts of criminology," and he displayed a resolute opposition to definitions of the normal and the pathological produced *in abstracto*. If crime was not a sickness, Durkheim asserted, then punishment could not be a remedy, and the functions of punishment must therefore lie outside the realm of penality. Additionally, Durkheim complained that criminologists were wrong to agree unanimously on the pathological or morbid nature of crime. What was abnormal from the perspective of biology or pathology was not necessarily so from that of sociology. For a sociologist a social fact "is normal for a given social type, viewed at a given phase of its development, when it occurs in the average society of that species, considered at the corresponding phase of its evolution."[94] Durkheim therefore pleaded for historical specificity in the understanding of social facts; in a specific social context, and against the background of a specific level of social development, the very generality of social facts is indicative of their normality. Social facts as such can never be abnormal; however, in a particular context their intensity, their presence or absence, could be abnormal and pathological phenomena. At any given moment every society will have an average or normal incidence of, for example, marriages, suicides, and sickness; it is only deviations from these averages that can be termed abnormal.

Durkheim makes three specific claims about the nature of crime. Firstly, crime is a thoroughly normal phenomenon. It occurs in all societies of all types, it is very closely related to the conditions of collective life, and its incidence tends to increase as societies evolve from lower to higher phases. This claim about the normality of crime Durkheim had, of course, advanced in considerably more depth in *The Division of Labor,* although now he suggests that "to classify crime among the phenomena of normal sociology is not merely to declare that it is an inevitable though regrettable phenomenon arising from the incorrigible weakness of man; it is to assert that it is a factor in public health, an integrative element in any healthy society."[95] Durkheim professes that his discovery of the normality of crime he at first found surprising and disconcerting. However, no society can ever be entirely free of crime; universal and absolute uniformity is impossible because each member of society is confronted with variation in "the immediate physical environment . . . hereditary antecedents . . . (and) social influences upon which we depend."[96] Hypothetically, even if the actions regarded as criminal at one moment ceased to exist, new forms of crime would at once be invented. Durkheim thus entreats his readers to imagine a community of saints in an exemplary and perfect monastery: "in it crime as such will be unknown, but faults that appear venial to the ordinary person will arouse the same scandal as does normal crime in ordinary consciences.[97]

To his counterfactual claim that crime is both necessary and normal, Durkheim additionally claims that crime is useful. This is so because crime is indispensible to the normal evolution of law and morality. If there were no crimes then the collective conscience would have attained an intensity unparalleled in history—crime is thus both a manifestation of individual originality and a preparation for, or a prelude to, changes in law and morality. Durkheim provides Socrates' crime of independent thought as an example of his second claim: Socrates' crime "served to prepare the way for a new morality and a new faith, which the Athenians then needed because the traditions by which they had hitherto lived no longer corresponded to the conditions of their existence."[98] Finally, Durkheim claims that crime is a social phenomenon whose ontological and cultural status is variable. He suggests that if because of increasing public sentiment against it, a particular category of crime (e.g., theft) becomes rarer, then the public reaction to and condemnation of lesser actions of the same sort (e.g., mere misappropriation), correspondingly, will intensify. Thus, dishonest contracts or those fulfilled dishonestly, which only incur public censure or civil redress, will become crimes. "Nothing," Durkheim claims, "is good indefinitely and without limits."[99]

The "Abnormality" of Crime: Tarde

Tarde's reactions to Durkheim's claims about the normality of crime were identical to those of many of the first readers of the *Rules*.[100] In his reply to Durkheim, Tarde was as concerned to rebut what he understood to be the major points of Durkheim's argument about crime as he was to advance the merits of his own views about the role of the individual in social development. His reply to Durkheim rested on three counterclaims about the nature of crime.

Firstly, Tarde takes issue with Durkheim's claim that crime is normal. Indeed, he objected to Durkheim—as he had to Lombroso—that this notion was expressed in "the increasing indulgence of judges and juries and in the relaxation of the fibres of indignation and of public contempt when confronted by certain criminal outrages [*attentats*]" (1895b; p. 138). Tarde applauds Durkheim ("the distinguished sociologist," "the learned professor from Bordeaux," "my subtle opponent") for posing frankly the question of whether it is true that "*in some respects crime, like misfortune, is good,* and that its extirpation is no more desirable than possible?"[101] But he suggests that Durkheim was wrong to equate normality with generality; it had already been demonstrated by Cournot that it was a mistake to confound the normal type with the average type.[102] Tarde asks us to consider a tribe where the average lifespan is less than the age of adulthood: it would follow that it would be normal for none of its members to reproduce! If "superior culture" is less widespread, then it would follow that ignorance and immorality would be healthy. Tarde suggests that the pathological could be defined as whatever diminishes the chances of an individual's success in the "struggle for existence," and the normal as that which is adapted to triumph in the struggle.[103] The abnormal, therefore, could be whatever renders an individual unable or less able to enter into an association and to fortify its bonds. Following Pasteur's theory of the origin of the

most serious illnesses, in which illness was understood to be a combat
between an army of cells and an army of microbes, a combat in which
our organism is simultaneously the stake and the battlefield, Tarde de-
fines criminality as

> a conflict between the great legion of honest men and the
> small battalion of criminals, and both act *normally* given the
> goal which each pursues. But, as their two goals are contrary,
> the resistance they mutually offer each other is perceived by
> each of them as a pathological state which, although perma-
> nent and universal, is still painful.[104]

Following J. S. Mill's dictum that an individual's normal state is
the highest state obtainable, it follows, Tarde suggests, that for a society "the normal is peace in justice and enlightenment, the complete
extermination of crime, vice, ignorance, misery and abuse."[105] Moreover, Tarde obligingly asserts that Durkheim's argument about the
normality of crime could perhaps be rescued if it was the coupling of
crime and punishment that was normal rather than crime itself. To this
Tarde replies that it is precisely the unprosecuted and unpunished
crime which plays a distinctive role in history: "this triumphant
crime, interred with royal or dictatorial honors, exalted in statues in
public places . . . this scourge . . . this poison a necessary and indispensable ferment of historical progress."[106]

Second, Tarde objects to Durkheim's notion that crime is useful.
The real agents of "human perfection" have not been the violent but
"apostles . . . the discoverers of truth, the inventors of useful things
and the collectors of artistic beauties."[107] How can low and rampant
crime ("the only type identified by M. Durkheim") be useful where it
produces nothing but the contagion of its own bad example? Only for
pursuit by the police is it useful.[108] Third, Tarde objects that Durkheim
was wrong to argue that an increase in morality will be followed by an
intensity in the reaction to what was previously categorized as moral
offences. Against Durkheim's error Tarde counters that if one exam-
ines the increasing lenience of the judiciary, the tendency to reduce
crimes to misdemeanors or to divert them to a civil status, and an increase in the rate of acquittals, then precisely the opposite is true. It is

not punitive severity but "the tribunal of public opinion" which would become rigorous, exacting and fastidious—"And would that be harmful?"[109]

In what amounted to little more than the clarifying of their own position and the correcting of that of their adversary, fueled by mutual animosity, the skirmish between Durkheim and Tarde continued unabated.[110] No clear victor emerged.

Crime and Penality: The Neoclassical Compromise

The major objects of Tarde's criminology, this chapter has thus far suggested, were constructed in the context of his debates with biological positivism, with moral statistics and with certain aspects of Durkheim's sociology. Each debate had originated in a very particular sociocultural configuration. Each differed from the other two in its objective focus, in its level of abstraction and, if resolved, in its point of insertion within the complex of penal strategies. Each debate had intense practical significance. Tarde engaged in these debates not simply because each encompassed one of the most pressing issues of penality in late nineteenth-century France, but because in combination all three seriously threatened the very core of French penality, namely, the responsible legal subject of classical jurisprudence. Quite simply, the positivist revolution portended the disintegration of the classical legal subject. As Garofalo had remarked, during the stormy sessions of the First International Congress of Criminal Anthropology in 1885, prior to the revision of the Italian penal code, the two cornerstones of penal law—moral responsibility and the proportionality of punishment to crime—had been proven obsolete by positivism.[111] Moreover, if the overdetermined subject of positivism was allowed to penetrate criminal law, Tarde thought that the direction of future penal strategies would be reduced to two, neither of which would reduce the imitative propagation of crime: either complete absolution of a crime or extermination of the criminal. Thus, Tarde warned,

> During a criminal trial it is becoming more and more easy for
> a lawyer, with the writings of alienists at his disposal, to dem-
> onstrate the irresistible nature of the criminal impulse which

carried his client off his feet; and for the jury, as for the legislator, the irresponsibility of the accused follows as a matter of
course. [112]

Tarde's criminology must ultimately be understood, I suggest, in the
overriding context of his attempt to establish a compromised terrain
between the unbridled subject of classical jurisprudence and the overdetermined object of positivism. To secure the importance of a neoclassical terrain between them, Tarde first attempted to vanquish the
sterile debate between the spiritualists and the materialists about the respective merits of the extremes of free will and determinism. Both
doctrines he castigated as metaphysical absolutes. Neither doctrine
was justified either theoretically or practically. The doctrine of free will
derived from ignorance and superstition, and posited the individual
agent as a volitional demigod. It let to barbaric forms of penality in-
congruous with the level of morality required by advanced civilization.
The latter had arisen, especially among the positivists and socialists of
the *nuova scuola,* largely as a misplaced reaction to the exaggerated individualism of classicists, such as Beccaria, and viewed the individual
as an automaton. In his several discussions of the penal implications of
extreme determinism, Tarde vociferously rejected the argument that
criminal responsibility should a priori be reduced if action is not based
entirely on free will. [113] On the one hand, Tarde argued, it was wrong
to claim, as the radical determinists consistently did, that the sole basis
of responsibility is free will. [114] That responsibility and free will are
inseparably associated was based on a misreading of classical penal theory by the determinists. On the other hand, Tarde bemoaned that notions of determinism contributed greatly to the crises in French
penality. The influence of these notions was manifest in the increasing
laxity shown criminals by prosecutors, judges, and juries. Nowhere
was this more visible than in the tendency to reduce charges from
crimes to misdemeanors which, Tarde argued, in turn caused more
than a threefold increase in the number of misdemeanors between 1835
and 1885. [115]

Neither the doctrine of free will nor that of determinsim, therefore,
was seen by Tarde as an adequate basis for a coherent system of penal
responsibility. The basis of penal responsibility Tarde held to be intimately connected to the philosophical search for the causes of action,

and the mistake of much contemporary discussion was its misplaced focus on the question, "Where is the cause of action?" rather than "What is the cause of action?" In addressing the what question, Tarde responded with an answer in two parts, respectively lodged at the psychological and sociological levels of action.

At the psychological level of action Tarde argued that penal responsibility is always in the nature of a debt, i.e., its nature is to produce a satisfaction judged to be useful to the person, or groups of persons, who have the right to invoke it. This penal utilitarianism Tarde based on a unity of the notions of "individual identity" and "social similarity": "responsibility has always been thus understood in every period by popular instinct."[116] By the notion of individual identity Tarde meant that personhood is a relatively enduring state of consciousness which, in its normal state, is possessed of various habitual and characteristic faculties that are susceptible of association with others. By the notion of social similarity Tarde assumed that the author of a criminal action is a member of a society which has common patterns of socialization, education, and values of imitative origin. In *Penal Philosophy* Tarde wrote that he agreed with "the socialists of the new school" on the "superiority of social causes over external causes; but instead of concluding from this, as they do, that society alone is guilty of every crime, I conclude from it that the individual is really and justly punishable."[117] Each person is thus responsible for his or her actions because only the individual can be the authentic cause of action and because association involves mutual obligation. Criminal responsibility can be "excused," or a crime can remain unprosecuted, only in such cases as when the memory of an actor is impaired by madness, epilepsy, or involuntary hypnosis.[118]

At the sociological level of action, Tarde suggested that the state itself is obliged to cultivate individual responsibility and that this duty increases with the progress of civilization. However, the possibilities for the exercise of individual responsibility had been seriously undermined by the imminent and pathological collapse of French morality. This collapse was especially manifest for Tarde in the rise of Marxism, which he saw as a major threat to the democratic rights of the citizen, and in the decay of Christian moral values.[119] Both resulted in the abrogation of individual moral responsibility. The chief barriers to the imitative propagation of crime, and the main hopes for its elimination, Tarde held to lie in the pursuit of two broad policies by the state. The first was the consolidation of existing counterweights in the realm of ideas and values. These included a revived Christianity, patriotism, and family sentiment. Against the spread of paganism, Tarde recommended the Christian virtues of charity, humility, the despising of riches, and self-purification through penance. Indeed, according to Tarde the rise of atheistic Marxism was not only a symptom of the decay of Christian morality but also a cause of it; moreover, "the thing which Karl Marx seems least anxious about is the problem of morality, which with him becomes confused with the problem of economics."[120] The second policy comprised the creation of a stable political system, prominent features of which would be a more powerful gendarmerie, a strong judiciary, and a vigorous system of punishment. In a discussion of crowd behavior, for example, Tarde urged the dissolution of the jury (that "useless institution") and its replacement by a criminal magistracy whose members should be "specially trained and recruited from the ranks of men who combine the necessary skills with exemplary personal qualities."[121]

Tarde's proposals for a renewed system of punishment were an often ambiguous, neoclassical amalgam of classical and positivist principles. These included:

1. *Equivalence.* There should be an equivalence between the seriousness of a crime and the degree of punishment awarded it. Punishment should be "exemplary" but not "vengeful," and should reflect both the mechanisms of the free market[122] and also the use of individualized treatment.[123]

2. *Deterrence.* All punishments should seek to deter future miscreants and should include elements of suffering and certainty. Deterrence is unworkable only for the criminally insane and the semi-insane.[124] On the anniversary of their misdeeds, criminals should be subject to public humiliation.[125]

3. *Imprisonment.* Although transportation and penal colonies should gradually be abolished, imprisonment must be the primary

form of punishment. Different penitentiary systems should be used. The criminally insane and recidivists should be isolated and segregated; other categories of prisoners should be placed in compulsory single cells by night; most prisoners, depending on their moral character and social origin, should be allowed in optional cells by day;[126] there should be increased use of visitation (by "the kindly disposed") and probation ("conditional liberation").[127]

4. *The Death Penalty.* The death penalty should be retained—and used sparingly, humanely, and without spectacle—or corporal punishment should be used.[128]

However, the implementation of Tarde's proposals notwithstanding, the prospects for France's recovery from its pathological and moral crises were not good. So serious were the effects of the decline in Christian belief and practice that Tarde compared late nineteenth-century France with the moral collapse that accompanied the decline of the Roman Empire and the turbulent period of the Reformation.[129] As the 1890s progressed, Tarde seems occasionally to have despaired of ever finding a "penal therapeutic" because the proliferation of crime seemed to be an inevitable, if paradoxical, accompaniment to the growth of civilization itself.[130] Sensationalistic journalism that associated heroism with violent actions, irresponsible economic and philosophical doctrines that focused on the exploitation of the working class, policies of military rearmament, and financial scandals in Parliament and elsewhere—these factors also contributed to the contagion of criminality for which, ultimately, every citizen was partly responsible.

Conclusion

The dense tapestry into which Tarde's discourse on crime and penality must eventually be woven is the compromise between classicism and positivism that emerged among sociologists and criminologists in the final quarter of the nineteenth century. More as preparation for this larger task than as an epilogue for the present chapter, a brief concluding comment is now in order about the peculiar nature of Tarde's intellectual legacy of which, except for the considerable influence his writings posthumously exerted among criminologists in the United States during the first two decades of the twentieth century,[131] very little has remained.[132]

This chapter has outlined the three major debates around which Tarde constructed the objects of his criminology. In attempting to rescue the volitional subject of classical jurisprudence, in constructing a sociological explanation of crime in which the individual criminal was ultimately the principal actor, and in suggesting forms of penality whose principles avoided the determinist implications of the positivist revolution—in these ways Tarde's criminology helped to forge the dominant features of the neoclassical terrain. However, against none of his three principal antagonists did Tarde exert decisive effects. Against Lombrosianism the apparent death knell was not to be sounded until a decade after Tarde's death and largely in isolation from Tarde's own labors. To French, British, and American criminologists, most of whom were entranced with the conceptual categories of medicine and psychiatry, it was not Tarde's work but rather the erstwhile scientific rigor of Goring's *The English Convict* of 1913, that was regarded—mistakenly so, as I argue in the next chapter—as the definitive refutation of atavistic notions of crime.[133]

Against Quetelet and the moral statisticians the fatal blows had already been delivered, in a domain whose technicalities still eluded criminologists, some three decades before Tarde's intervention. While Tarde was the first criminologist roundly to castigate the antitheoreticism of moral statistics, his own criticisms of this enterprise had been largely preempted by French statisticians such as Cournot, Bertillon, and Bertrand. Finally, the increasing subordination of serious intellectual concerns to those of personal animosity in his debates with Durkheim, coupled with the subsequent classical status accorded Durkheim's vast corpus, ensured not only for Tarde's criminology but also for his general system of sociological theory, an uninfluential silence when the historical landmarks of criminology were later reconstituted.[134]

Moreover, almost to the end of his life Tarde was unique among French academics in that, despising the intellectual domination of the metropolis, he had no secure position within the all-powerful French university system. By 1890 some of Tarde's friends were displeased that the high position occupied in the scientific world by the examining magistrate from Sarlat was not recognized by his professional superiors. In 1891 his friends procured employment for him (which Tarde was persuaded to accept) at the Ministry of Justice in Paris. Here, from 1891 to 1896, he directed the statistical bureau that produced the annual *Compte général de l'administration de la justice criminelle*. Between 1896 and 1900 Tarde taught several courses in an informal capacity at the *École Libre des Sciences Politiques* and the *Collège Libre des Sciences Sociales*. Not until 1900 was Tarde elected to, and did he deign to accept, the chair of modern philosophy at the College de France. An isolated and often better antagonist, he cultivated neither the allies nor the disciples required of a systematic intellectual legacy. He died, exhausted, in 1904.

Notes

1. Detailed accounts of Tarde's early career as poet and playwright, of the series of chronic illnesses that plagued him in his provincial habitat, including bronchitis, asthma, and severe difficulties with his eyes, and of the interesting—if unsubstantiated—links between his family history and subsequent intellectual output can be found in Lacassagne (1904), "Gabriel Tarde, 1843–1904"; Geisert (1935), op. cit., pp. 1–22; and his son G. Tarde (1909), *Tarde. Introduction et pages choisies par ses fils,* pp. 7–70. Brief intellectual histories of the formative years of Tarde's work can be found in Bouglé (1905), "Un Sociologue individualiste: Gabriel Tarde"; and Worms (1905), "La philosophie sociale de G. Tarde."

2. The standard French commentary on Tarde's criminology by Geisert is now very outdated (Geisert, 1935, "Le système criminaliste de Tarde"). Moreover, there is no sustained treatment of Tarde's criminology in English. Only a small part of his voluminous output on crime and penality is readily available to an English-language audience. The commentary on these writings in English is often not especially helpful; see, for example, Vine (1972), "Gabriel Tarde"; and Jones (1986), *History of Criminology: A Philosophical Perspective,* pp. 159–61. The few useful commentaries are, in different ways, intentionally limited in their respective scopes—see Clark (1968), "Gabriel

Tarde"; Lukes (1973), *Emile Durkheim: His Life and Work,* pp. 302–14; and Lukes and Scull (1983), "Introduction to Durkheim", pp. 15–19.

3. It is important to note that Tarde's legal career began as a *juge d'instruction,* a position within the French legal system whose activities were predicated on the rigorous acceptance of the classical doctrine of free will. Robert Nye has stressed that the task of the Napoleonic *juge d'instruction,* whose role combined those of prosecutor, investigator, and judge in bringing indictments and assembling evidence, lay in "extracting the motives for a crime in direct confrontation with the accused [and which] operated as a working presumption of the existence of reason and conscious responsibility" (1984, *Crime, Madness, and Politics in Modern France,* p. 119).

4. See further Perrot (1975), "Délinquance et système pénitentaire en France au XIXe siècle."

5. Duesterberg (1979), "Criminology and the Social Order in Nineteenth-Century France," p. 89.

6. Wright (1983), *Between the Guillotine and Liberty: Two Centuries of the Crime Problem in France,* p. 50.

7. *Compte général* (1936), p. 46; Nye (1984), op cit., pp. 58–59.

8. Duesterberg (1979), op. cit., p. 301.

9. Nye (1984), op. cit., p. 59.

10. *Compte général* (1881), p. 83.

11. Tarde (1890b), *Penal Philosophy,* p. 312.

12. Tarde's arguments on this point can be found in Tarde (1886b), "La statistique criminelle du dernier demi-siècle"; and Tarde (1890a), *The Laws of Imitation.*

13. In accounting for this process of the medicalization of deviance, Nye writes that "degeneration was the perfect expression of a hygienic medicine whose primary concern was the health and moral well-being of a whole population" (1984), op. cit., p. 45, and that "the binary term 'normal-pathological' could be used to sanction social norms and social fears deeply felt by the masses with the approval of medical science. The terminology could also be used effectively to enlighten or persuade a nonscientific public because it is conceptually isomorphic with so many other binary terms that regulate the perception of social life: moral-immoral, criminal-honest, sane-insane, violent-passive" (p. 48).

14. Of the numerous accounts of Lombroso's theory of the born criminal available in English, the three best are Kurella (1911), *Cesare Lombroso: A Modern Man of Science;* Wolfgang (1972), "Cesare Lombroso;" and Pick (1989), *Faces of Degeneration: A European Disorder, c.1848–c.1918,* chapter 5. Kurella'a

account is quite comprehensive, but very dated in its interpretation and most partisan. A dimension missing from Wolfgang's excellent essay (and also, incidentally, from the narrow focus on racism and scientism of Marxist critics such as Lukács, 1952, *The Destruction of Reason,* pp. 667–761) is Lombroso's adamant rejection of any form of idealism, his virulent opposition to which, in turn, explains much of the vehemence directed against him by Tarde.

15. Silvani (1976), "Lavori recenti su Lombroso."

16. Gramsci (1926), "Some Aspects of the Southern Question," p. 444. Moreover, Gramsci condemned the incipient racism of the Socialist Party and of southern intellectuals who have "a fierce antipathy to the working peasant . . . [and who] acquire an atavistic, instinctive feeling of crazy fear of the peasants with their destructive violence" (*ibid.* p. 455). See also the polemical remarks of Georg Lukács against biologism, and in particular against social Darwinism and Lombrosianism, in Lukács (1952, op. cit., pp. 667–761); and Togliatti's comments of 1919 quoted in Piccone (1983, *Italian Marxism,* p. 112, n. 15).

17. The first edition of *l'Uomo delinquente* has never been published in English, and most English-language commentaries on it have been forced to rely on Lombroso's considerably modified work (translated from French and published in English in 1918) *Crime: its Causes and Remedies* (1899). The quotation above is taken from the first Italian edition, an English translation of which (chap. 1 and 2 and the summary) was generously provided me by Professor Leonard Savitz. Other chapters of the first Italian edition dealt with such matters as tattooing, the emotions and passions, religion, jargon, and the handwriting of criminals.

18. Ferri (1884), op. cit.

19. Garofalo (1885), *Criminologia.*

20. Duesterberg (1979), op. cit., pp. 319–21.

21. See Tarde (1888), "Les actes du congrès de Rome."

22. See *Actes du deuxième congrès international de l'anthropologie criminelle* (1890), especially Tarde's comments at pp. 199–200 and his "Dixième question: les anciens et les nouveaux fondements de responsabilité morale," pp. 92–105.

23. See *Actes du troisième congrès de l'anthropologie criminelle.* Brussels, 1893.

24. See Tarde (1895c), "Criminalité et santé sociale."

25. Tarde (1885), *Le type criminel,* pp. 9–10.

26. Tarde (1890b), op. cit., p. 65.

27. Ibid., p. 220.

28. Ibid., p. 226.

29. Ibid., p. 237.

30. "What did Fustel de Coulange find in his voyage of discovery about the origins of the family in our higher races? An intensity of domestic and religious life, an energy of patriarchal virtue, of filial piety and of elementary justice . . . without which the ancient household—let alone the ancient city— is neither possible nor conceivable" (Tarde, 1889a, "L'atavisme moral," p. 259).

31. Ibid., p. 257.

32. Tarde (1886c), "Problèmes de pénalité," pp. 155–56.

33. Tarde (1890b), op. cit., p. 66. See also Tarde's interesting comments on prison diets (ibid., p. 65) and on the Mafia (ibid., pp. 279–84).

34. See further Nye (1982a), "Heredity, Pathology and Psychoneurosis in Durkheim's Early Work." Ultimately, it is not surprising to discover the pervasive "biologism" in Durkheim's early work. In the *Division of Labor*, for example, Durkheim draws upon Féré's (1889) *Dégénérescence et criminalité* to argue both that "the propensity to wrongdoing in general is often hereditary" (1893, p. 258) and that "organic and psychological" influences are themselves often produced from the social environment (*ibid.*, pp. 258–67).

35. Duesterberg (1979), op. cit., pp. 271–89, 319–29.

36. Lombroso (1899), *Crime: Its Causes and Remedies,* p. 1.

37. Tarde (1890b), op. cit., p. 8.

38. It is important to note that, in part precisely because it lacked explanatory power, moral statistics was not incompatible with other avowedly antitheoretical discourses such as biological determinism. Indeed, Quetelet's distinction of the 1840s between "normality" and "deviation," for example, was itself in part predicated on a latent biologism that he had borrowed from early phrenologists such as Gall and Spurzheim.

39. Marx (1853), "Capital Punishment," p. 229; Durkheim (1897), op. cit., p. 300.

40. About the value of the moral statisticians, Tarde wrote, for example, "If however they have so far given us nothing more than an outline, if they have not worked for a common object, though they have limited themselves to working out a few isolated problems of social arithmetic . . . the relations between certain facts which they have established are valuable acquisitions to science" (1890b, op. cit., pp. 295–96).

41. Tarde (1887), "Positivisme et pénalité," p. 33; and Tarde (1890b), op. cit., pp. 120–32.

42. To Cournot's memory Tarde dedicated his *Laws of Imitation* and, after severe problems with his vision, he (Tarde, 1890a, op. cit., p. xi) wrote that he owed to Cournot his salvation from death by mental starvation. On the

intellectual relationship between Tarde and Cournot, see further Davis (1909, "Gabriel Tarde: Psychological Interpretations of Society," pp. 109–12). A condensed account of Tarde's sociological project can be found in Logue (1983, *From Philosophy to Sociology: The Evolution of French Liberalism, 1870–1914*, pp. 117–28).

43. Tarde (1890b), op. cit., p. 299.

44. See ibid., pp. 294–302.

45. Tarde (1886a), *La criminalité comparée*, p. 64.

46. See Zehr (1975), "The Modernization of crime in Germany and France, 1830–1913"; Wright (1983), op. cit., pp. 95–99. This is not the place to enter the debate about whether the increased rate of recorded crime reflected an actual increase in the crime rate; for a brief review of this debate in the context of nineteenth-century France, see *supra*, pp. 70–71, p. 99 n.23.

47. *Compte général* (1937), pp. 46–48; Nye (1982a), op. cit., pp. 107–8.

48. Tarde (1890a), op. cit., pp. 114–20.

49. Tarde (1886c), op. cit., p. 132.

50. See, for example, Quetelet (1831b), *Research on the Propensity for Crime at Different Ages*, pp. 37–38.

51. Tarde (1890b), op. cit., pp. 375–80.

52. Tarde (1897a), *Universal Opposition*, p. 265.

53. Tarde (1890b), op. cit., p. 390.

54. Ibid.

55. Ibid., p. 321.

56. Tarde (1884), "Qu'est-ce qu'une société?" p. 501.

57. Tarde (1890b), op. cit., p. 322.

58. Tarde was one of the first French theorists to apply the notion of imitation to "normal" social phenomena, but his application of it to the growth of crime followed the tradition established for the analysis of "abnormal" life by penologists such as Sighele, Prosper Lucas, de Boismont, Jolly and Despine. See further Davis (1909), op. cit., pp. 115–18.

59. Throughout his sociological writings Tarde was rarely explicit about whether voluntarism or coercion exerted primacy in imitation, although at one point, inconclusively, he retorted: "I must point out one thing, once and for all. Imitation in the social life, I mean normal, and not sickly imitation, is to a great extent voluntary, even with respect to language and custom, but it is nonetheless a determining factor" (1890b, op. cit., p. 302, n. 1).

60. Tarde never adequately responded to the problem of explaining the dominance, the triumph, of either good or of evil. Like the source of Hegel's dialectic in the Absolute Idea, Tarde tended to resort to metaphysics and argued

that the result of the incessant struggle between opposite attractions is, for example, "the result of logic" (1890b, op. cit., p. 375).

61. Tarde (1890a), op. cit., pp. 331–38.

62. Tarde (1890b), op. cit., p. 332.

63. Ibid., p. 256.

64. Ibid.

65. Ibid., p. 261.

66. Ibid.

67. Ibid., p. 263.

68. Ibid.

69. Ibid.

70. Ibid., p. 264.

71. Ibid., p. 266.

72. Durkheim (1893), *The Division of Labor in Society,* pp. 256–57.

73. Tarde (1890b), op. cit., pp. 266–68.

74. Against one unfortunate Lombrosian who had tried to turn Tarde's notion of the criminal as a professional type into a defense of the born criminal, see Tarde's scathing reply in Tarde (1893a), "Biologie et sociologie: Réponse au Dr. Bianchi."

75. This subdivision Tarde attempted briefly to illustrate with the motivating factors, and professional coherence, of such groups as rural brigands and urban assassins, the forms of criminality peculiar to the countryside and the city; both forms stemmed from imitation (Tarde, 1890b, op. cit., pp. 275–92).

76. Ibid., pp. 348–62.

77. Ibid., p. 359.

78. Tarde himself engaged in a vitriolic squabble with Sighele about the intellectual ownership of the new field of crowd behavior. The squabble ended in 1895, when Tarde was confronted with a more formidable antagonist in Emile Durkheim. A good example of the extent to which crowd psychology was used to interpret the crises of mass democracy in the Third Republic is the account of the trial of Gabrielle Bompard given in Harris (1985), "Murder under hypnosis in the case of Gabrielle Bompard: Psychiatry in the courtroom in *Belle Epoque* Paris." On the changing fortunes of the analysis of crowd behavior in late nineteenth-century France, see further the excellent discussion in Barrows (1981), *Distorting Mirrors: Visions of the Crowd in Late Nineteenth-Century France,* pp. 137–61.

79. Tarde (1892), "Les crimes des foules," p. 358.

80. Tarde (1890b), op. cit., p. 323.

81. Tarde (1892), op. cit., pp. 372–73.

82. Ibid., p. 373.

83. Ibid., p. 377; and Tarde (1893c), *Les transformations du droit: étude sociologique.* See further Perrot (1978, "Delinquency and the Penitentiary System in Nineteenth-Century France," pp. 240–41), who argues that with the exception of libertarians such as Kropotkin, the organized labor movement was generally uninterested in questions of crime and penality.

84. Tarde's equation of "feminine" and "fickle" derived from his general belief about the necessary domination of women in the patriarchal family. See also Tarde's correlative view, which he held in common with Lombroso, that after puberty the crimes of women were caused by masculine contagion (1890b, op. cit., p. 320). Later, Tarde (1893d, "Foules et sectes au point de vue criminel") suggested that their domestic subjugation was a fortunate fact for women because their opportunities to commit crime were thereby restricted.

85. Tarde (1893b), "Questions sociales," p. 626, n. 1.

86. The concept of *lutte pour la vie* was widely used by biologists and social theorists in the late nineteenth century and, according to Nye (1982a, op. cit., p. 111), usually referred to the struggle of an individual organism to adjust its organic economy to the requirements of a successful adaptation. Tarde himself tended to posit this struggle at the cerebral level—in *Social Laws,* for example, he typically concluded that "the great struggle for existence, through which the least adapted beings are eliminated, is waged between competing dreams and rival projects, rather than different beings" (1899a, p. 211).

87. Tarde (1893b), op. cit., pp. 628–29.

88. Durkheim (1894), *The Rules of Sociological Method,* p. 102.

89. Ibid., p. 59.

90. Ibid.

91. Ibid., p. 70.

92. Ibid., p. 52. Lukes (1982) has perceptively pointed out how imprecisely Durkheim's notion of "constraint" operates in the first chapter of the *Rules.* In a single paragraph this notion abruptly shifts from "the authority of legal rules, moral maxims and social conventions . . . to the need to follow certain rules or procedures to carry out certain activities successfully" (p. 4).

93. Durkheim (1894), op. cit., p. 59.

94. Ibid., p. 97.

95. Ibid., p. 98.

96. Ibid., p. 100.

97. Ibid.

98. Ibid., p. 102.

99. Ibid., p. 101.

100. Tarde (1895c), "Criminalité et santé sociale." See further Lukes (1973), op. cit., p. 314.

101. Tarde (1895c), op. cit., p. 139.

102. Here Tarde refers to Cournot's criticisms of Quetelet's concept of the *l'homme moyen:* the "average man" determined from the physical averages of many men would simply be *un homme impossible.* See Cournot (1843), *Exposition de la théorie des chances et des probabilités,* p. 210.

103. Tarde (1895c), op. cit., p. 152.

104. Tarde (1895b), "Revue critique: congrès de sociologie," pp. 152–53. Elsewhere, Tarde was careful to modify this sweeping statement by distinguishing between crime, misdemeanors, and simple offences; see, for example, Tarde (1895d), "Crimes, délits, contraventions," pp. 322–25.

105. Tarde (1895c), op. cit., p. 55.

106. Ibid., pp. 140–41.

107. Tarde (1895b), op. cit., p. 79.

108. Tarde (1895c), op. cit., p. 141.

109. Ibid., p. 143.

110. It can be traced in Durkheim (1895), "Crime and social health"; Tarde (1898), *Études de psychologie sociale,* pp. 158–61; Durkheim (1897), *Suicide: A Study in Sociology,* pp. 123–34 and pp. 140–42; Tarde (1901b), "La réalité sociale"; Durkheim (1901a), "Two Laws of Penal Evolution." Durkheim and Tarde finally confronted each other in lectures given in 1903–4 at the *École des Hautes Études Sociales.* On this confrontation see Lukes (1973), op. cit., pp. 312–13; and Clark (1969), *Gabriel Tarde on Communication and Social Influence,* pp. 136–40.

111. Garofalo's remarks can be found in *Actes du premier congrès international d'anthropologie criminelle: Rome 1885* (1886), pp. 173–75. A summary of the Congress can be found in Nye (1984), op. cit., pp. 103–6.

112. Tarde (1890b), op. cit., p. 16. From the 1832 Penal Code onward, various inroads had already been made by the positivists into the purity of the classical legal subject. These inroads included pleas of "mitigating" and "extenuating" circumstances, and the increasing visibility in courts of doctors and psychiatrists as witnesses "expert" in the understanding of "state of mind"; see further Wright (1983), op. cit., pp. 114–15. However, the extreme determinism of the biological positivists challenged the distinctions and gradations of the medical experts. The latter therefore united against the positivists with the criminal magistrates and the free-will jurists. This unity continued the tradition of *politique criminelle.* About this tradition see further Radzinowicz (1962), *In Search of Criminology,* pp. 65–67; and Nye (1984), op. cit., pp. 110–13.

113. Tarde (1886b), op. cit.; Tarde (1886c), op. cit., pp. 122–50; Tarde (1889a), op. cit.; Tarde (1890b), op. cit., pp. 83–214.

114. Tarde (1887), op. cit.; Tarde (1889b), "Sur la responsabilité morale (rapport sur la xième question)," pp. 356–57.

115. Tarde (1886b), op. cit., pp. 63–71; this should be compared with Donovan (1981), "Justice Unblind: The Juries and the Criminal Classes in France, 1825–1914."

116. Tarde (1890b), op. cit., p. 134.

117. Ibid., pp. 301–2.

118. Ibid., p. 213.

119. Ibid., passim; and Tarde (1901a), "La criminalité et les phénomènes économques."

120. Tarde (1890b), op. cit., p. 11, n. 1.

121. Tarde (1892), op. cit., p. 385.

122. Tarde (1890b), op. cit., pp. 40–41.

123. Ibid., pp. 489–502; and Tarde (1891), "Études criminelles et pénales." Raymond Saleilles, one of Tarde's few protégés, soon became the most prominent representative of the movement for individualized treatment and punishment. See Saleilles (1898), *The Individualization of Punishment*.

124. Tarde (1890b), op. cit., pp. 474–87, 526.

125. Ibid., p. 516.

126. Ibid., pp. 511–27.

127. Ibid., pp. 511–27.

128. At one point in *Penal Philosophy*, Tarde discussed putative justifications for castrating criminals, and declared, "from the *utilitarian* point of view I can find no answer to such arguments" (ibid., p. 526).

129. Ibid., pp. 375–76; and Tarde (1897a), *L'opposition universelle*, pp. 266–68.

130. See, for example, Tarde (1893d), op. cit.

131. See Vine (1972), op. cit., pp. 292–94.

132. Tarde's widespread influence in the formative years of criminology in the United States is attested to by the fact that in 1912 his book *Penal Philosophy* was one of the few European works translated into English under the auspices of the American Institute of Criminal Law and Criminology.

133. Remembering Tarde's contribution to criminology, Durkheim's (quoted in Nye, 1984, op. cit., p. 117, n. 60) comments of 1915 are quite appropriate here: "To understand its full significance, it is necessary to place it in the epoch in which it was conceived. This was the time when the Italian school of criminology exaggerated positivism to the point of making it into a kind of

materialistic metaphysics which had nothing scientific about it. Tarde demonstrated the inanity of these doctrines and reemphasized the essentially spiritual
character of social phenomena."

134. Tarde's criminology has thus been understood with a progressive
amnesia, and most recent histories of criminology ignore his pivotal contributions altogether. Marginal exceptions are provided by Taylor, Walton, and
Young (1973, *The New Criminology*, p. 227), who refer to Tarde in the context
of their prior concern with the Dutch socialist Willem Bonger; and by Vold and
Bernard, who conclude briefly that "[Tarde's] theory was important at the
time for its role in opposing Lombroso's theories. . . . The major problem
with the theory is that it was based on such a simplistic model of learning"
(1986, *Theoretical Criminology*, p. 209).

Chapter 6

Science, Statistics and Eugenics In Charles Goring's *The English Convict* (1913)

His figure such as might his soul proclaim,
One eye was blinking and one leg was lame,
His mountain shoulders half his breast o'erspread,
Thin hairs bestrewed his long mis-shapen head.

—Homer

Much of the lengthy intellectual history of criminology has been dominated by the belief that physical features are external signs of inner and spiritual darkness. In this history few books have commanded such gargantuan esteem as Charles Goring's *The English Convict: A Statistical Study* of 1913.[1] Fewer still have exerted such decisive intellectual effects. Upon publication *The English Convict* at once entrenched itself as a methodological classic. Among many prison officials, statisticians, and criminologists its 528 oblong folio pages, 286 methodological tables and separate schedule of measurements and general anthropological data were taken as a staunch, positivist bulwark against the theoretical superstitions of Lombrosianism. Prison Commissioner Ruggles-Brise recorded simply that *The English Convict* was "a great step forward."[2] In his introduction to the abridged edition of *The English Convict*,[3] the eminent statistician Karl Pearson enthused that "it is not too much to say that in the early chapters of Goring's work he clears out of the way for ever the tangled and exuberant growths of the Lombrosian School."[4] In such laudatory terms *The English Convict*'s august analysis of the Lombrosian notion of the born criminal has consistently been appraised. *The English Convict* was "the most comprehensive and painstaking of all existing refutations [of Lombrosianism]" recorded Mannheim;[5] three decades later, to Albert Cohen, *The English Convict* remained "a devastating critique."[6] In a recent essay about the origins of scientific criminology it has even been claimed that "positivism, within the Lombrosian context, simply ceased to function as a serious explanation of crime with the publication of *The English Convict*."[7]

My intention in this chapter is neither to cast doubt on the practical importance of *The English Convict* within official investigations of criminality prior to World War I nor to dispute Goring's status as perhaps the first recognized major figure in British criminology.[8] Rather, it is to take issue, on a number of fronts, with the legendary view that *The English Convict*'s intervention in criminology chiefly represented a definitive refutation of Lombrosianism. About a second view of *The English Convict*'s intervention, historians of criminology have tended to retain a collective amnesia.[9] Leading members of the British eugenics movement, for instance, regarded *The English Convict* as strong evidence for the view that the "criminal character" is an inherited condition.[10] Although many of Lombroso's opponents saw in *The English Convict* the death knell of the anthropological criminal type, simultaneously, Lombroso's disciples regarded *The English Convict* as a complete vindication of the views of their master.[11]

In the annals of criminology, then, there coexist two opposed assessments of *The English Convict*'s confrontation with Lombrosianism.[12] This chapter will suggest not only that both views are false but that, paradoxically, they have considerable, if partial, merit in concert. However, neither singly nor in concert have assessments of *The English Convict* done much to establish either the specific technical content of its discourse or the conceptual and theoretical sources on which Goring relied in his confrontation with Lombosianism. The findings of *The English Convict,* and its ambivalent reception upon publication, cannot be understood apart from the fact that the objects of its discourse were erected on a radical and unacknowledged dualism. *The English Convict*'s intent was to challenge both Lombrosian and environmental theories of crime. The intellectual context in which this double intent unfolded was provided for by Goring's reliance on the methods of evolutionary and mathematical zoology and by his insertion of their claims about organic maladaptations in animal evolution into the class and racist propaganda of the eugenics movement. Its institutional context was the Biometric Laboratory of University College—founded by Galton, strongly influenced by W.F.R. Weldon's investigations of evolutionary development in crustaceans, and directed (after 1906) by Pearson.

Against this background, I will claim that for a variety of reasons Goring's critical engagement with Lombrosianism must be considered somewhat of a failure.

Let me offer two caveats about the procedure of what follows. First, I will not insert the arguments of *The English Convict* into the discourses of the various social programs (including criminology) that contributed to the general restructuring of social regulation in late Victorian and Edwardian Britain. That ambitious task has already been accomplished in David Garland's brilliant study *Punishment and Welfare*. What follows here is largely limited to *The English Convict*'s confrontation with Lombrosianism, and to Goring's conflation of that project with his support for the application of eugenics to "criminality."

My second caveat refers to the theoretical status of the widespread predominance of empiricist methodologies in English criminology at the turn of the century. The criminological field which Lombrosianism entered in England at this time differed vastly from the terrain elsewhere; in France, for example, Lombrosianism had been strenuously and widely resisted as early as the mid-1880s. It is difficult to establish precisely why the forms of social thought in England were so different from much of continental Europe, but from the late eighteenth century on, different they were in the conscious importance attached to epistemological issues, in their focal concerns and, with the notable exceptions of Spencer and L. T. Hobhouse, in their levels of abstraction. At least until 1914, British social thought, dominated by positivist individualism, ignored or avoided issues of structured social inequality and directed itself instead to narrow social reforms.[13] British criminology, also, was more committed than its continental counterparts to a belief in the superiority of statistical empiricism over theoretical "speculation." Nowhere was this belief more pronounced than in *The*

English Convict. However, I am not inclined to argue here that statistical instruments necessarily rest on theoretical or even ideological presuppositions. Although the positivist distinction between theoretical and observational categories cannot ultimately be maintained, no general objections can be made against the use of statistics as such. In this I follow Barry Hindess, who argues that a rational evaluation of statistical arguments hinges on the recognition of the theoretical interests of the science in question.[14] It is to the overdue recognition of the influence of certain theoretical interests on the apparently contradictory findings of *The English Convict* that this chapter principally attends.

Calculations of Criminality: The Lombrosian Challenge

The structure of argumentation and much of the substantive content of *The English Convict* conjoined some of the focal concerns of several hitherto more or less separate domains of activity. To begin with, *The English Convict* continued the English tradition of prison research pursued by medical doctors such as J. Bruce Thomson, David Nicolson, and John Baker. This tradition pursued the empirical calculation of "criminal propensities" within the discourse of phrenology and psychiatry; to it Goring's innovative contribution was the measurement of criminality with the instruments of another tradition, namely, those deriving from the statistical techniques established by Quetelet, Francis Galton, and Karl Pearson. *The English Convict*'s initial object was the combination of these two traditions for the avowed purpose of testing the concept of "born criminality" invented by Lombroso and his followers. However, it must be stressed that *The English Convict*'s point of engagement with Lombrosianism—itself not an unproblematic discourse and of which, it will be shown, Goring's understanding was far from complete—was governed not only by the temporary union of the traditions of prison research and statistics but also by Goring's understanding of the debate between the respective traditions of hereditarianism and environmentalism.

This debate, for Goring, involved a theoretical dispute between the tenets of Lombrosianism and the analysis of crime that was prefigured in Quetelet's "social mechanics" and which was later lodged in the sociology of Tarde and Durkheim. The debate between this emergent sociological tradition (with which Goring had only crude familiarity) and hereditarianism was itself traversed by an empiricist debate about the methodological utility of statistics in the identification of law-like human behavior. In this debate, also, Quetelet's methods provided a central referent. [15] Therefore, I now turn to the influence of the outcome of the unwritten debate between Lombroso and Quetelet—the latter as the intellectual mentor and, with Malthus, Babbage, and Drinkwater, one of the founders of the Statistical Society of London. [16]

Quetelet's criminology had been one effect among many of the failure of the stated reformative object of the new carceral institutions in France. As we saw in Chapter 3 above, the epistemological basis of Quetelet's efforts to understand crime lay in his belief that the same law-like regularities which existed in the mechanics of nature also existed in the world of social facts; the greater the number of empirical observations, the more visible these regularities would become. He calculated that young males, the poor, the uneducated, and those without employment or in lowly occupations have greater propensities than others to commit crimes and to be convicted of them. Because he saw crime as a constant feature of social life, Quetelet intimated that society itself must be one of its causes. However, lacking the techniques of analysis of variance and believing that crime had an infinitude of possible causes, he felt unable to unravel the respective powers of different causal factors; seldom did he compare more than two factors at a time. Eventually, Quetelet presented both the mean of a scale of given characteristics and also the upper and lower limits within which individuals oscillated. Minor or "natural" variation around the mean he then identified as deviation attracting no unusual attention; extraordinary variation he saw not only as unusual deviation from the mean but also as "preternatural" and "monstrous."

Additionally, Quetelet perceived that variation around the mean occurred not at random but in a determinate order that approximated the principle of the normal distribution in celestial mechanics. His application of this principle to crime led directly to his erection of a rigid binary opposition between the statistical mean and unusual deviation.

Though he inferred from the normal distribution that everyone has a certain propensity to break the laws, he also believed that the criminal propensities of the "average man" were rarely actualized. Against the virtues of the "average man" he juxtaposed the criminality of the "inferior classes" and "inferior moral stock." In keeping with a pervasive emphasis on the biological basis of social facts, Quetelet finally argued that criminal morality was manifest in physical defects, that those with such defects had very high criminal propensities, and that crime was sometimes "hereditary."

It should be noted that Quetelet could not identify the precise point at which variations from the physical norm reached into the alien world of abnormality and defect. The impetus to make such a distinction was largely afforded by the public hysteria about the increasing rates of recidivism, confirmed by the *Compte* throughout the nineteenth century. These publicized increases fostered a pervasive belief in habitual and born criminality of which, in France, the most prevalent explanation was a biomedical amalgam of native, Lamarckian heredity theory and the notion of a degenerative organism, itself created by a strict rupture in medicine and elsewhere between the "normal" and the "pathological." Within this amalgam, normality was defined, following Quetelet's lead in part, in terms of statistical averages. Pathological states were statistical deviations from the norm that were invested with a weight of moral condemnation by a bewildering variety of quasi-medical discourses whose influence persisted largely unchallenged until the objections of Tarde and Durkheim in the 1890s.

Into this receptive atmosphere the notion of the born criminal was inserted by Lombroso's *l'Uomo delinquente*. With the aid of the notorious "scientific" data lodged in this book, Lombroso claimed that his autopsies of male criminals revealed "significant" atavistic deviations—features which he saw as similar to those displayed by a variety of other categories, especially "prehistoric man." Another group, selected from "among the most notorious and depraved" of male and female criminals, revealed an even greater range of anatomical deviations. This second group was then compared with Italian soldiers and with "lunatics." From these data Lombroso concluded that many of the characteristics found in "savages and among the colored races" are also to be found in habitual criminals. The causes of criminality, in other words, lay not in the realm of social matter but in that of bodily constitutions.

Enthusiasm for the Lombrosian notion of the "born criminal" was far from universal, and a noisy offensive against it reached a climax in Paris in 1889 at the Second International Congress of Criminal Anthropology. There Garofalo proposed that a commission of seven anthropologists, which included representatives from both the classical and the new schools of criminology—Lombroso, Lacassagne, Benedickt, Bertillon, Manouvrier, Magnan, and Lemal—engage in comparative family case studies of 100 born criminals, 100 persons with criminal tendencies, and 100 honest persons.[17] Lombroso defiantly agreed to retract his notion of born criminality if the physical, mental, and psychological characteristics of the first group proved identical with either of the others. This plan was accepted but not effected because, according to the anthropologist Manouvrier's report at the following Congress,[18] it was found impossible—"a pretext" complained Gina Lombroso-Ferrero[19]—for anyone to distinguish among the three groups with sufficient accuracy. The mounting campaign of empirical criticism compelled Lombroso to dilute the atavistic basis of born criminality with an expanded categorization of criminal types whose genesis also lay in epilepsy and insanity. This wider basis of criminality Lombroso now held to explain various pathological states that he recognized as contributing to criminality but which were not revealed solely through the phenomena of atavism.[20]

Lombrosianism was eagerly introduced to a British audience in 1890, in the pages of Havelock Ellis's *The Criminal*,[21] and recommended to the government for further investigation by Prison Inspector Arthur Griffiths.[22] The mantle of the Lombrosian challenge was assumed in 1901 by G. B. Griffiths, deputy medical officer of Parkhurst Prison, and by a small cohort of medical and prison officials. Plans were then made to subject to Lombrosian measurements 3,000 English prisoners who had been convicted of similar offences in order to determine if they deviated from the nonconvicted population. In 1902 Griffiths' efforts were noticed by Sir Bryan Donkin, visiting director of prisons, and Sir H. Smalley, medical inspector of prisons, of the Prison Inspectorate. Attempts were made to organize the collection of similar data at Parkhurst, Portland, Dartmoor, and Borstal prisons, and an initial report was published.[23] This report included the preliminary methods ("the larger scheme not having been completely formulated") of measuring 100 "ordinary" and 30 "Lunatic" criminals who were serving sentences of three or more years. Griffiths' and Donkin's measurements included the anteroposterior curve; the horizontal curve; the height, length, and breadth of the cranium; face length and breadth; and facial symmetry.

In 1903 Griffiths was succeeded as coordinator of the project by the junior medical officer at Broadmoor, Charles Goring.[24] Between 1904 and 1908 Goring expanded the subject population to 4,000 prisoners, made 1,500 observations himself, and added more physical and mental characteristics to the measurement schedule. On the advice of Karl Pearson, Goring analyzed his data with the biometric method, the preliminary results appearing in the "Studies in National Deterioration" series of the Biometric Laboratory at University College.[25] Such data, thought Goring, would eventually offer a decisive answer to the question "does crime have social or biological causes?" In so doing, of course, they would arbitrate the competing views of the traditions championed, respectively, by Quetelet and Lombroso.

The English Convict 1: Confronting Lombrosianism

> We owe much to the experimental methods of investigating natural phenomena in plants and animals; but in the future our debt will be as great to the statistical method.
>
> —*The English Convict*, p.27

Introduction: Biometrics

From the 1830s onward the primary object of the British movement in "state-istics" had been the quantification of social facts in order to address a wide range of divisive social issues—poor law, combinations, public health, child labor, emigration, factory conditions, education, and crime. As Philip Abrams has recorded, the practice of statistics was institutionalized under the direct patronage of the British political elite and with the active participation of its most distinguished members.[26] While the statistical movement was oriented to the empiricist gathering of facts, in some respects its recommendations about state policy preceded its conceptual development.

By the 1890s the statistical movement found itself embroiled in a deep intellectual fissure. On one side were those like Booth and Rowntree, whose investigations tended to reveal the structural connections of poverty and its extent. On the other side were those who wished to concentrate on the refinement of statistical techniques. In this latter group some, including luminaries like Galton and Pearson, were as keen to develop the conceptual aspects of statistics as they were to harness their creations to an already given political and social agenda. An integral part of this agenda was the eugenics program, a vehicle that largely expressed the fears and aspirations of the professional middle class, and to which proper due will be given shortly. Within this program the statistical creations of Galton and Pearson led to the convoluted formation of the biometric school.

It should be noted that for his knowledge of the properties of the normal curve Galton was specifically indebted to Quetelet's display of the "curve of possibility" in Downes's English translation of the latter's book *Lettres . . . sur la théorie des probabilités*. Indeed, a concerted attempt to isolate the specific weights of the various causes that produced the seductively regular patterns in Quetelet's normal distributions permeated much of Galton's statistical work on ancestral resemblance, especially as it appeared in his books *Hereditary Genius* and *Natural Inheritance*. With good reason, then, his pupil Karl Pearson recollected that Galton's "mind had been so deeply stirred by his greatest forerunner, Quetelet."[27] In moving beyond Quetelet's crude moral statistics, Galton's "statistics of inter-comparison" spawned the methods of reversion, co-relation, reversion, and regression.

Another factor in the development of biometrics and in the imminent merger of biometrical and eugenist concerns, was the mathematical calculations of the effects of variation, selection, and heredity on the processes of organic evolution in animals by W.F.R. Weldon, a zoologist at University College London. Initially, in two papers published in the early 1890s in the *Proceedings of the Royal Society of London,* the core of Weldon's calculations involved the application of Galtonian statistics to evolutionary theory.[28] Weldon suggested that rather than construct an ideal type of a species, as did anatomists, biologists should try to identify the average physical characteristics of a species. With the use of Galton's statistical methods biologists could identify and focus on an actual average type and the extent and sort of variation from it.

Weldon reported to the Royal Society in 1895 his findings about the selective destruction of crabs. He suggested that he had demonstrated a high positive correlation between the carapace lengths (and smaller variation in the right dentary margins) of crabs and their death rates; in this he followed Charles Darwin's metaphysical wager that "individuals [of any species] . . . born with parts diminished in size and efficiency, on which the welfare of the species depended, would be eliminated; those individuals alone surviving in the long run which possessed such parts of the proper size."[29] The larger the variation in carapace lengths the higher and the earlier the death rate. Thus, for Weldon the Darwinian hand of natural selection operated as a conservative mechanism in that crabs with characteristics deviant from the mean were selected for early destruction.[30] Additionally, Weldon argued that the evolutionary questions raised by Darwinism were purely statistical. The biometric method could therefore properly be applied to evolutionary theory, or at least to the rate and direction of evolution, without any theoretical knowledge of the mechanics of heredity:

> Knowing that a given deviation from the mean character is associated with a greater or less percentage death rate in the animals possessing it, the importance of such a deviation can be estimated without the necessity of inquiring how that increase or decrease in the death rate is brought about, so that all ideas of "functional adaptation" become unnecessary.[31]

More dramatic still was Weldon's argument that his findings about crabs could also be applied to species such as moths, sweet peas, and even humans. The natural correlation between physical deviation and early death rate was also present in humans, he suggested, but it occurred naturally only when the process of selective destruction was uninterrupted by "civilization." The parallel between crabs and humans would thus cease to hold wherever

> there is considerable protection of the physically unfit; and that here, as in other civililised countries, any influences which might in a savage race produce selective destruction are reduced to a minimum, whereas in the case of the crabs such selective influences are active.[32]

Among biologists the controversy that erupted over Weldon's findings centered on rival interpretations of his use of evolutionary theory (de Vries's *mutationstheorie* and Mendelian genetics—both forcefully championed by Bateson) and on the adequacy of his statistical techniques. During the 1890s Weldon sought advice about the proper statistical techniques for his project from Karl Pearson, and it was through Weldon that Pearson met Galton. His inquiries stimulated Pearson (appointed Chair of Applied Mathematics and Mechanics at University College in 1884) to depart from his eclectic interests in mathematics and the history of science and to concentrate on the application of statistical methods to questions of heredity and eugenics.[33] In less than two decades Pearson produced dozens of essays on statistical techniques and his invention of standard deviations, correlation, and regression coefficients, skewed distributions, and chi squares provided statistics, or "biometrics," with a large measure of intellectual autonomy.[34]

The institutional facility for the practical application of biometrics to social matters was initiated by Pearson and Weldon in 1901 with their founding of *Biometrika,* a journal devoted solely to biometrical work. In 1906 a small grant from the Worshipful Company of Drapers established the Biometric Laboratory within the Department of Applied Mathematics at University College; its object was to further research on the inheritance of various pathologies and on the relative influence of heredity and environment on school children.[35] Galton then engineered the installation of Pearson as director of the new Galton Eugenics Laboratory, also at University College; its object was to act as the research arm of the national eugenics movement. In concert, the Biometric Laboratory and the Galton Eugenics Laboratory instructed students in biometrics, assisted the projects of visiting research scientists, and issued joint publications.

It was at the Galton Eugenics Laboratory that Goring studied biometry, under the tutelage of Pearson—*cher maître,* as Goring addressed him.[36] The likely direction of influence on Goring's studies exerted by Pearson can be surmised from methodological caveats inscribed in the latter's essay, "Nature and Nurture: The Problem of the Future," published in the *Eugenics Laboratory Lecture Series* in 1910. In this essay Pearson indicated:

> up to the present time no satisfactory treatment of crime is really possible, because there has been no scientific investigation as to whether crime is correlated with any peculiar physical or mental characters; in reality nobody knows whether crime is associated with general degeneracy, whether it is a manifestation of certain hereditary qualities or whether it is a product of environment or tradition.

Such caution did not, however, deter Pearson from the bold conclusion:

> I think it quite safe to say that the influence of environment is not one-fifth that of heredity, and quite possibly not one-tenth of it. There is no real comparison between nature and nurture; it is essentially the man who makes his environment, and not the environment which makes the man.[37]

Between May 1909 and November 1911, Goring analyzed his data at the Eugenics Laboratory and prepared them for publication. Some preliminary results of his investigations appeared in 1909, in one of the laboratories' publications, the *Studies in National Deterioration* series. In this study ("On the Inheritance of the Diatheses of Phthisis and Insanity"), Goring attempted to determine the relative intensity of heredity and environment in the transmission of tuberculosis (phthisis) and insanity. His method was a correlational analysis of a random sample (the families of 1,500 nonlunatic criminals) of the general population divided into disease-present and disease-absent groups. Diseased children were significantly more likely (tuberculosis, r = 0.43; insanity, r = 0.50) to have diseased parents than children in whose parents the diseases were absent. These associations, Goring concluded, showed that tuberculosis and insanity were transmitted in the same way as physical characteristics—through heredity rather than through "contagion, infection . . . class distinctions or social conditions."[38] Discarding other possible explanations of these data, and ignoring contrary evidence, such as sewage treatment programs that reduced the incidence of tuberculosis, Goring adduced, "[The] ultimate extinction [of disease] will depend upon an inherited improvement in the human stock, and not upon hygiene."[39]

Let us now turn to *The English Convict*.

The English Convict: Introduction

In his brief introduction to *The English Convict* Goring suggested that scientific criminology had been warped by superstitious dogma, chief among which was Lombroso's notion of the born criminal. In this opening foray, and with the authority of the British statistical movement behind him, Goring adamantly opposed any investigation (such as Lombrosianism) lacking a proper statistical analysis of a large series of carefully collected data. Such analysis was indispensable because it generated knowledge about organic beings as solid and reliable as in the natural sciences and because "it records facts in their original crudity, unaffected by partisanship or any particular system or theory."[40] "What we have to do," Goring insisted,

> all that can be done, is to measure, by the statistical method of averaging large numbers, the extent to which an increasing tendency to commit anti-social acts is correlated with different degrees or variations of the personal, economic, and social conditions under investigation.[41]

Goring thus objected to the reigning conclusions of criminal anthropology. Previous calculations were useless because the raw material from which their means were derived was never published; their probable errors were never given with the recorded means; no measure was obtained of the variability of the series of measurements whose mean value had been investigated; no allowance was made for the confounding effects of factors such as differences in the age, stature, and intelligence of the populations compared; and there was no controlled comparison between the criminal and noncriminal populations.

> The "facts" of criminal anthropology, gathered by prejudiced observers employing unscientific methods, are inadmissable as evidence either for, or against, [Lombroso's criminal] type. The criminal type may be a real thing; but if so, it is real despite of, and not because of, the spurious evidence of its supporters; its existence may be scientifically proved by future investigation. [42]

To these introductory caveats Goring attached his own preliminary understanding of crime and normality, all this set against the background of Lombroso's claims about the various bases of born criminality. His outline was given at two distinct, almost irreconcilable levels. At one level Goring warned that his use of the term *criminal* only designated the legal fact of an individual who had been imprisoned. He suggested that no quality in human actions inherently branded them as criminal: "whatever difference there may be underlying the acts of the law-breaker and those of the law-abiding person, the difference is one of degree only, and not of kind."[43] Moreover, he objected to "the unfortunate tendency to theorise as to the existence of abnormal types of human beings."[44] Although the types of "mentally defective," "degenerate," and "criminal" conveniently stated certain facts, they were only constructs and, as such, derived from theories that presuppose that human qualities markedly deviant from the average necessarily indicate defect or disease. For Goring, statistically unusual (i.e., rare) qualities, however, are not always abnormal ones, with only the latter implying unnaturalness and morbidity: "Now any judgement of abnormality presupposes a definition of what is normal. . . . Criminologists, although they make frequent use of some standard, have consistently evaded its definition" and, like Lombroso, have confounded "normality" with "statistical average."[45] He suggested instead that, although the normal and the abnormal do not gradually merge into each other and that the one is always separated from the other by a definite, abrupt line of demarcation, the criminal nevertheless cannot be viewed a priori as anything other than a "normal" being from whom the righteous and iniquitous are distinguished only by degree.

A second level of commentary infiltrated these otherwise[46] unobjectionable remarks. While reiterating that "some people are technically designated as criminal," Goring added that "these ['normal' criminals] are to be distinguished from those who are specifically criminal in constitution."[47] It is thus difficult for the reader to avoid Goring's equation of "criminal in constitution" and "abnormality." "However criminality may be analysed," he continued,

> we must assume [the possibility] that constitutional, as well as environmental factors, play a part in the production of criminality. In other words we are forced to an hypothesis of the possible existence of a character in all men which, in the absence of a better term, we call the criminal diathesis.[48]

Goring argued that the "criminal diathesis" is a hypothetical character or constitutional proclivity, either mental, moral, or physical, present to a certain degree in everyone. But the diathesis was only manifest, like Quetelet's propensity for crime, in its supposed effects on the "abnormal character" or after interference in "the natural physiological and psychological laws of existence."[49] In the same way that Quetelet had held criminal propensities to be incapable of direct measurement, so too, for Goring direct quantification of the criminal diathesis was impossible because it was not within reach of the senses. "Our object will be to find out," Goring declared, "how far this criminal diathesis, as measured by criminal records, is associated with environment, training, stock, and with the physical attributes of the criminal."[50] Thus, the existence of the diathesis could be traced

backward through its effects, but the causes of its activation were to be
identified through its relationship with a plethora of associated factors.

The English Convict: Testing Lombrosianism

Goring's investigation of Lombrosianism per se had three phases: (1) a
statistical analysis to detect the presence of Lombrosian characteristics
in the criminal population,[51] (2) a comparison of the findings in (1)
above with the characteristics of the noncriminal public,[52] and (3) an
analysis of the general physique of criminals.[53] These sections of *The
English Convict,* although quite complicated, are relatively well
known, and can be summarized as follows:

(1) The first phase involved statistical observation of 2,348 male
convicts, embracing the mean values, standard deviation and frequency
distributions of thirty-seven Lombrosian characteristics (e.g., length,
breadth, and circumference of the head). Goring selected these convicts
as they first entered Parkhurst prison, and they included prisoners
ranging from first offenders ("star class") convicted of serious crimes
to "pronounced" habitual offenders.[54] He stratified the convicts according to the length of their sentences and the gravity of their offences,
assuming that if a criminal type did exist it would be more visible the
more heinous the crime or the more habituated the criminal.

Goring's analysis revealed that only 10 of the 37 characteristics had
correlations with a given crime greater than 0.1; of these only three
(right-handedness, shade of hair, and tattooing) were above 0.2, and
only one (tattooing) was above 0.3. Although physical differences existed among types of criminals, these were not to be explained by differences in "criminality," Goring surmised, but by the skewing effects
of differences in "age, stature, intelligence, [and] the different social
classes from which [criminals] are drawn."[55] Although some minor
physical differences existed between frauds and other criminals, for example, such differences were less significant than the additional finding
that convicted frauds and other criminals together "are drawn from extremely differentiated classes of the general community."[56] The lack of
significant physical differences between fraudulent offenders and habitual offenders marked "singularly strong evidence against the alleged

existence of any physical criminal type."[57] Further, the average association [$r = 0.15$] between physical characteristics and type of crime, Goring concluded, was also insignificant.

(2) Goring strongly criticized Lombroso's failure to compare the characteristics of criminals with those of noncriminals.[58] So next he compared the physical characteristics of "criminals as a class" with those of the "non-criminal public," reasoning that, by itself, the finding that criminals were not physically differentiated among themselves individually did not argue either for or against the conclusion that criminals were not differentiated as a class. Goring's sample of the noncriminal public was based largely on convenience and ease of access, on his own copious measurements and interviews, and on prior work in criminal anthropology (some of it conducted as far afield as New South Wales). His motley sample included a company of the Royal Engineers; undergraduates from Oxford, Cambridge, and Aberdeen; staff at University College; inmates at Middlesex General Hospital; and criminals and the insane in Scotland. He found no significant differences between the average physical characteristics of criminals and those of his control groups:

> In the present investigation we have exhaustively compared . . . criminals as a class, with the law-abiding public. . . . *No evidence has emerged confirming the existence of a physical criminal type, such as Lombroso and his disciples have described—our inevitable conclusion must be that there is no such thing as a physical criminal type.*[59]

Thus far, Goring reasoned not that criminals were a physically undifferentiated class, but that no physical characters peculiar to criminals were explicable by differences in factors such as age and stature. Although he found no physical stigmata among criminals, the physical differences that did emerge were

> of interest sociologically; and the interpretation of these differences in terms of the varying ages, stature, intelligence, and social class of the subjects under investigation, should help to

throw light upon the nature and origin of criminals, and aid the construction of sound criminological theory.[60]

(3) Next, Goring compared convicts' physique with that of the general population. Controlling for age, social class, and the effects of imprisonment, he compared prisoners' height, weight, arm span, general health, physical constitution, muscularity, and degree of obesity with those in the noncriminal public. He found, first, criminals to be differentiated among themselves in stature and weight according to the types of crime they had committed. This differentiation was accounted for by their different age distributions and by their class origins. Second, except for convicted frauds, criminals were "markedly" physically inferior—less tall (by 1.4 to 1.8 inches) and less heavy (by 4.3 to 7.3 pounds)—to the general population. These two findings were "the facts—*they are the sole facts at the basis of criminal anthropology.*"[61]

How did Goring interpret criminals' physical "inferiority"? From a strict empiricist mode he now entered the wider latitudes of theory. With some hesitation, and with little persuasiveness, he argued that "physique selects crime." Specific crimes likely entailed the presence of certain physical attributes or the absence of others, e.g., violent crimes were more likely to be committed by the more muscular. Criminals as a class were likely to be physically inferior to the law-abiding citizenry because "the acts of potential law-breakers, as well as the proclivities of those who have broken the law . . . are influenced in the long run by physique."[62] Moreover, those with inferior physiques were less likely to avoid arrest, especially so since the police were appointed only from among those with superior physiques.

On the merits of Goring's attempted dissolution of Lombroso's born criminal, I will, for the moment, refrain from comment. Let us only record Goring's ominous conclusion to his test of Lombrosianism, the first object of *The English Convict:*

The inferior stature and weight of criminals is the result of selection, and is not an inbred criminal trait. A possibility, however, not to be lost sight of is that this physical inferiority,

although originating in and fostered by selection, may tend
with time to become an inbred characteristic of the criminal
classes.[63]

The English Convict 2: Mental Hereditarianism and Eugenics

The principal constitutional determinant of crime is mental defectiveness—which, admittedly, is a heritable condition."

—*The English Convict*, p. 372

Introduction: Eugenics

It was mentioned earlier that assessments of *The English Convict* invariably assume Lombroso's born criminal to have been the sole object of Goring's discourse. For Lombroso's contemporaries, it must be
noted, Quetelet's statistical labors in the new field of positivist criminology seemed to provide an anticipatory "environmental" account of
criminality opposed to Lombrosianism but with which, it transpired,
Goring also took issue. Although *The English Convict*'s initial object
was ostensibly Lombrosianism, it was equally concerned with the ad-
versarial arguments of Lombrosianism as they were marshaled within
the late nineteenth-century debate about the relative influences of heredity and environment. Against biological determinism the conceptual points of this debate were chiefly fixed, as *The English Convict*'s
textual sources and references indicate, by the arguments not of English
criminology but of French sociology, and of which Quetelet's social
mechanics was the chief precursor.

Having apparently disposed of Lombroso's born criminal, Goring
abruptly engaged *The English Convict*'s second object, namely, environmentalism. This he tried to accomplish by the insertion of his statistical empiricism into the discourse of the program in *eugenics,* a term
which, along with *race-betterment* and *viriculture,* Galton had coined to
refer to "the science of improving stock."[64] It must be noted that this
program's literary output was avowedly based on a critical assumption. In some works it was made quite explicit; in others it festered

arrogantly beneath the surface. This assumption was that eugenics research based on the biometric method was independent of theoretical categories. At times, this assumption was articulated in terms of the notion that facts could be conceived of through the technical instruments of statistics, in isolation from the forces which generated them and without theoretical mediation. Other times, it was invoked in terms of the kindred assumption that science was concerned with the factual identification and description of uniformities rather than metaphysical explanations of them. At still other times, it was argued that the eugenist approached empirical data without prejudice or preconceived notions.

Within the texts of the eugenics program this scientism naturally led to the presumption that the distribution of social, moral, and intellectual qualities in humans could be discerned with the very procedures used to identify the distribution of physical qualities in the world of nature. Accordingly, it seemed to follow that the natural human talents comprising "civic worth" in any nation are distributed according to certain statistical laws, among them the normal law of frequency. Each citizen was held to have received at birth a definite endowment of talents and to be personally accountable for its profitable use. Hence, the distribution of natural talents could be constructed as a normal distribution around the mean that varied from "extremely high" to "extremely low."

A further assumption permitted the eugenist to move from the imprecise notion of "civic and national worth" to the creation and recognition of its specific manifestations. The distribution of "worth" was assumed to be spread throughout the class structure and to manifest its presence or absence in social indicators such as wealth and pathologies, respectively. This claim was developed by appropriating relevant empirical findings of government enquiries, such as the Royal Commission on the Feeble-Minded, and of private investigators like Booth and Rowntree.

In these findings the eugenist discovered confirmation of the normal distribution of civic and national worth. In his *Hereditary Genius*, Galton, for example, had first suggested, with retrospective confirmation sought from his cousin Darwin's *Origin of Species,* that it was

almost exclusively the naturally "worthy" who achieved social prominence and this despite whatever obstacles they might encounter.
Among them lay "The brains of the nation," and they should be provided with inducements to propagate.[65] Conversely, the naturally
"worthless" never succeeded in rising above their lowly stations in life,
and this despite all state and private provision of encouragement. Thus,
"it would be an economy and a great benefit to the country if all habitual criminals were resolutely segregated under merciful surveillance
and peremptorily denied opportunities for producing offspring."[66] In
the works of yet others, this vision of negative eugenics included isolation, sterilization, castration, and death.[67]

The English Convict: Mental Hereditarianism and Eugenics

The second object of *The English Convict*'s discourse unfolded against
this background of the British eugenics program. Fully two-thirds of
the authorities cited in *The English Convict* were taken from British biometric and eugenic literature, either the publications of the Galton Eugenics Laboratory, including the works of Galton and Pearson, or the
populist, crusading literature of the Eugenics Education Society[68] such
as *The Eugenics Review.*[69]

   The English Convict's point of entry into the discourse of the eugenics program was the social distribution of "mental qualities."[70]
Among the specific attributes of these Goring included "tempera-
ment" and "intelligence" or "mental capacity." With regard to "tem-
perament," he found that among criminals the only distinguishing
features were that (1) fraudulent and sexual offenders tend to be more
egoistic than other offenders and (2) criminals convicted of violent
crimes were distinguished by "hot and uncontrolled" tempers and by
increased suicidal tendencies. "Other differences of temper . . . depend
entirely upon the grade of [their] general intelligence." However, in relation to the estimated 0.45 percent of mental defectives in the general
population,[71] Goring asserted that 10 to 20 percent of the criminal
population had some degree of mental defect and that all criminals displayed a decadence in general intelligence very similar to their increasing physical defectiveness.[72] With typical eugenist flourish, Goring

then linked these findings to the distribution of socioeconomic indicators of worth. "In every class and occupation of life, it is the feeble-minded and the inferior forms of physique—the less mentally and physically able persons—which tend to be selected for a criminal career."[73] The consistent regression of crime with mental capacity was thus consistent with the declining existence of worth "as we pass down the economic scale."[74] Moreover, because he found such a high correlation ($r = 0.64$) between crime and defective intelligence, Goring concluded it very probable that, if reducible to one condition, mental defectiveness would prove to be the common antecedent of other pathologies such as alcoholism, epilepsy, insanity, and sexual profligacy.[75]

While most eugenists dismissed altogether the relevance of sociological factors, Goring also engaged in an analysis of the relative potencies of several "adverse environmental conditions" (nationality, employment, education, family life, and social class), of mental defectiveness and of heredity upon the recidivism of convicts and the types of their crimes.[76] This analysis was the second object of Goring's discourse. Within criminology a definite line of demarcation had been drawn between constitutional and environmental factors in the genesis of crime, between Lombroso's criminal as an anthropological phenomenon and the "social" criminal in the tradition (as Goring incompletely understood it) of Quetelet, Ferri, and Lacassagne. Goring understood both parties to this dispute to have based their arguments not on sound statistical facts but on metaphysical assumptions. However, he too employed his instruments with an overarching conceptual assumption largely shared not only by both parties to this dispute but also by British eugenists: mental capacities and heredity, on the one hand, and the social environment, on the other, were independent of each other. For Goring, it followed that in order to measure the effect of one factor, the effect of the other had merely to be controlled, or eliminated, through partial correlations.[77] Additionally, Goring also assumed, like Weldon before him, that in the evolutionary causal schema "maladaptive," "deviant" or "defective" qualities of individuals in a given species existed without the mediation of environmental factors.

The operationalization of these assumptions occured in the three final stages of *The English Convict*. First, Goring found that a variety of "adverse environmental conditions" (defective education, irregular employment, and low standard of living of parents) were much more strongly correlated with convicts' intelligence than with the degree of their recidivism or the types of their crimes.[78] Mental defectiveness of the convict," Goring inferred, "is antecedent to his environmental misfortunes."[79] Thus,

> Our interim conclusion is that, relative to its origin in the constitution of the malefactor, and especially in his mentally defective constitution, crime in this country is only to a trifling extent (if to any) the product of social inequality, of adverse environment, or of other manifestations of what may be comprehensively termed the "force of circumstances."[80]

Second, Goring examined whether the criminal diathesis could be inherited, and in doing so he juxtaposed the concepts of differential fertility, hereditability, and family "contagion" while eschewing analysis of the putative underlying mechanisms of inheritance: "the problem of heredity rests upon a statistical basis."[81] The first part of his argument addressed differential fertility. Goring found that "criminals are a product of the most prolific stocks in the community,"[82] that prior to incarceration criminals were precisely as fertile as the general population,[83] and that unimprisoned criminals were twice as fertile as criminals who had been frequently in prison. Habitual criminals, therefore, had a lower fertility than the general population, but this was not because they shared in the relative sterility of all degenerate stocks but because they were adversely affected by the psychological and social consequences of prison. Goring found through analysis of family histories that the percentage of criminal offspring increased progressively according to whether neither parents, the mother only, the father only, or both parents were criminal. Although criminals comprised only 4 percent of the general population, as many as 68 percent of the male offspring of criminals themselves became criminal.[84] "The tendency

for crime to recur in families is . . . [thus] an indisputable statistical
fact."[85] However, this did not, as Goring realized, prove an inherited
criminal resemblance; it might have resulted from family "contagion."
He therefore attempted to disentangle the factor of criminal heredity
from that of family contagion. Controlling for the influence of contagion, he found the intensity of inheritance in criminality to be $r =$
0.45 to 0.5 but of criminal contagion to be insignificant ($r = 0.05$ to
0.1).[86] He concluded:

> A comparison of the results that have emerged from the
> present investigation . . . leads to two very definite general
> conclusions. The one is that the criminal diathesis, revealed by
> the tendency to be convicted and imprisoned for crime, is in-
> herited at much the same rate as are other physical and mental
> qualities and pathological conditions in man. [Second] the in-
> fluence of parental contagion . . . is, on the whole, inconsid-
> erable, relatively to the influence of inheritance, and of mental
> defectiveness: which are by far the most significant factors we
> have been able to discover in the etiology of crime.[87]

Finally, Goring offered some familiar eugenist proposals for the
crusade against crime, such as appropriate education to modify criminal tendencies; segregation and supervision of the unfit to modify the
opportunities for crime; regulation of the reproduction of constitutional qualities ("feeble-mindedness, inebriety, epilepsy, deficient social
instinct, etc.") which foster crime; and more statistical research into offenders' lives outside prison and into the experiments of the modern re-
formatory system "dealing with the child-criminal of the race."[88]

A Reconsideration of *The English Convict*

This chapter began by noting that the conclusions of *The English Convict* at once provoked heated dispute. On one side were those who held
that *The English Convict*'s findings disposed of Lombrosianism. On the
other were those who argued that Goring's chief accomplishment was
its confirmation. My argument here indicates that both views were

(and are) mistaken. They were mistaken because both assumed *The English Convict* to have had a unitary object, namely, Lombrosianism. However, it has been shown that *The English Convict*'s discourse was erected *ab initio* on a duality of objects that derived from a merger in the traditional focal concerns of prison research, statistics, evolutionary and mathematical zoology, and eugenics. Under their combined influence, Goring's engagement with Lombrosianism was transformed, first, into opposition to environmentalism and, second, into what ultimately became a psychiatric concern with the criminal diathesis and its heritable reproduction. Indeed, it was precisely this duality that permitted such ambivalent interpretations of *The English Convict*'s findings.

Although thus far I have not strictly been concerned with the putative merits of *The English Convict*'s critical engagement with Lombrosianism, let me now suggest two reasons why his apparent refutation of it must be considered largely a failure.

First, the same sorts of empirical criticisms of the concept of the born criminal made by Goring had already been marshalled against Lombrosianism by French anthropologists and sociologists in the 1880s and 1890s, three decades before the appearance of *The English Convict*. The origins of this criticism, as we have seen, were threefold: disagreement with the adequacy of Lombroso's sampling procedures, i.e., that he had failed to compare the physical characteristics of criminals with those of a control group of noncriminals; empirical disputation of Lombroso's data relating to the external physical manifestations of the born criminal; and a rejection, often for nonscientific reasons, of the rigidity underlying Lombroso's original classification of criminal types. In common with most proponents of these criticisms, and with sampling procedures as deficient as Lombroso's but with other sophisticated instruments unavailable to Lombroso and his French critics, *The English Convict*'s achievement was to deny the inheritance of certain physical features attributed to criminals by Lombroso but to affirm other physical features claimed by Lombroso to be peculiar to criminals, namely, inferior stature and physique.

Second, it is fair to say that Goring attempted to undermine a position that Lombroso himself had long since repudiated, a complaint

that was justly leveled at *The English Convict* by Lombroso's support-
ers. Indeed, although the 1876 first edition of *l'Uomo delinquente* had
argued that all criminals are born to their misdeeds, the subsequent intellectual development of Lombrosianism was increasingly dominated
by the commonplace belief that attributed to crime an infinitude of
possible causes and to criminals a variety of moral characters which, in
principle, encompassed the whole range from normal to pathological.
In response to the widespread rejection of monocausal theories of
crime, Lombroso adopted a multicausal approach to criminality based
on a cumulative mixture of hereditable and environmental factors.
Lombroso's admission to the influence of environmental and social
factors first appeared in the 1878 second Italian edition of *l'Uomo delinquente*. In 1899, in the course of Lombroso's last major statement on
the causes of crime and on the priority of atavism within them, the notion of born criminality barely survives amid "environmental" influences such as meteorology, climate, race, civilization, population
density, alcoholism, education, economic conditions, religion, and
imitation.[89]

About these modifications *The English Convict* displayed a per-
plexing ignorance. Goring's three primary references to Lombrosianism included *L'Homme criminel,* which was a French edition of *l'Uomo
delinquente* that omitted much of Lombroso's recognition of social factors; Lombroso and Ferrero's *The Female Offender,* which was an
abridged English translation of those portions of *La Donna delinquente*
dealing with female criminality; and Lombroso's speech at the 1906
Turin Congress of Criminal Anthropology, which merely reiterated
his discovery of anomalous cadavers found in Pavia in 1870. It is likely
that Goring's scanty understanding of Lombrosianism, and of the many
criticisms made of it, especially in France, derived from the shortcom-
ings of his secondary sources. *The English Convict's* references suggest
that chief among these was Maurice Parmalee's *The Principles of Anthropology and Sociology in Their Relations to Criminal Procedure* of 1912
and Gina Lombroso-Ferrero's *Lombroso's Criminal Man* of 1911. Parmalee's account of Lombrosianism was quite limited in that it offered
no account of Lombroso's recognition of social factors; its discussion of
criticisms of Lombrosianism was conducted almost exclusively at the

methodological level, and except for some passing anthropological comments, no mention is made of the serious sociological objections to biologism made by those such as Durkheim. Moreover, Lombroso-Ferrero's book was a congratulatory, uncritical summary of her father's writings on atavism, insanity, and crime. With his dependence on sources such as these, only slightly did Gina Lombroso-Ferrero exaggerate, therefore, when concluding that "Goring is more Lombrosian than Lombroso."[90] Indeed, not long before his death Goring was discussing with Karl Pearson the possibility of a series of essays on criminal psychology.[91]

Ironically, *The English Convict*'s dubious merit was to have replaced Lombroso's criminal—an unfortunate genetically stamped with atavistic physical features—with a convict born with inferior weight, stature, and mental capacity. Despite its rhetorical asides to the contrary, within the psychologistic notion of "character" *The English Convict* allowed a definite space for the intersection of rigidly determinist concepts of criminality and abnormality. Goring's determinist proposition that the criminal diathesis was inherited—which led directly to his fatalistic eugenist proposals—created a considerable problem, if accepted, for a pragmatic penal establishment directed to the moral reformation of character.[92] Alerted to this danger, Prison Commissioner Ruggles-Brise warned in his preface to *The English Convict* that Goring's general theory of defectiveness "must not be pressed so far as to affect the liability to punishment of the offender for his act. . . . Punishment must be individualized."[93] The Prison Commissioner, almost alone, clearly understood that the findings of *The English Convict* should not be considered a progressive advance on Lombrosianism but a parallel movement in the same operative movement as that initiated by Lombroso himself.

Notes

1. Charles Buckman Goring (1870–1919) was a distinguished student, and later Fellow, of University College, London. In 1893 he was awarded the John Stuart Mill Studentship in Philosophy of Mind and Logic, probably the only

occasion on which it had fallen to a medical exhibitioner. His early career included both service as a medical officer on a hospital ship during the Boer War, and the study of nervous diseases at Saltpêtrière and other hospitals in Paris. For *The English Convict* Goring was awarded the Weldon Medal and premium by Oxford University in 1914. He died on 5 May 1919, trying to curb a bout of influenza at Strangeways Prison in Manchester; see K. M. Goring (1919), "Letter to Karl Pearson, May 7th." Accounts of Goring's life can be found in several eulogies: Anon. (1919), "Obituary: Charles Buckman Goring"; Lucas and Goring (1919), "Appreciations of Charles Goring"; Pearson (1919b), "Charles B. Goring"; and Harris (1920), "Charles Buckman Goring."

2. Ruggles-Brise (1913), "Preface [to Goring, *The English Convict*]" p. 9; and see Ruggles-Brise (1921), *The English Prison System,* pp. 198–215.

3. *The English Convict* was originally published by His Majesty's Stationery Office (London) in 1913 in two separate volumes: (1) *The English Convict. A Statistical Study,* with a preface by Prison Commissioner Sir Evelyn Ruggles-Brise, and (2) *The English Convict: A Statistical Study. Schedule of Measurements and General Anthropological Data. The English Convict* then appeared in two abridged versions, in 1915 and 1919 respectively, the latter with an introduction by Karl Pearson, which was probably solicited by Ruggles-Brise (1919), "Letter to Professor Pearson, September 2nd." In 1972 a useful reprint edition was published by Patterson Smith that contained both volumes of 1913, Pearson's introduction of 1919 and a new introductory essay by Edwin D. Driver.

4. Pearson (1919a), "Charles Goring and his Contribution to *Criminology*," p. xviii; and see Pearson (1919b), op. cit., p. 299.

5. Mannheim (1936), "Lombroso and His Place in Modern Criminology," pp. 32–36.

6. A. K. Cohen (1966), *Deviance and Control,* p. 50.

7. Savitz, Turner, and Dickman (1977), "The Origin of Scientific Criminology: Franz Joseph Gall as the First Criminologist," p. 53; and see Marsh and Katz (1985), *Biology, Crime and Ethics,* p. xix.

8. Appreciative but critical comments on Goring's work can be found in Garland (1985a), *Punishment and Welfare: A History of Penal Strategies,* p. 179; and in S. Cohen (1974), "Criminology and the Sociology of Deviance in Britain: A Recent History and a Current Report," p. 6.

9. *Pace* Sellin (1931), "Charles Buckman Goring," p. 703; and Driver (1972), "Introductory Essay," p. xii.

10. For example, L. Darwin (1914), "The Habitual Criminal."

11. For example, Ferri (1914), "The Present Movement in Criminal Anthropology Apropos of a Biological Investigation in the English Prisons,"

pp. 226–27. In a special issue of the *Journal of the American Institute of Criminal Law and Criminology*. Gina Lombroso-Ferrero (Cesare Lombroso's daughter) proclaimed that *The English Convict* "marks an epoch in the history of the new science and must be considered one of the most important and best arguments in favor of criminal anthropology, which the author tried to refute" (1914, "The Results of an Official Investigation made in England by Dr. Goring to Test the Lombroso Theory," p. 209); and similarly, see *inter alia* de Sanctis (1914), "An Investigation of English Convicts and Criminal Anthropology," p. 233–36.

12. To these two views of *The English Convict* a third should be added. This view, which I do not consider here, encompasses a set of specifically methodological criticism that focus on the nonrandom nature of *The English Convict*'s sampling techniques and on Goring's mistaken strategy of eliminating the confounding effects of "environmental" factors. Good examples of this third view include Hooton (1939), *The American Criminal: An Anthropological Study*, pp. 18–31; and Sutherland and Cressey (1960), *Principles of Criminology*, pp. 99–101.

13. Swingewood (1970), "Origins of Sociology: The Case of the Scottish Enlightenment," p. 165; and see Hickox (1984), "The Problem of Early English Sociology."

14. Hindess (1973), pp. 12, 44–45.

15. Goring himself admitted that, methodologically, his work was "inspired by the genius of Francis Galton, and of Quetelet . . . [and] the brilliant mathematical researches of one master [i.e., Pearson] who has recently reduced to order the previous chaos of statistical science" (*The English Convict*, p. 27).

16. On 27 June 1833 in Cambridge, Quetelet communicated "some of the results of his inquiries into the proportion of crime at different ages and in different parts of France and Belgium" to the inaugural meeting of the Committee of the Statistical Section of the British Association (Drinkwater, 1833, "Note Book, 27th June 1833—8th March 1834"). Among those present at this meeting were Malthus, Babbage, and Drinkwater (the secretary, who took minutes). At a second meeting on the same day, Mr. Richard Jones (Professor and Chair of Political Economy at King's College London) observed that "this was the first meeting in England of this sort, and it was specially indebted to the presence and the influence of Quetelet" (ibid.). An account of how Quetelet was invited to address this meeting is given by Cullen (1975), *The Statistical Movement in Early Victorian Britain*, pp. 78–83, and 171, n. 12.

17. *Actes du Deuxième Congrès d'Anthropologie Criminelle* (1889), p. 406. For a slightly different account, see Ferri, *Criminal Sociology* (1917), p. 26–27.

18. *Actes du Troisième Congrès d'Antropologie Criminelle* (1892), pp. 171–82.

19. Lombroso-Ferrero (1914), op. cit., p. 207.

20. Lombroso (1896), 2:60.

21. While it rehearsed many of the extant French methodological criticisms of *l'Uomo delinquente,* and even applauded Quetelet's and Tarde's "social factor," Ellis's *The Criminal* was nevertheless based on Lombrosian categories which "render the criminal a proper object of scientific study" (1890, p. 43). Its first two editions involved an enthusiastic rendition of Lombrosianism "balanced" by the recognition of social factors. In the third and fourth editions, Ellis (by then a prominent eugenist) agreed that criminality resided in defective, savage, and abnormal characters whose bearers should be compulsorily sterilized in their own and in society's interests.

22. Major Arthur Griffiths—His Majesty's Inspector of Prisons between 1878 and 1896—was the sole English delegate at the 1897 International Congress of Criminal Anthropology in Geneva. For his detailed recollections of Lombroso at the Congress, see Griffiths (1904), *Fifty Years of Public Service,* pp. 380–84. About Griffiths's recommendations to the government, see Radzinowicz and Hood (1986), "The Emergence of Penal Policy," p. 20. Interestingly, Griffiths later wrote that "the conclusions of the Italian school have been warmly contested and on very plausible grounds. If the doctrines be fully accepted the whole theory of free-will breaks down, and we are faced with the paradox that we have no right to punish an irresponsible being who is impelled to crime by congenital causes, entirely beyond his control" (1910), "Criminology," p. 464.

23. Griffiths and Donkin (1904), "Measurements of One Hundred and Thirty Criminals." Upon his appointment as coordinator of the project, Goring at once expanded the number of subjects to 300, and correlations were made in 1906 between "shape of forehead" and "intelligence." These 300 subjects were then rolled over into Goring's larger study; see further *The English Convict,* pp. 28–29.

24. Goring did not always view his erstwhile government overseers favorably. In a letter to Pearson, for example, he referred to Smalley as "that unenlightened gentleman," and he voiced his depression with, and personal bitterness against, "the reckless pretensions and native inefficiency, and cynical selfishness [of the Prison Inspectorate]" (Goring, 1912a, "Letter to Professor Pearson, April 21st," pp. 1–3).

25. Goring (1909), "On the Inheritance of the Diatheses of Phthisis and Insanity." The laboratories' joint publications included a lengthy "memoir" se-

ries that focused on the inheritance of pathologies, a lecture series, and combined studies on "Questions of the Day and of the Fray" and on "National Deterioration."

26. Abrams (1968), *The Origins of British Sociology: 1834–1914*, pp. 13–52.

27. Karl Pearson (1924), *The Life, Letters and Labours of Francis Galton*, 2:424; see also Anon. (1911), "Obituary of Sir Francis Galton," p. 315. "As a statistician," confirms Stephen Stigler, "Galton was a direct descendant of Quetelet (1986, *The History of Statistics: The Measurement of Uncertainty before 1900*, p. 267). Galton's union of the technical development of statistics with the concerns of the eugenics program for national improvement is the focus of Cowan (1985), *Sir Francis Galton and the Study of Heredity in the Nineteenth Century*.

Like those of his Belgian mentor, Galton's intellectual interests were pursued on an encyclopaedic scale. One of these first surfaced in a paper that he delivered to the Anthropological Institute in 1879, and which explicitly reveals that Galton's concept of a "composite portrait" was self-consciously derived from Quetelet's concept of the "average man." Here Galton elaborated on an idea that had first been suggested to him by Herbert Spencer. Galton made it clear that he believed typical (or "composite") facial characteristics of criminals could be obtained by combining the photographs of two or more criminals who differed in minor respects. With the aid of a stereoscope, Galton displayed for his audience the composite portrait provided by photos of criminals convicted of murder, manslaughter, or robbery accompanied by violence. About this portrait he declared (Galton, 1879a, "Composite Portraits," p. 135; and see Galton 1879b, "Generic Images," p. 162): "It will be observed that the features of the composites are much better looking than those of the components. The special villainous irregularities in the latter have disappeared, and the common humanity that underlies them has prevailed. They represent, not the criminal, but the man who is liable to fall into crime. All composites are better looking than their components, because the averaged portrait of many persons is free from the irregularities that variously blemish the looks of each of them."

Galton had been provided with photographs of criminals by Sir Edmund Du Cane, Director General of Prisons, during the course of the latter's investigations of the distinguishing features of criminals and "their inferior mental and bodily organisation" (1879), op. cit., p. 143; and see Pearson (1924), op. cit., 2:228–33, 283–86. In 1898 Weldon, Galton and Professor E. B. Poulton participated in a new committee of the British Association "to promote the

systematic collection of Photographic and other Records of Pedigree Stock"
(cited in Pearson, ibid., 2: 321).

28. Weldon (1892), "Certain Correlated Variations in *Crangon Vulgaris*";
and Weldon (1893), "On Certain Correlated Variations in *Carcinus Moenas.*"

29. C. Darwin (1873), "On the Males and Complemental Males of Certain Cirripedes, and on Rudimentary Structures," p. 432. According to
George Darwin (1873, "Variations of Organs," p. 505), Charles Darwin explicitly traced his work on the measurement of the rates of natural selection and
elimination in all species to Quetelet's notion that all physical characteristics in
people vary according to the principle of the normal distribution.

30. Weldon's findings strongly implied that the early destruction of crabs
with deviant carapace lengths was caused by functional maladaptation. He
gradually retracted this claim after biologists' criticisms that changes in the size
of the frontal portion of crabs could themselves be caused by such physiological factors as increased silting of the beaches where the crab samples had been
collected, differences in water temperature, and the action of the preservatives
in which the sample crabs had been stored. See, for example, Weldon (1898),
"Presidential Address to Section D, Zoology"; and see Farrall (1969), *The Origins and Growth of the English Eugenics Movement, 1865–1925*, pp. 78–86.

31. Weldon (1894–95), "An Attempt to Measure the Death-Rate due to
the Selective Destruction of *Carcinus Moenas* with respect to a Particular Dimension," p. 381.

32. Ibid., p. 368. At the same time, from February to June 1895, Weldon
was discussing in some detail with Karl Pearson Bertillon's method of anthropometric measurements. See, for example, Weldon, "Weldon to Pearson, 9th
June 1895."

33. Norton (1978), "Karl Pearson and Statistics: The Social Origins of
Scientific Innovation."

34. Stigler (1986), op. cit., pp. 326–61.

35. On the founding of the Biometric Laboratory, see Farrall (1969), op.
cit., pp. 103–11. It should be noted that Galton had earlier established an "Anthropometric Laboratory." This was a simple room with a battery of anthropometric measuring devices, which began its life at the International Health
Exhibition in London in 1884, and which then moved to the Science Museum
in South Kensington before finding more permanent quarters at University
College London. According to a penny pamphlet of some fourteen pages, the
purpose of the Laboratory at the 1884 Exhibition was "to ascertain whether the
growth of a child or youth is proceeding normally, and to draw attention to
defects with a view to their being remedied; and . . . to discover the efficiency

of a nation as a whole and of its several parts, and the direction in which it is changing, whether for better or worse" (quoted in Pearson, 1924, op. cit., 2: 370).

36. Goring (1912b), "Letter to Professor Pearson, October 2nd." Pearson's great influence on Goring can be appreciated even more from the intimate correspondence between them which survives in the *Pearson Papers* in the University College London Archives.

37. Ibid., p. 27.

38. Goring (1909), op. cit., p. 24. Galton himself had earlier undertaken research on the physiognomical characteristics of the phthisical diathesis of hospital patients in London. See, for example, Galton and Mahomed (1882), "An Inquiry into the Physiognomy of Phthisis by the Method of Composite Portraiture"; see also Pearson (1924), op. cit., 2: 291–93.

39. Ibid., p. 19. Goring would doubtless have been fascinated, although not perhaps with any lingering sense of its importance, by a gift that Karl Pearson received in 1911 on behalf of the Museum of the Galton Eugenics Laboratory. The gift (the Robert Noel Collection of Original Casts) was provided by Mary Caroline Milbanke, the Countess of Lovelace, whose husband Lord Lovelace had acquired it from the phrenologist Major Robert Noel, his cousin and, incidentally, the grandson of the poet Byron. The gift, whose macabre contents were collected during Noel's travels in Europe between 1837 and 1845, consisted of about fifty original casts of the heads (both living and dead—of the famous and infamous and were intended by their collector to illustrate head types with high and low intelligence. Next to each head is a short informative commentary by Noel. For example, about the head of a woman who had callously and horribly murdered the youngest of her three children, Noel had observed "Unmarried woman, anxious to marry." Detailed information on the collection and its background can be found in *The Daily News,* 14 October 1896; and Murray Watson, "If you Want To Get Ahead," *University College London Bulletin,* November 1980. I am grateful to Francesca Emous at the Slade School of Fine Art for alerting me to this important gift, whose contents now inhabit the basement of the Slade School, in appropriate proximity to the imposing remains of Jeremy Bentham at University College.

40. *The English Convict,* p. 27.

41. Ibid., p. 20.

42. Ibid., p. 18.

43. Ibid., p. 21. One of Goring's colleagues at the Biometric Laboratory asked him about his proposed book, "Why is this to be *The English Convict* instead of *The English Criminal?*" to which Goring instantly replied, "Perhaps

some of them are not criminals, only convicts" (Harris, 1920, op. cit., p. 134). Analytically, Goring never applied this insight: throughout *The English Convict* he conflated the terms *criminal* and *convict* and juxtaposed *criminals* with the *noncriminal public* and the *law-abiding community*.

44. Ibid., pp. 23–24.

45. Ibid., pp. 22–23, and see Garland (1985b), "Politics and Policy in Criminological Discourse: A Study of Tendentious Reasoning and Rhetoric," pp. 15–16.

46. *Pace* Ferri (1914), op. cit., p. 224.

47. *The English Convict*, p. 21.

48. Ibid., pp. 26–27.

49. Ibid., p. 23.

50. Ibid., p. 27.

51. Ibid., pp. 28–139.

52. Ibid., pp. 139–73.

53. Ibid., pp. 174–201.

54. "The population at Parkhurst prison . . . is very heterogeneous compared with that at other stations. Parkhurst is the station for the weak-minded, the epileptic, the insane, the tubercular, the diseased generally; there is also a large population of star-class convicts at Parkhurst; and all the Jews are located there" (ibid., p. 74).

55. Ibid., p. 139.

56. Ibid., p. 138.

57. Ibid.

58. In fact, in his book *The Female Offender* of 1893, written with his son-in-law William Ferrero, Lombroso had tried—unsuccessfully—to juxtapose the characteristics of a control group of "normal women" with those of "female criminals."

59. Ibid., p. 173.

60. Ibid., p. 174.

61. Ibid., pp. 201–2.

62. Ibid., p. 197.

63. Ibid., p. 200.

64. Galton (1883), *Inquiries into Human Faculty and Its Development*, pp. 24–25; and see Galton (1904), "Eugenics: Its Definition, Scope and Aims," p. 35; and Pearson (1924), op. cit., 2: 119.

A good account of Galton's views on race improvement and eugenics is given by Forrest (1974), *Francis Galton: The Life and Work of a Victorian Genius*, pp. 245–64. Farrall (1969, op. cit.) provides an excellent guide to the internal contours of the English eugenics movement; its relations with contemporary political issues are discussed in Searle (1976), *Eugenics and Politics in Britain 1900–1914;* and with criminology by Garland (1985a), op. cit., pp. 142–52, 178–80.

65. Galton (1901), "The Possible Improvement of the Human Breed, Under the Existing Conditions of Law and Sentiment," p. 11.

66. Ibid., p. 20.

67. See further Garland (1985a), op. cit., p. 149. The articulation of these assumptions was demonstrated in Galton's Huxley Lecture to the Royal Anthropological Institute. This lecture was delivered in 1901, at a time when it was widely argued that the British army had failed to gain complete victory in the Boer War because so many of its recruits were physically and mentally unfit. Indeed, on a global scale the eugenics movement—including Pearson, a rabid supporter of British imperialism; see Collini (1979, *Liberalism and Sociology,* p. 177)—wished to address the causes of Britain's declining position in the imperialist world and to identify the means of its social regeneration. In this lecture, which Galton regarded as an additional chapter to his (Galton, 1869, *Hereditary Genius;* Galton, 1889, *Natural Inheritance*) earlier works on heredity and as an important plea for eugenics, he relied on evidence in Charles Booth's *Life and Labour of the People in London* showing that the "highest (i.e., so-called worthy) classes" constituted 0.97 percent of the population. The proportion of the highest classes in Booth's data, Galton continued, matched almost identically the proportion of the lowest: 0.94 percent of London's population comprised criminals, semicriminals, loafers, the casually poor and those whose poverty stemmed from shiftlessness, idleness, and drink (Galton, 1901, op. cit., pp. 8–11).

In this lecture Galton argued that important and as yet unanswered questions remained: What are the respective costs and benefits to national performance of raising children in the lowest and highest sections of society? What is the association between promise of civic worth in youth and actual performance in adult life? How can the fertility of the lowest sections best be reduced, and that of the highest sections raised? Galton (ibid.) concluded by urging that "to no nation is a high human breed more necessary than to our own, for we plant our stock all over the world and lay the foundation of the dispositions and capacities of future millions of the human race" (p. 34).

68. The Eugenics Education Society was formed in 1907 by eugenists in the Moral Instruction League and the Sociological Society. See Farrall (1969), op. cit., p. 206); and Abrams (1968), op. cit., pp. 108–13. The branches of the Eugenics Education Society spanned much of England and extended quickly to

Ireland, Scotland, New Zealand, and Australia. After 1909 its influential membership included Cyril Burt, Neville Chamberlain, J.B.S. Haldane, A. J. Balfour, Francis and Horace Darwin, Havelock Ellis, Patrick Geddes, John Maynard Keynes, and Harold Laski.

69. *The Eugenics Review* was the official journal of the Eugenics Education Society. According to Farrall's analysis of its contents up to 1921, " a main theme running through the Review was that a number of social problems— poverty, mental illness, criminality and alcoholism—were the result of the hereditary constitutions of the individuals found in [the] problem classes" (1969, op. cit., p. 237). Those unfortunates with hereditary disorders (chiefly manifest in alcoholism, criminality, and feeble-mindedness) had much larger families than "sound stock." For a contemporary assessment of the Eugenics Review, see Hobhouse (1911), *Social Evolution and Political Theory*, p. 72. In a Columbia University lecture series, Hobhouse engaged in a sophisticated and concerted debate with eugenists in which he challenged them on their own empirical terrain and, in opposition especially to Pearson, argued that social progress could not adequately be measured in terms of social and biological health but, rather, in those of justice and equity (ibid., especially pp. 55ff, 64–79).

70. Recognizing that the measurement of these qualities was less precise than that of physical qualities, Goring nevertheless asserted that "personal estimations of . . . mental attributes . . . if carefully made and recorded by an unbiased and disinterested investigator . . . [are] of equal value scientifically, as that produced by measurement" (*The English Convict*, p. 237).

Incidentally, Goring was aware of Galton's address to the Anthropological Department of the British Association, delivered in Plymouth in 1877, in which he argued that criminal traits were hereditable and that the so-called ideal criminal has various peculiarites of character; these included a deficient conscience, vicious instincts, and weak self-control (see Galton, 1879a). That Goring undoubtedly took note of Galton's argument here is borne out by Pearson's "confirmation" of the former's conclusions by explicit reference to the latter's *The English Convict* (Pearson, 1924, op. cit., 2: 228–33).

71. *The English Convict*, pp. 254–56.

72. Ibid., p. 244.

73. Ibid., p. 261.

74. Ibid.

75. Ibid., p. 262.

76. Ibid., pp. 263–89.

77. On this point, at least, it is difficult to disagree with the Harvard anthropologist E. A. Hooton's caustic remark about this aspect of *The English*

Convict's method that is marked "a triumphant demonstration of the obvious fact that if due allowance be made for all of the physical and mental differences between criminals and noncriminals, the former are not different from the latter" (1939), op. cit., pp. 23–24.

78. Goring displayed a woeful lack of familiarity with the contemporary sociological literature (Durkheim, Tarde, etc.) on crime and "the force of circumstances" which, precisely because much of it was directed against biologism, in turn helps to explain his inadequate understanding of the various "environmental" concessions made by the Lombrosians. Goring's knowledge of the "social factors in crime" seems to have relied heavily on *Punishment and Reformation* by the American penologist Wines (1910). Wines's book was based on a multifactorial approach in which mental deficiency played a central role: "Intellectually and morally, criminals are for the most part weak. Their mental feebleness is sometimes so marked as to produce the impression of partial imbecility" (p. 264).

79. *The English Convict*, p. 287.

80. Ibid., p. 288.

81. Ibid., p. 340.

82. Ibid., p. 334.

83. Ibid., pp. 290–306.

84. Ibid., p. 356.

85. Ibid., p. 364.

86. Ibid., p. 367.

87. Ibid., p. 368.

88. Ibid., p. 373. To this very problem, in the context of a heated exchange with Donkin, Goring responded that *The English Convict*'s statistical findings should not be assessed in terms of their penological relevance: "Criminology is not part of a propagandistic movement for regulating conduct. It is a Science, critical of the ideas by which conduct is being regulated" (1918, "The Aetiology of Crime," p. 130). See Donkin (1917), "Notes on Mental Defect in Criminals"; and Donkin (1919), "The Factors of Criminal Actions."

89. *Crime: Its Causes and Remedies* (Lombroso, 1899) originally appeared in Paris in 1899, and was included by Lombroso as the fourth volume of the fifth and last Italian edition of *l'Uomo delinquente*: it was published in English translation in 1918. Its precise position within Lombroso's total output is unclear. Differing views on its position can be found in Lindesmith and Levin (1937), "The Lombrosian Myth in Criminology," p. 666, n. 21; and in Wolfgang (1972), "Cesare Lombroso," p. 237. In the preface to this book Lombroso himself wrote that "I attempt by means of facts to answer those who, not having ready my *Criminal Man* (of which it is the necessary

complement . . . accuse my school of having neglected the economic and social causes of crime, and of having confined itself to the study of the born criminal, thus teaching that the criminal is riveted to his destiny" (1899, p. xxxiii).

90. Lombroso-Ferrero (1914), op. cit., p. 210.

91. See Pearson (1919a), op. cit., p. 297.

92. A good example of the extent of this problem is indicated by a typically belligerent statement from Garofalo (1914, *Criminology*): "Let me also say that a standard reply to the charge of fatalism levelled against the positivists is that 'it has been thought that we believe man, and consequently the criminal, to be incapable of transformation and never to act except in a determined direction.' No such error has at any time found place in our views. What experience has demonstrated is that the individual acts always in the same direction, so long as his intellectual and moral conditions remain unchanged and he finds himself in the same external circumstances. This is why we deem it the height of folly to hope for the reformation of the criminal by imprisonment or any other kind of punishment, if, as soon as it is ended, he is remitted to the same environment and the same conditions of existence as before. But by no means do we believe it impossible *to transform the activity of the offender*" (p. xxxii).

93. Ruggles-Brise (1913), op. cit., p. 8. Other members of the British penal establishment were less circumspect in their criticism. H. B. Simpson of the Home Office, for example, held that *The English Convict* was "a striking example of methods borrowed from Germany where facts are lost sight of in a cloud of highly debateable figures" (quoted in Radzinowicz and Hood, 1986, op. cit., p. 25). Later, Ruggles-Brise was able to modify the determinist implications of Goring's conclusions about the inherited nature of mental defect in criminals. Indeed, he inferred that Goring's findings confirmed: (1) the Borstal system was the most effective way of tackling crime by focusing on those aged 16 to 21, (2) imprisonment does not have adverse physical and mental results, (3) the "mentally defective" need better care, and (4) the "criminal problem" can best be solved by considering the criminal population itself first and foremost (Ruggles-Brise, 1921, op. cit., pp. 214–15).

Chapter 7

Epilogue

Less by way of conclusion to the rather narrowly focused chapters of this book than as an invitation to further thought, two general comments can now usefully be made about the broad periods of classical criminology and positivist criminology. One concerns the alleged epistemological rupture between them, the other the correct periodization of the emergence of positivism.

Concept formation in modern criminology is conventionally held to have been made possible only with the successful transformation from the worldview of classical criminology to that of positivist criminology. When discourse about crime emerged from the darkness of the far side of that divide and entered the positivist light of its near side in the nineteenth century, only then, in Foucauldian terms, did *Homo criminalis* become a definite object in the field of knowledge. According to David Matza, in the brilliant opening chapter of his book *Delinquency and Drift* (1964), the history of modern criminology is intimately wrapped up with—indeed, actually *is*—the increasing triumph of positivist criminology over the entire range of its intellectual competition, especially classicism. To Matza, to Foucault, and in every standard textbook treatment of the subject, this history is one in which positivist criminology effects a complete break with the classical framework of its intellectual past.

> Modern criminology is the positive school of criminology. According to most scholars, it begins with the views of Lombroso, which consisted of a rather fundamental repudiation of the earlier classical viewpoint of Beccaria, Bentham, Carrara, and others. This fundamental shift, signaled by Lombroso and

225

largely carried through by Ferri, laid the basic assumptions of criminological thought, and these assumptions persist to this day.[1]

One can disagree about the essential characteristics of positivism, about whether its ascendancy is more or less regrettable, and about whether its alleged epistemological limitations can be avoided or overcome by the revival of a modified version of classicism. But we cannot do that here. Moreover, there is no need to dispute the contention that the rise of positivism and the development of modern criminology are by and large one and the same historical enterprise. With the exception of a now distant, liberal moment in the 1960s and 1970s—when criminologists attributed the possibility of authentic action to their objects of study—the march of positivism in criminology has continued almost unchecked. What it does seem appropriate to comment on here, however, is the time-honored claim that between classical and positivist criminology there is a complete epistemological rupture or, in Matza's words above, a "fundamental shift . . . [in] the basic assumptions of criminological thought."

At root, the claim of a fundamental epistemological rupture between classical criminology and positivist criminology derives from an uncritical consensus about their respective cognitive assumptions. According to this consensus, the objects of classical criminology are erected on a combination of voluntarism, humanism, and rationalism, while those of positivist criminology derive from its fundamental scientism. Rarely, if ever, has this radical cognitive separation of classicism from positivism been questioned. Indeed, in the context of my own project of trying to uncover the intellectual and social roots of concept formation in modern criminology, I confess that my longstanding preference was to leave the study of classical criminology until last, thinking that classicism was a movement whose contours had already been accurately mapped and that its discursive objects had quite appropriately been relegated to criminology's prehistory.

But it is worth comparing the discourse of the central text of classical criminology, *Dei delitti e delle pene* (see Chapter 2 above) with that of the positivism in Quetelet's social mechanics (see Chapter 3) or Guerry's social cartography (see Chapter 4). Such comparisons cast some doubt on the extent of the epistemological break which is alleged to have occurred between classical criminology and positivist criminology. In my analysis of *Dei delitti e delle pene* I have not denied the conventional view that Beccaria's advocacy of voluntarism, of humanism and of legal rationality are important features of his treatise. Rather, I suggest that neither the method of *Dei delitti* nor its object can be understood in terms of these tendencies alone. An altogether different tendency, veiled and incompletely developed, actually comprised the kernel of Beccaria's discourse—the application to crime and penality of key principles in the protopositivist "science of man." In the framework of this new science the two major themes of *Dei delitti* (the "right to punish" and "how to punish") are couched, as are Beccaria's advocacy of deterrence and his opposition to capital punishment and judicial torture.

Contrary to prevailing opinion, the discourse of *Dei delitti* is not erected exclusively on the volitional conduct of the subject of classical jurisprudence, or "free will," as it is nowadays popularly termed. Precisely how Beccaria viewed volitional conduct in *Dei delitti* will probably never be known, but it is likely that, in common with many of his contemporaries in the eighteenth-century Enlightenment who saw in this no contradiction, he adhered to a notion of human agency simultaneously involving free rational calculation and determined action. The presence of determinism in *Dei delitti* should really come as no great surprise, since Beccaria's view of human agency was guided by the discourse of the "science of man." Throughout *Dei delitti* the rigidly determinist principles of that science are displayed in the doctrines of probabilism, associationism, and sensationalism. The warriors and wretches who stalk its pages are thus not volitional agents, as the conventional view of classicism would have it, but creatures trapped in a web of determinism. The potential criminals in Beccaria's schema "act" like automata; in effect, they are recalcitrant objects who, in the administrative interests of a model bourgeois society, must be angled, steered, and forced into appropriate and law-abiding behavior. The classical juristic concept of an unfettered free will must therefore be relegated along with humanism and legal rationality to the margins of *Dei delitti*.

If the discourse of *Dei delitti* is not couched in the rhetoric of classical jurisprudence, if its chief object (the construction of a rational and efficient penal calculus) is not directed to the actions of volitional subjects but to those of automata given by the "science of man," if humanism is a minor rather than a major feature of this discourse, then what is left of the orthodox view of the classical edifice? Perhaps very little. At the very least, these questions imply that the position of *Dei delitti* in intellectual history does not lie at the center of classical criminology as it is conventionally understood. The very existence of classical criminology, in other words, therefore needs to be reconsidered. Indeed, as an identifiable set of assumptions about crime and punishment, classical criminology was not actually denominated as such until the 1870s, and then by another generation of Italian theorists—by militantly positivist criminologists such as Lombroso, Garofalo, and Ferri. These thinkers were keenly interested in distinguishing *their* invention of a scientific criminology from that of Beccaria's "outmoded" discourse of free will, either because they failed properly to understand the arguments of *Dei delitti* or, more likely, because it did not suit their own interests to do so. As such, perhaps classical criminology is no more than the retrospective invention of distorted scholarly self-aggrandizement.

Despite how tempting it is to focus on Beccaria's predeliction for the "science of man," his discourse should not be placed, however precariously, at the beginning of the tradition to which it is commonly opposed, namely positivist criminology. Beccaria's utterances on crime and punishment were never intended—nor could they have been—to inhabit the same positivist terrain as that so eagerly tenanted a century later by the biologism of his compatriot Lombroso.[2]

The still widely held opinion that the early history of positivist criminology begins with the writings of Lombroso and Ferri also needs to be revised. As has been documented extensively here, there existed in France and Belgium in the 1830s a presociological tendency whose positivist discourse flourished some forty years before the appearance of Lombroso's *l'Uomo delinquente* and which, especially in its scientific ambitions, was far more advanced than the crude biologism of the latter's criminal anthropology.

The criminology of the Franco–Belgian moral statisticians included some of the focal concerns in penality and the statistical movement. During the Restoration these domains coincided in a common issue, namely, the regulation of the dangerous classes. The apparent failure of French penal strategies to regulate the conduct of the dangerous classes, when conjoined with an expansion in the scope of the statistical movement to include empirical social research, provided the structure and much of the substantive content of the criminology of the moral statisticians, especially so in the case of Adolphe Quetelet's social mechanics of crime. Its structure was formed by the relentless application of the methods of the natural sciences to the moral phenomena lodged in the official records of crime. Its content comprised an empirical examination of the effects of different social environments on those individuals—drawn largely from the "dangerous classes"—who passed through the successive layers of the administration of justice.

In this examination neither his colleagues nor Quetelet himself made any theoretical distinction between their own observational categories and those of the state officials who constructed the data in the *Compte général*. Nor did they even contemplate such a distinction. The object of their criminology was therefore the already constituted problem of the dangerous classes. Its outcome was a positivist discourse about *Homo criminalis* which included such concepts as criminal character and propensities and which looked to the causal influence on crime of such factors as age, sex, class, and race. Eventually, it nurtured a rigid binary opposition between normality and deviation.

However, if classical criminology was less voluntaristic than is generally supposed, then at least in the minds of some of its practitioners, so too was the positivist criminology of the Franco–Belgian moral statisticians less deterministic. It is true that they were involved in the same search for law-like regularities as Beccaria's heir and their mentor Condorcet, who observed that "in meditating on the nature of the moral sciences, one cannot help but see that, if they depend on the observation of facts, like the physical sciences, they would follow the same method, acquire a language equally exact and precise, and attain the same degree of certitude."[3] But members of the Franco-Belgian school were not unmitigated positivists and, like Laplace, they wished to combat superstition yet not to overthrow religion. Like Laplace, they participated in the metaphysical wager that "the beauty of the universe and the order of celestial things force us to recognize some superior nature which ought to be remarked and admired by the human race."[4]

Quetelet's analysis of crime, in particular, contained, and maybe even fostered, many of the uncertainties of the inconsistencies associated with the transitional phase in French penality between the voluntarism of classical jurisprudence and the embryonic hard determinism of positivism, between the unbridled legal subject of the former and the overdetermined object of the latter. At most, Quetelet was a reluctant determinist who neither disowned the juristic doctrine of free will nor denied the determinate character of social behavior. Indeed, over and over again, in a variety of ways often tinged with a mixture of bewilderment and poignancy, Quetelet's ambivalence pervades the positivist discourse of all the moral statisticians, including A. M. Guerry,[5] Adolphe d'Angeville,[6] and others. In the soul of Quetelet's criminal, as in that of Victor Hugo's ex-convict Jean Valjean in *Les Misérables,* there dwelled a primitive spark, a divine element, incorruptible in this world and immortal in the next, which could be kindled, lit up, made radiant by good, and which evil could never entirely extinguish.

Notes

1. David Matza (1964), *Delinquency and Drift,* p. 3.

2. So also I must resist, even in the relative security of a footnote, the intriguing temptation of arguing that *Dei delitti* should be seen as the first link in a chain that proceeds to Condorcet's obscure *Essai sur l'application de l'analyse à la probabilité des décisions rendues à la pluralité des voix* (1785) and his *Tableau général de la science* (1795b)—See also Condorcet (n.d.), "Essai sur les probabilités en fait de Justice"—and concludes with the rise of well-formed, presociological analyses of crime as found in the 1830s in the discourse of moral statistics. Some of the groundwork for such an argument—were it to be at-

tempted—has been prepared by Lottin (1912), *Quetelet: statisticien et sociologue,* p. 362; Baker (1975), op. cit., pp. 227–42; and Hankins (1985), op. cit., pp. 182–83.

3. Condorcet (1782), "Discours prononcé dans l'Académie française le jeudi, 21 février 1782," p. 392.

4. Laplace (1814), *A Philosophical Essay on Probabilities,* p. 175.

5. For example, in discussing the patterned and predictable regularity of judicial statistics, Guerry argued, "If we now consider the infinite number of circumstances which can lead to a crime, including both the exterior and the purely personal influences which determine its character, we could not possibly imagine how constant are the results; acts of free will develop in a fixed order and they are confined to very narrow limits." See Guerry (1833), *Essai sur la statistique morale de la France,* pp. 11–12.

6. The apparent rigidity of the moral order posed an obvious contradiction for the moral statisticians who believed in free will. For example, in commenting on the extraordinary constancy of crime rates recorded in the *Compte,* d'Angeville (1836, pp. 95–96) wrote in his famous *Essai sur la statistique de la population française . . .* that "it is impossible not to recognize that the facts of the moral order occur in the domain of statistics, just like those in the physical order. This is a disheartening thing for those who seek human perfection. In effect, it would seem that free will exists only as a theory, and that in the midst of each society are the germs of evil which develop without check. Fortunately, this opinion is contradicted by experience, and, above all, by reason."

Appendix

The Invention of the Term *Criminology*

It may with confidence be said that, etymologically, the term *criminology* derives from the Latin word *crimen*, a category of Roman law that is variously translated into English as "judgment," "accusation," and "offense." However, why, by whom, in what intellectual or social context, and precisely when the term was invented have never been firmly established. This appendix tries to clarify what is known about the origin of the term *criminology*, although to identify anything more than its etymological origins is inevitably somewhat of a speculative task, albeit an interesting one.

There is no recorded instance of the term *criminology* ever having been used before the final quarter of the nineteenth century. According to a consensus of opinion which has persisted since the early 1890s, the term was invented in 1889 by the anthropologist Paul Topinard, the director of the *École anthropologie* in Paris.[1] At that time, and in the decade immediately prior to it, a large number of terms jostled noisily together as descriptive indicators of the presociological terrain of criminology. In France alone, these terms included *anthropologie criminelle, science criminelle, anthropologie juridique,* and *anthropologie et le droit.* By the early 1880s, a measure of dominance over its competitors had been achieved by *anthropologie criminelle,* a term that, in relation to the study of crime and criminality, designated the total complex of individual, biological, and sociological factors associated with the general notion of humanity. At first, doubtless, *anthropologie criminelle* was able to assert its dominance precisely because its all-encompassing, and therefore ill-defined, frame of reference afforded more shelter to a wide variety of methodologies and theoretical perspectives than did other terms. It was embraced by authors of widely divergent and often incompatible views, including Gabriel Tarde, Alexandre Lacassagne, and Cesare Lombroso. It was, additionally, officially adopted by several international congresses, most notably the First International Congress of Criminal Anthropology, held in 1885 in Rome, and by the Second Congress of Criminal Anthropology, held in 1889 in Paris.

However, not long after the widespread acceptance of *anthropologie criminelle* during the mid-1880s, the stability of this broad-based union was threatened and then ruptured by a group of French lawyers, anthropologists, and sociologists who sought to distance their several objects of study from the exclusively biological one which was then espoused by Lombrosianism. In short, it was mounting opposition to the Lombrosian notion of the "born criminal," and the search for a countervailing explanation of crime and criminality, that supplied the primary context for the invention of an alternative term to the Lombrosian-dominated discourse signified by *anthropologie criminelle*.

In 1887, in the course of a review of a French translation (*l'Homme criminel*) of the fourth Italian edition of Lombroso's *l'Uomo delinquente*, Topinard pondered a number of alternatives to *anthropologie criminelle*, including *sociologie criminelle* and *criminalogie*. He suggested that Lombroso's book *l'Homme criminel* could just as accurately have been entitled *criminalogie:*

> Its title, *l'Homme criminel*, perfectly reflects its content. It could just as well be entitled *"La criminalogie"* unless we wish that practical applications, professional jurisprudence, the question of prevention and punishment, not enter into the subject. It does not make any claim—a claim which could not be justified in any case—to be about anthropology.[2]

Moreover:

> To accept as true the concept of atavism—i.e., that certain individuals are predestined to commit crime or that they possess

a physical and mental constitution which leads to crime—
would be to undermine at its foundation the new branch of applied science which has been developed under the name of
criminalogie.[3]

Only after he had rejected *criminalogie* did Topinard use the term
criminologie. According to Joseph van Kan,[4] Topinard's term *criminalogie,* was etymologically mistaken because it had been developed from
a false analogy with *criminality. Criminalogie* was abandoned by its inventors (*inventeurs*), van Kan rather unhelpfully suggests, "from the
moment when the correction '*criminologie*' made them understand their
error."[5] In any event, it is at this point that Topinard is held to have
corrected the error with *criminologie,* specifically at the Second Congress of Criminal Anthropology held in Paris in August, 1889.[6]
Among the many early sources that implicitly support Topinard's can-
didacy are the English periodical *The Athenaeum,* in which an anonymous reviewer of 1890 observed about Havelock Ellis's book *The
Criminal:*

> It is curious that in Britain, which claims to be preeminently
> a country of practical people, so little should have been done,
> and so little should be known of what has been done else-
> where, in that branch of the anthropological sciences which has
> the best promise of affording results of immediate practical
> value—criminology. We share Dr. Topinard's dislike of the
> term "criminal anthropology," and may adopt the term
> "criminology" till a better can be found.[7]

However, as it stands, this account of the invention of the term
criminology must be firmly rejected. There are two pieces of evidence
that support this conclusion, the one quite compelling, the other bi-
zarre but suggestive.

Topinard's priority was in fact preceded by the title of an Italian
book of 1885 by the sociologist Baron Raffaele Garofalo, namely,
Criminologia. Indeed, Topinard himself stated at the 1889 Second Congress of Criminal Anthropology that "the legitimate title of our

science is that which M. Garofalo has given it, namely, *criminology*
[*criminologie*].[8] It is not known (at least not by me) explicitly how or
why Garofalo produced this title, although it is worth noting that Garofalo, who wrote the preface to this book in Naples in July 1884,
stated that a major influence on his thinking was the book *Socialismo e
Sociologia criminale* of 1884 by the Italian socialist sociologist Napoleone
Colajanni.[9] Colajanni's book is distinguished by its pre-Durkheimian
mission of founding a scientific sociology;[10] like many early socialists,
Colajanni's book embraced a primitive multifactorial combination of
social, economic, biological, and meteorological influences on crime.

Rather bizarrely, it seems that the term *criminology* was predated by
the term *criminologist*. In an anonymous review ("Felons and Felon
Worship") of the also anonymous book *Dark Deeds* of 1857 in the conservative periodical *The Saturday Review*, the reviewer wrote, "In the
author of *Dark Deeds*, we have a criminologist of a third sort."[11] Precisely what in this context the reviewer intended by the term *criminologist* remains a mystery, in part because each of the three sorts of
criminologist reviewed was allegedly writing descriptive accounts of
crime. It is likely that by *criminologist* the reviewer—who was almost
certainly John Ormsby (1829–95),[12] author of papers of travel and
well-known to readers of *The Saturday Review*—referred, quite
loosely, to no more than someone, like himself, who writes about
crime and criminals.

It should also be noted that the anonymous author of *Dark Deeds*
was the Reverend Erskine Neale. His book is a rogue's gallery of
eighteen criminal portraits, each written by Neale himself. Nowhere
in this book did Neale himself use the term *criminology*, nor did he do
so in his book of 1847 *Experiences of a Gaol Chaplain*. Interestingly, in
his preface there occurs the idea,

> Society itself must produce the germs of guilt, and offer the
> facilities necessary for their development. Every social condi-
> tion and state contain within themselves a certain number, and
> a certain order of offences, which result as necessary conse-
> quences from their organization.[13]

These lines, written either by an anonymous editor or else by Neale himself, were taken unacknowledged from *Physique sociale*,[14] the pioneering book of 1835 written by the young Belgian astronomer Adolphe Quetelet. Moreover, it was Quetelet who, by embarrassing Auguste Comte, was vicariously responsible for inventing the neologism *sociology*.[15]

Notes

1. For example, see van Kan (1903), *Les Causes économiques de la criminalité*, p. 2; and Nye (1984), *Crime, Madness, and Politics in Modern France*, p. 107.

2. Topinard (1887), "L'Anthropologie criminelle," p. 659. Topinard's proposed term *criminalogie* was repeated the following year in an article by Colajanni that addressed problems of "criminality": see Colajanni (1888), "Question contemporaine de la crimnalité," p. 59.

3. Ibid., p. 684.

4. Van Kan (1903), p. 2.

5. Ibid.

6. See Topinard (1889), "Criminologie et anthropologie."

7. Anon. (1890), "Review of Havelock Ellis' *The Criminal*," p. 325.

8. Topinard (1889), p. 496.

9. However, as an alternative to *sociologie criminelle*, the term *criminalogie* was still being used by Colajanni in his 1888 work (p. 59).

10. See especially Colajanni's (1884) book *Il Socialismo: Socialismo e sociologia criminale*, 1: 267–306. Durkheim's first usage of the term *criminologie* occurred in 1894—the year before Garofalo's *Criminologie* made its appearance in French translation—in his *Rules of Sociological Method* (1894), pp. 70–79, 83, 97–100).

11. Anon. (1857a), p. 271. A brief reference to this review is contained in the Compact Edition of the *Oxford English Dictionary* (1971), 1: 604. The reviewer also commented on two books in addition to *Dark Deeds:* J. B. (1857) and Anon. (1857b). Neither the Library of Congress nor the British Library nor the Cambridge University Library contains a catalogue reference to either of these two books.

12. Evidence that points to John Ormsby as the anonymous reviewer can be found in Bevington (1941), *The Saturday Review 1855–1869*, p. 365.

13. Neale (1847), *Experiences of a Gaol Chaplain*, 1: vii–viii.

14. See Quetelet (1835), *Sur l'homme et sur les développements de ses facultés, ou Essai de physique sociale.* It is also quite possible that Neale borrowed Quetelet's phrase from Quetelet's *A Treatise on Man* (1842, p. 108), an English-language version of *Sur l'homme*.

15. See further *supra,* p. 103, n.49.

Bibliography

Author's Note: some entries have two publication dates. The first refers to the original publication date, the second to the edition used here and to which page citations in the text refer.

Unpublished Items

Bentham, Jeremy (1831a). "Untitled Manuscript," *Bentham Papers,* no. 149 (238), University College London archives.

Bentham, Jeremy (1831b). "Untitled Manuscript," *Bentham Papers,* no. 149 (237), University College London archives.

Drinkwater, John Elliott (1833). "Note Book, 27th June 1833 to 8th March 1834," *Royal Statistical Society,* London archives.

Duesterberg, Thomas J. (1979). "Criminology and the Social Order in Nineteenth-Century France. Unpublished Ph.D. diss., Indiana University.

Geisert, M. (1935). "Le système criminaliste de Tarde," University of Paris, Ph.D. diss., Paris: Domat-montchrestien.

Goring, Charles (1912a). "Letter to Professor Pearson, April 21st," *Pearson Papers,* University College London archives.

Goring, Charles (1912b). "Letter to Professor Pearson, October 2nd," *Pearson Papers,* University College London archives.

Goring, Katie MacDonald (1919). "Letter to Karl Pearson, May 7th," *Pearson Papers,* University College London archives.

Guerry, André-Michel (1834). "Letter to Edwin Chadwick, May 14th, 1834," *Chadwick Papers,* no. 905, University College London archives.

Ruggles-Brise, Evelyn (1919). "Letter to Professor Pearson, September 2nd," *Pearson Papers,* University College London archives.

Weldon, W.F.R. (1895). "Weldon to Pearson, 9th June 1895," *Pearson Papers,* no. 891, University College London archives.

Zeman, Thomas Edward (1981). "Order, Crime and Punishment: The American Criminological Tradition," unpublished Ph.D. diss. in the History of Consciousness (Political and Social Thought), University of California at Santa Cruz.

Primary Literature

Actes du Premier Congrès International de l'Anthropologie Criminelle (1886). Turin: Bocca.

Actes du Deuxième Congrès International de l'Anthropologie Criminelle (1889). Lyons: A. Storck.

Actes du Troisième Congrès d l'Anthropologie Criminelle (1892). Brussels: Hayez.

Alembert, Jean Le Rond d' (1765) (1965). "Lettera a Paolo Frisi," pp. 312–14, in Venturi (ed.), *Cesare Beccaria, Dei delitti e delle pene.* Turin: Giulio Einaudi.

Alembert, Jean Le Rond d' (n.d.1) (1821–22). "De l'abus de la critique en matière de religion." *Oeuvres complètes de d'Alembert* (Paris: A. Belin, 5 vols.), 1: 547–72.

Alembert, Jean Le Rond d' (n.d.2) (1921–22). "Explication détaillée du système des connaissances humaines," *Oeuvres complètes de d'Alembert (Paris: A. Belin, 5 vols.), 1: 99–114.*

Angeville, Adolphe d' (1836) (1969). *Essai sur la statistique de la population française, considérée sous quelques-uns des ses rapports physiques et moraux.* The Netherlands: Mouton and Maison des Sciences de l'Homme.

Anon. (1857b). *The Lamentation of Leopold Redpath.* Catnach, Seven Dials.

Bacon, Francis (1632). *The Essayes or Counsels Civill and Morall, of Francis Lo[rd] Verulam.* London: John Haviland.

Balbi, Adriano (1822). *Essai statistique sur le royaume de Portugal et d'Algarve, comparé aux autres états de l'Europe.* 2 vols. Paris: Rey and Gravier.

Balbi, Adriano (1826). *Introduction à l'atlas ethnographique du globe.* Paris.

Balbi, Adriano, and André Michel Guerry (1829). *Statistique comparée de l'état de l'instruction et du nombre des crimes dans les divers Arrondissemens des Académies et des Cours Rles de France.* Paris: Renouard.

Balzac, Honoré de (1829) (1973). *Code pénal des honnêtes gens.* In *Oeuvres complètes de M. de Balzac* (Paris: Delta), 25: 385–484.

Beccaria, Cesare (1762a) (1958). "Del disordine e de' rimedi delle monete nello stato di Milano nell' anno 1762," in Sergio Romagnoli (ed.), *Cesare Beccaria: Opere.* Florence: Sansoni, 1: 7–34.

Beccaria, Cesare (1762b) (1958). "Tentativo analitico su i contrabbandi," in Sergio Romagnoli (ed.), *Cesare Beccaria: Opere.* Florence: Sansoni, 1: 164–66.

Beccaria, Cesare (1764) (1986). *On Crimes and Punishments,* trans. David Young. Indianapolis: Hackett.

Beccaria, Cesare (1765a) (1958). "A Jean-Baptiste Le Rond d'Alembert," in Sergio Romagnoli (ed.), *Cesare Beccaria: Opere.* Florence: Sansoni, 2: 859–61.

Beccaria, Cesare (1765b) (1958). "All' arciduca Ferdinando d'Austria, duca di Modena, governatore della Lombardia," in Sergio Romagnoli (ed.), *Cesare Beccaria: Opere.* Florence: Sansoni, 2: 858–59.

Beccaria, Cesare (1765c) (1958). "Frammento sullo stile," in Sergio Romagnoli (ed.), *Cesare Beccaria: Opere.* Florence: Sansoni, 1: 167–74.

Beccaria, Cesare (1766) (1958). "Ad André Morellet, le 26 janvier," in Sergio Romagnoli (ed.), *Cesare Beccaria: Opere.* Florence: Sansoni, 2: 862–70.

Beccaria, Cesare (1770) (1984). "Ricerche intorno alla natura dello stile," in Firpo (ed.), *Cesare Beccaria: Opere.* Milan: Mediobanca, 2: 63–206.

Beccaria, Cesare (1792). "Voto per la riforma del sistema criminale nella Lombardia Austriaca riguardante la pena di morte," in Sergio Romagnoli (ed.), *Cesare Beccaria: Opere.* Florence: Sansoni, 2: 735–41.

Beccaria, Cesare (1804) (1958). "Elementi di economia pubblica," in Sergio Romagnoli (ed.), *Cesare Beccaria: Opere.* Florence: Sansoni, 1: 379–649.

Beccaria, Cesare (n.d.) (1984). "Estratti da Bacone: Nota al testo, materiali non pubblicati," in Firpo (ed.), *Cesare Beccaria: Opere.* Milan: Mediobanca, 2: 457–73.

Bentham, Jeremy (1776) (1988). *A Fragment on Government.* Cambridge: Cambridge University Press.

Bérenger, A. M. (1818). *De la justice criminelle en France.* Paris.

Bertrand, Joseph (1889). *Calcul de probabilités.* Paris: Gauthiers-Villers.

Blackstone, Sir William (1769) (1978). *Commentaries on the Laws of England,* 4 vols. London: Garland.

Bulwer, Henry Lytton (1834). *France, Social, Literary, Political*, 2 vols. London: Richard Bentley.

Candolle, Alphonse de (1830). "Considérations sur la statistique des délits," *Bibliotèque universelle des sciences, belles-lettres et arts*, 1: 159–86.

Châteauneuf, Benoiston de (1842). "Sur les résultats des comptes de l'administration de la justice criminelle en France, de 1825 à 1839," *Séances et travaux de l'Académie des sciences morales et politiques, compte rendu*, 1: 324–41.

Colajanni, Napoleone (1884). *Il Socialismo: Socialismo e Sociologia Criminale*, 3 vols. Catania: Filippo Tropea.

Colajanni, Napoleone (1888). "Question contemporaine de la criminalité," *Revue socialiste*, 7: 59–68.

Compte général de l'administration de la justice criminelle en France. Paris: L'Imprimérie royale.

Comte, Auguste (1838) (1869). *Cours de philosophie positive*, 6 vols. Paris: J. B. Baillière.

Condillac, Etienne Bonnot, Abbé de (1754) (1982). *A Treatise on the Sensations*, pp. 175–339 in *Philosophical Writings of Etienne Bonnot, Abbé de Condillac*, trans. Franklin Philip. Hillsdale, N.J.: Lawrence Erlbaum.

Condorcet, Marie-Jean-Antoine-Nicolas Caritat (1782) (1847). "Discours prononcé dans l'Académie française le jeudi 21 février 1782," in A. Condorcet-O'Connor and M. F. Arago (eds.), *Oeuvres de Condorcet*, 1: 389–415. Paris: Firmin Didot.

Condorcet, Marie-Jean-Antoine-Nicolas Caritat (1785) (1788). "Letter to King Frederick II of Prussia, 2 May 1785," in *Oeuvres posthumes de Frédéric II, roi de Prusse*, 13: 268–73. Berlin: Voss.

Condorcet, Marie-Jean-Antoine-Nicolas Caritat (1795a) (1900). *Tableau historique des progrès de l'esprit humain*. Paris: G. Steinheil.

Condorcet, Marie-Jean-Antoine-Nicolas Caritat (1975b). "Tableau général de la science qui a pour objet l'application du calcul aux sciences politiques et morales," in A. Condorcet-O'Connor and M. F. Arago (eds.), *Oeuvres de Condorcet*, 1: 539–73. Paris: Firmin Didot.

Condorcet, Marie-Jean-Antoine-Nicolas Caritat (n.d.) (1804), "Essai sur les probabilités en fait de Justice," in *Oeuvres complètes de Condorcet*, 6: 390–92. Paris: Viewed.

Danjou, E. (1821). *Des prisons, de leur régime et des moyens de l'améliorer*. Paris.

Darwin, Charles (1873). "On the Males and Complemental Males of certain Cirripedes, and on Rudimentary Structures," *Nature,* 8(44): 431–32.

Darwin, George (1873). "Variations on Organs," *Nature,* 8(44): 505.

Darwin, Leonard (1914). "The Habitual Criminal," *The Eugenics Review,* 6(3): 204–18.

Despine, Prosper (1868). *Psychologie naturelle.* Paris: Savy.

Dexter, Edwin Grant (1904). *Weather Influences: An Empirical Study of the Mental and Physiological Effects of Definite Meteorological Conditions.* London: Macmillan.

Diderot, Denis (1771). "Des recherches sur le style par Beccaria," *Diderot: Oeuvres complètes,* 4: 60–63. Paris: Garnier.

Dupin, Charles (1827a). *Forces productives et commerciales de la France,* 2 vols. Paris: Bachelier.

Dupin, Charles (1827b). *Carte figurative de l'instruction populaire de la France.* Paris.

Durkheim, Emile (1893) (1986). *The Division of Labor in Society.* Trans. W. D. Halls. New York: Free Press.

Durkheim, Emile (1894) (1982). *The Rules of Sociological Method.* Ed. Steven Lukes, trans. W. D. Halls, London: Macmillan.

Durkheim, Emile (1895) (1983). "Crime and social health," *Revue philosophique,* 39: 518–23. (Translated into English in Lukes and Scull [1983], pp. 92–101.)

Durkheim, Emile (1897) (1951). *Suicide: A Study in Sociology.* Trans. J. A. Spaulding and George Simpson. New York: Free Press.

Durkheim, Emile (1901a) (1983). "Two Laws of Penal Evolution," in Steven Lukes and Andrew Scull (eds.), *Durkheim and the Law,* pp. 102–32. New York: St. Martin's.

Durkheim, Emile (1901b). "Lettre au directeur la *Revue philosophique,*" *Revue philosophique,* 52: 74.

Durkheim, Emile (1915). "La Sociologie," in Durkheim, *La Science française.* Paris: Ministère de l'Instruction Publique et des Beaux-Arts.

Durkheim, Emile, and Paul Fauconnet (1903) (1982). "Sociology and the Social Sciences," in E. Durkheim, *The Rules of Sociological Method,* pp. 175–208. (ed. Steven Lukes, trans. W. D. Halls.) London: Macmillan.

Ellis, Havelock (1890). *The Criminal.* London: Walter Scott.

Facchinei, Ferdinando (1765) (1965). "Note ed osservazioni sul libro intitolato 'Dei delitti e delle pene,' " in Franco Venturi (ed.), *Cesare Beccaria, Dei delitti e delle pene*, pp. 164–77. Turin: Giulio Einaudi.

Féré, Charles (1887). "Dégénérescence et criminalité," *Revue philosophique*, 24: 337–77.

Féré, Charles (1889). *Dégénérescence et criminalité*. Paris: Alcan.

Ferri, Enrico (1884) (1917 rev. ed.). *Criminal Sociology*, trans. J. I. Kelly and J. Lisle. Boston: Little, Brown.

Ferri, Enrico (1914). "The present movement in criminal anthropology apropos of a biological investigation in the English prisons," *Journal of the American Institute of Criminal Law and Criminology*, 5(2): 224–27.

Fletcher, Joseph (1843). "Progress of Crime in the United Kingdom," *Journal of the Statistical Society of London*, 6: 218–40.

Fletcher, Joseph (1847). "Moral and Educational Statistics of England and Wales," *Journal of the Statistical Society of London*, 10: 193–242.

Fletcher, Joseph (1849). "Moral and Educational Statistics of England and Wales," *Journal of the Statistical Society of London*, 12: 151–76.

Frégier, Honoré-Antoine (1840). *Des classes dangereuses de la population dans les grandes villes, et des moyens de les rendre meilleurs*, 2 vols. Paris: Baillière.

Gall, Franz Joseph (1806) (1835). *On the Origin of the Moral Qualities and Intellectual Faculties of Man, and the Conditions of their Manifestation*, trans. Winslow Lewis, 6 vols. Boston: Marsh, Capen and Lyon.

Galton, Francis (1869). *Hereditary Genius*. London: Macmillan.

Galton, Francis (1879a). "Composite Portraits," *Journal of the Anthropological Institute*, 8: 132–42.

Galton, Francis (1879b). "Generic Images," *Proceedings of the Royal Society*, 9:161–70.

Galton, Francis (1883). *Inquiries into Human Faculty and Its Development*. London: Macmillan.

Galton, Francis (1888). "Co-relations and their measurement, chiefly from anthropometric data," *Proceedings of the Royal Society of London*, 45: 135–45.

Galton, Francis (1889). *Natural Inheritance*. London: Macmillan.

Galton, Francis (1901). "The Possible Improvement of the Human Breed, under the Existing Conditions of Law and Sentiment," in

Galton, *Essays in Eugenics*, pp. 1–34. London: Eugenics Education Society.

Galton, Francis (1904). "Eugenics: its Definition, Scope and Aims," in Galton, *Essays in Eugenics*, pp. 35–43. London: Eugenics Education Society.

Galton, Francis (1909). *Essays in Eugenics*. London: Eugenics Education Society.

Galton, Francis, and F. A. Mahomed (1882), "An Inquiry into the Physiognomy of Phthisis by the Method of Composite Portraiture," *Guy's Hospital Reports*, 25: 1–18.

Garofalo, Raffaele (1880). *Di un criterio positivo della penalità*. Ed. Vallardi. Naples.

Garofalo, Raffaele (1885). *Criminologia*. Turin: Bocca.

Goring, Charles (1909). "On the Inheritance of the Diatheses of Phthisis and Insanity," *Studies in National Deterioration*, no. 5, Biometric Laboratory, University College London.

Goring, Charles (1913). *The English Convict: A Statistical Study*. London: His Majesty's Stationery Office.

Goring, Charles (1918). "The Aetiology of Crime." *Journal of Mental Science*, (April), 129–46.

Gramsci, Antonio (1926) (1978). "Some Aspects of the Southern Question," in *Gramsci: Selections from Political Writings (1921–1926)*, pp. 441–62. Trans. Quintin Hoare. New York: International Publishers.

Greg, William Rathbone (1835). *Social Statistics of the Netherlands*. London: Ridgway and Sons.

Griffiths, Arthur (1904). *Fifty Years of Public Service*. London: Cassell.

Griffiths, Arthur (1910). "Criminology," *Encyclopaedia Brittanica*, 7: 464–65.

Griffiths, G. B., and H. B. Donkin (1904). "Measurements of One Hundred and Thirty Criminals," *Biometrika*, 3(1): 60–62.

Grimm, Melchior (1765a) (1878). "Sur le traité des *Délits et des Peines, par Beccaria*," *Correspondance littéraire, philosophique et critique*, 6: 329–38. Paris: Garnier.

Grimm, Melchior (1765b) (1878). "Examen de la traduction du *Traité des Délits et des Peines de Beccaria par Morellet*," *Correspondence littéraire, philosophique et critique*, 6: 422–29. Paris: Garnier.

Guerry, André-Michel (1829). *Statistique comparé de l'état de l'instruction et du nombre des crimes*. Paris.

Guerry, André-Michel (1831). "Letter to Quetelet, September 11th." Trans. Sawyer Sylvester in Quetelet (1831b), pp. 70–78.

Guerry, André-Michel (1832a). "Motifs des crimes capitaux, d'après le compte de l'administration de la justice criminelle," *Annales d'hygiène publique et de médecine légale*, 8: 335–46.

Guerry, André-Michel (1832b). "La statistique comparée de l'état de l'instruction et du nombre des crimes," *Revue encyclopédique*, 55: 414–24.

Guerry, André-Michel (1833). *Essai sur la statistique morale de la France*. Paris: Crochard.

Guerry, André-Michel (1864). *Statistique Morale de l'Angleterre comparée avec la Statistique Morale de la France*. Paris: Bailliére.

Hegel, G.W.F. (1821) (1967). *The Philosophy of Right*, trans. T. M. Knox. London: Oxford University Press.

Helvétius, Claude-Adrien (1758). *De l'esprit*. Paris: Durand.

Herschel, John (1850). "Review," *Edinburgh Review*, 92(185): 1–57.

Hobhouse, Leonard T. (1911). *Social Evolution and Political Theory*. New York: Columbia University Press.

Hooton, Earnest A. (1939). *The American Criminal: An Anthropological Study*. Cambridge: Harvard University Press.

Humboldt, Alexander von (1811) (1966). *Political Essay on the Kingdom of New Spain*, trans. John Black, 4 vols. New York: AMS Press.

Humboldt, Alexander von (1817). "Mémoire sur les lignes isothermes." *Annales de Chimie et de Physique*, 5: 102–11.

Hume, David (1739) (1967). *A Treatise of Human Nature*. Oxford: Clarendon Press.

Hutcheson, Francis (1725a) (1738). *An Inquiry into the Original of our Ideas of Beauty and Virtue, in Two Treatises*. London: printed for D. Midwinter, A. Bettesworth and C. Hitch.

Hutcheson, Francis (1725b) (1973). *An Inquiry Concerning Beauty, Order, Harmony, Design*. The Hague: Martinus Nijhoff.

Hutcheson, Francis (1755). *A System of Moral Philosophy*. London: A Millar and T. Longman.

Jaucourt, Chevalier de (1751) (1969). "Crime (faute, péché, délit, forfait)," *Encyclopédie, ou dictionnaire raisonné des sciences, des arts et des métiers* (Diderot and d'Alembert, eds.), 1: 466–70. New York: Pergamon.

Jevons, W. Stanley (1873) (1958). *The Principles of Science: A Treatise on Logic and Scientific Method.* New York: Dover.

John, Victor (1898). *Quetelet bei Goethe.* Jena: Fischer.

Kant, Immanuel (1797) (1965). *The Metaphysical Elements of Justice* (Part I of *The Metaphysics of Morals*), trans. John Ladd. Indianapolis: Bobbs-Merrill.

Lafargue, Paul (1890). "Die Kriminalität in Frankreich von 1840–1886," *Die Neue Zeit,* 8(1): 11–23.

Lamarck, Monet de (1802) (1964). *Hydrogéologie,* trans. Albert V. Carozzi. Urbana: University of Illinois Press.

Laplace, Pierre Simon de (1814) (1951). *A Philosophical Essay on Probabilities,* trans. F. W. Truscott and F. L. Emory. New York: Dover.

LeBon, Gustave (1895). *La Psychologie des foules.* Paris: Alcan.

Locke, John (1689) (1727). "Essay Concerning Human Understanding," 1: 1–342, and "Of the Conduct of the Understanding," 3: 389–428, in *The Works of John Locke.* London: printed for Arthur Bettesworth.

Locke, John (1695). *Further Considerations Concerning Raising the Value of Money.* London: printed for A. and J. Churchill.

Lombroso, Cesare (1876). *L'Uomo delinquente.* Milan: Hoepli.

Lombroso, Cesare, and Guglielmo Ferrero (1893). *La Donna delinquente.* Turin: Roux. Partially translated into English as *The Female Offender* (1895, London: T. Fisher Unwin).

Lombroso, Cesare (1899) (1918). *Crime: Its Causes and Remedies,* trans. Henry P. Horton. Boston: Little, Brown.

Lombroso-Ferrero, Gina (1911) (1972). *Lombroso's Criminal Man.* Montclair, N.J.: Patterson Smith.

Lombroso, Ferrero, Gina (1914). "The results of an official investigation made in England by Dr. Goring to test the Lombroso theory," *Journal of the American Institute of Criminal Law and Criminology,* 5(2): 207–23.

Lucas, Charles (1827). *Du système pénal et du système répressif en général, de la peine de mort en particulier.* Paris.

Lucas, E. V., and Katie Macdonald Goring (1919). "Appreciations of Charles Goring," *Biometrika,* 12: 300–307.

Lukács, Georg (1952) (1981). *The Destruction of Reason,* trans. "P.R.P." London: Merlin.

Marx, Karl (1853) (1956). "Capital Punishment," *New York Daily Tribune*, February 18, 1853, reprinted in T. B. Bottmore and M. Rubel (eds.), *Karl Marx: Selected Writings in Sociology and Social Philosophy*, pp. 228–30. New York: McGraw-Hill.

Montesquieu, Charles-Louis de Secondat (1721) (1960). *Lettres persanes*. Paris: Garnier.

Montesquieu, Charles-Louis de Secondat (1748) (1973). *De l'esprit des lois*, 2 vols. Paris: Garnier.

Morris, Terence (1957). *The Criminal Area*. London: Routledge and Kegan Paul.

Neale, Erskine (1847). *Experiences of a Gaol Chaplain*, 3 vols. London: Richard Bentley.

Neale, Erskine (1857). *Dark Deeds*. London: George Vickers.

Oëttingen, Alexander von (1882). *Die Moralstatistik in ihrer Bedeutung für eine Socialethik*. Erlangen: Andreas Deichert.

Parent-Duchâtelet, Alexandre J. -B. (1836). *De la Prostitution dans la ville de Paris*, 2 vols. Paris: Baillière.

Pearson, Karl (1903). "On the Inheritance of the Mental and Moral Characters in Man, and Its Comparison with the Inheritance of the Physical Characters," *Journal of the Anthropological Institute of Great Britain and Ireland*, 33: 179–237.

Pearson, Karl (1910). "Nature and Nurture: The Problem of the Future," *Eugenics Laboratory Lecture Series*, no. 6, University of London.

Pearson, Karl (1919a). "Charles Goring and his Contribution to *Criminology*," pp. xv–xx, in Goring (1919, abridged edition of *The English Convict*).

Pearson, Karl (1919b). "Charles B. Goring," *Biometrika*, 12: 297–99.

Pearson, Karl (1924). *The Life, Letters and Labours of Francis Galton*, 2 vols. Cambridge: Cambridge University Press.

Petty, William (1662) (1899). "A Treatise of Taxes and Contributions," in Charles Henry Hall (ed.), *The Economic Writings of Sir William Petty*, pp. 1–97. Cambridge: Cambridge University Press.

Playfair, William (1786). *The Commercial and Political Atlas*. London: Wallis.

Plint, Thomas (1851). *Crime in England, Its Relation, Character, and Extent, as Developed from 1801 to 1848*. London: Charles Gilpin.

Porter, G. R. (1837). "On the Connexion Between Crime and Ignorance, as Exhibited in Criminal Calendars," *Transactions of the Statistical Society*, 1(1): 97–103.

Quetelet, Adolphe (1826). "Mémoire sur les lois des naissance et de la mortalité à Bruxelles," *Nouveaux Mémoires de l'Académie Royale des Sciences et Belles-Lettres de Bruxelles,* 3: 495–512.

Quetelet, Adolphe (1827). "Recherches sur la population, les naissances, les décès, les prisons, les dépots de mendicité, etc., dans le royaume des Pays-Bas," *Nouveaux mémoires de l'Académie Royale des Sciences et Belles-Lettres de Bruxelles,* 4: 116–74.

Quetelet, Adolphe (1828). *Instructions populaires sur le calcul des probabilités.* Brussels: Tarlier.

Quetelet, Adolphe (1829a). "Recherches statistiques sur le royaume des Pays-Bas," *Nouveaux mémoires de l'Académie Royale des Sciences et Belles-Lettres de Bruxelles,* 5: 25–38.

Quetelet, Adolphe (1829b). "Du nombre des crimes et des délits dans les provinces du Brabant méridional, des deux Flandres, du Hainaut et d'Anvers, pendant les années 1826, 1827 et 1828," *Correspondance mathématique et physique,* 5: 177–87.

Quetelet, Adolphe (1830a). "Sur la constance qu'on observe dans le nombre des crimes qui se commettent," *Correspondance mathématique et physique,* 6: 214–17.

Quetelet, Adolphe (1830b). "Relevé des crimes et délits commis dans les provinces du Brabant méridional, des deux Flandres, du Hainaut et d'Anvers, pendant l'année 1829," *Correspondance mathématique et physique,* 6: 273–75.

Quetelet, Adolphe (1831a). *Recherches sur la loi de la croissance de l'homme.* Brussels: Hayez.

Quetelet, Adolphe (1831b) (1984). *Research on the Propensity for Crime at Different Ages,* trans. Sawyer F. Sylvester. Cincinnati, Ohio: Anderson.

Quetelet, Adolphe (1835). *Sur l'homme et sur les développements de ses facultés, ou Essai de physique sociale.* Paris: Bachelier.

Quetelet, Adolphe (1842). *A Treatise on Man,* trans. R. Knox and T. Smibert. Edinburgh: William and Robert Chambers.

Quetelet, Adolphe (1846). *Lettres à S.A.R. Le Duc Régnant de Saxe-Coburg et Gotha sur la Théorie des Probabilités.* Brussels: Hayez.

Quetelet, Adolphe (1848a) (1984). "Sur la statistique morale et les principes qui doivent en former la base," *Déviance et société,* 8(1): 13–41.

Quetelet, Adolphe (1848b). *Du système social et des lois qui le régissent.* Paris: Guillaumin.

Quetelet, Adolphe (1851). "Sur la statistique criminelle du Royaume-Uni de la Grande Bretagne, Lettre à M. Porter à Londres," *Bulletin de la Commission centrale de statistique*, 4: 109–21.

Quetelet, Adolphe (1869). *Physique sociale, ou Essai sur le développement des facultés*. Brussels: C. Murquardt.

Quetelet, Adolphe (1871a). "Des lois concernant le développement de l'homme," *Annuaire de l'observatoire de Bruxelles*, 38: 205–16.

Quetelet, Adolphe (1871b). *Anthropométrie, ou mesure des différentes facultés de l'homme*. Brussels: C. Muquardt.

Ramsay, Allan (n.d.). "Lettre à A. M. Diderot," *Diderot: Oeuvres complètes*, 4: 52–60. Paris: Garnier.

Rawson, Rawson W. (1839). "An Enquiry into the Statistics of Crime in England and Wales," *Journal of the Statistical Society of London*, 2: 316–44.

Rawson, Rawson W. (1841). "An Enquiry into the Condition of Criminal Offenders in England and Wales, with respect to Education; or, Statistics of Education among the Criminal and General Population of England and other Countries," *Journal of the Statistical Society of London*, 3: 331–52.

Ruggles-Brise, Evelyn (1913). Preface, in Goring (1913) [1972], pp. 6–9.

Ruggles-Brise, Evelyn (1921). *The English Prison System*. London: Macmillan.

Saleilles, Raymond (1898) (1911). *The Individualization of Punishment*, trans. Rachel Szold Jastrow; introduction by Gabriel Tarde. Boston: Little, Brown.

Sanctis, Sante de (1914). "An Investigation of English Convicts and Criminal Anthropology," *Journal of the American Institute of Criminal Law and Criminology*, 5(2): 228–40.

Servin, Antoine Nicholas (1782). *De la législation criminelle*. Basel: Schweigenhauser.

Sighele, Scipio (1892). *La foule criminelle, essai de psychologie collective*, trans. P. Vigny. Paris: Alcan.

Spencer, Herbert (1850) (1896). *Social Statics*. New York: Appleton.

Spurzheim, J. G. (n.d.) (1817). *Observations on the Deranged Manifestation of the Mind, or Insanity*. London: Baldwin, Cradock and Joy.

Sutherland, Edwin H., and Donald R. Cressey (1960). *Principles of Criminology*. Chicago: J. D. Lippincott.

Taillandier, A. H. (1824). *Réflexions sur les lois pénales de France et d'Angleterre*. Paris.

Taillandier, A. H. (1827). "Review of *Compte général de l'administration de la justice criminelle en France, pendant l'année 1825,*" *Revue encyclopédique,* 34: 360–74.

Tarnowsky, Pauline (1888) (1889). *Etude anthropométrique sur les prostituées et les voleuses.* Paris.

Tarde, Gabriel (1884). "Qu'est-ce qu'une société?," *Revue philosophique,* 18: 501.

Tarde, Gabriel (1885) (1902). *Le type criminel,* pp. 9–61, in Tarde (1886a).

Tarde, Gabriel (1886a) (1902). *La criminalité comparée.* Paris: Alcan.

Tarde, Gabriel (1886b). "La statistique criminelle du dernier demi-siècle," pp. 61–121, in Tarde (1886a).

Tarde, Gabriel (1886c). "Problèmes de pénalité," pp. 122–211, in Tarde (1886a).

Tarde, Gabriel (1887). "Positivisme et pénalité," *Archives de l'anthropologie criminelle,* 2: 32–51.

Tarde, Gabriel (1888). "Les actes du congrès de Rome," *Archives de l'anthropologie criminelle,* 3: 66–80.

Tarde, Gabriel (1889a). "L'atavisme moral," *Archives de l'anthropologie criminelle,* 4: 237–65.

Tarde, Gabriel (1889b). "Sur la responsabilité morale (rapport sur la xième question," *Archives de l'anthropologie criminelle,* 4: 356–69.

Tarde, Gabriel (1890a). *The Laws of Imitation,* trans. E. Parsons New York: Henry Holt.

Tarde, Gabriel (1890b) (1912). *Penal Philosophy,* trans. R. Howell. Boston: Little, Brown.

Tarde, Gabriel (1891). "Études criminelles et penales," *Revue philosophique,* 32: 483–517.

Tarde, Gabriel (1892). "Les crimes des foules," *Archives de l'anthropologie criminelle,* 7: 353–86.

Tarde, Gabriel (1893a). "Biologie et sociologie: Réponse au Dr. Bianchi," *Archives de l'anthropologie criminelle,* 8: 7–20.

Tarde, Gabriel (1893b). "Questions sociales," *Revue philosophique,* 35: 618–38.

Tarde, Gabriel (1893c). *Les transformations du droit: Étude sociologique.* Paris: Alcan.

Tarde, Gabriel (1893d). "Foules et sectes au point de vue criminel," *Revue des deux mondes,* 120: 349–87.

Tarde, Gabriel (1894). "Address to the First International Congress of Sociology in October, 1894," translated as "Sociology, Social Psychology and Sociologism," pp. 112–35, in Clark (1969).

Tarde, Gabriel (1895a). *La Logique sociale*. Paris: Alcan.

Tarde, Gabriel (1895b). "Revue critique: Congrès de Sociologie," *Archives de l'anthropologie criminelle*, 10: 206–7.

Tarde, Gabriel (1895c). "Criminalité et santé sociale," *Revue philosophique*, 39: 148–62. Reprinted in Tarde (1898), pp. 138–61.

Tarde, Gabriel (1895d). "Crimes, délits, contraventions," pp. 309–26 in Tarde (1898).

Tarde, Gabriel (1897a). *L'Opposition universelle*. Paris: Alcan.

Tarde, Gabriel (1897b). "Criminal Youth," translated in Clark (1969), pp. 255–73.

Tarde, Gabriel (1898). *Études de psychologie sociale*. Paris: Giard and Brière.

Tarde, Gabriel (1899a). *Social Laws: An Outline of Sociology*, trans. N. C. Warren. London: Macmillan.

Tarde, Gabriel (1899b). *Les transformations du pouvoir*. Paris: Alcan.

Tarde, Gabriel (1901a). "La criminalité et les phénomènes économiques," *Archives de l'anthropologie criminelle*, 16: 565–75.

Tarde, Gabriel (1901b). "La réalité sociale, *Revue philosophique*, 52: 457–79.

Tarde, Gabriel (1909). *Tarde. Introduction et pages choisies par ses fils*. Paris: Louis-Michaud.

Taylor, Ian, Paul Walton, and Jock Young (1973). *The New Criminology*. London: Routledge and Kegan Paul.

Topinard, Paul (1887). "L'anthropologie criminelle," *Revue d'anthropologie*, 2: 658–91.

Topinard, Paul (1889) (1890). "Criminologie et anthropologie," *Actes du Deuxième Congrès Internationale d'Anthropologie Criminelle (1889, Paris)*, pp. 489–96. Lyons: A. Storck.

Treviranus, Gottfried Reinhold (1802). *Biologie, oder Philosphie der lebenden Natur für Naturforscher und Aertze*, 6 vols. Göttingen.

Verri, Pietro (1763). *Meditazioni sulla felicità*. Milan: Galeazzi.

Vico, Giambattista (1709) (1965). *On the Study Methods of Our Time*, trans. Elio Gianturco. Indianapolis: Bobbs-Merrill.

Vico, Giambattista (1725) (1970). *The New Science*, trans. T. G. Bergin and M. H. Fisch. Ithaca, N.Y.: Cornell University Press.

Villermé, Louis René (1820). *Des prisons telles qu'elles sont et telles qu'elles devraient être: Ouvrage dans lequel on les considère par rapport a l'hygiène à la morale et à l'économie politique*. Paris: Mequignon-Marvis.

Voltaire, François-Marie Arouet de (1762a) (1879). "Lettre à M. d'Alembert," *Oeuvres Complètes de Voltaire* (Paris: Garnier), 42: 78–79.

Voltaire, François-Marie Arouet de (1762b). "Lettre à M. d'Alembert," *Oeuvres Complètes de Voltaire* 42: 167–68. Paris: Garnier.

Voltaire, François-Marie Arouet de (1763) (1879). "Traité sur la tolérance à l'occasion de la mort de Jean Calas," *Oeuvres Complètes de Voltaire*, 25: 18–118. Paris: Garnier.

Weisser, Michael R. (1979). *Crime and Punishment in Early Modern Europe*. Atlantic Highlands, N.J.: Humanities Press.

Weldon, W.F.R. (1892). "Certain Correlated Variations in *Crangon Vulgaris*," *Proceedings of the Royal Society of London*, 51: 2–21.

Weldon, W.F.R. (1893). "On Certain Correlated Variations in *Carcinus Moenas*," *Proceedings of the Royal Society of London*, 54: 318–29.

Weldon, W.F.R. (1894–95). "An Attempt to Measure the Death-Rate due to the Selective Destruction of Carcinus Moenas with respect to a Particular Dimension," *Proceedings of the Royal Society of London*, 57: 360–82.

Weldon, W.F.R. (1898). "Presidential Address to Section D, Zoology," *British Association Report*, pp. 887–902.

Secondary Literature

Abrams, Philip (1968). *The Origins of British Sociology: 1834–1914*. Chicago: University of Chicago Press.

Ackerknecht, Erwin H. (1952). "Villermé and Quetelet," *Bulletin of the History of Medicine*, 26: 317–29.

Ackerknecht, Erwin H., and Henry V. Vallois (1956). "Franz Joseph Gall, Inventor of Phrenology and his Collection," *Wisconsin Studies in Medical History*, no. 1.

Anon. (1833). "Guerry on the Statistics of Crime in France," *Westminster Review*, 18 (April): 353–66.

Anon. (1857a). "Felons and Felon Worship," *Saturday Review*, 3 (March 21): 270–72.

Anon. (1866a). "Guerry (André-Michel)," *Grand Dictionnaire universel du XIXe siècle*, 8: 1604. Paris: Larousse.

Anon. (1866b). "Balbi (Adrien)," *Grand Dictionnaire universel du XIXe siècle*. 2: 91. Paris: Larousse.

Anon. (1890). "Review of Havelock Ellis' *The Criminal*," *The Athenaeum*, 6 September, pp. 325–26.

Anon. (1911), "Obituary of Sir Francis Galton," *Journal of the Royal Statistical Society,* 74: 314–20.

Anon. (1919). "Obituary: Charles Buckman Goring," *The Lancet,* 24 May, p. 914.

Baker, Keith Michael (1975). *Condorcet: From Natural Philosophy to Social Mathematics.* Chicago: University of Chicago Press.

Barrows, Susanna (1981). *Distorting Mirrors: Visions of the Crowd in Late Nineteenth-Century France.* New Haven: Yale University Press.

Beattie, J. M. (1986). *Crime and the Courts in England 1660–1800.* Princeton: Princeton University Press.

Becker, Carl L. (1932). *The Heavenly City of the Eighteenth-Century Philosophers.* New Haven: Yale University Press.

Beirne, Piers, and Alan Hunt (1990). "Lenin, Crime, and Penal Politics, 1917–1924," in Piers Beirne (ed.), *Revolution in Law: Contributions to Soviet Legal Theory, 1917–1938,* pp. 99–135. Armonk, N.Y.: M. E. Sharpe.

Berlin, Isaiah (1960). "The Philosophical Ideas of Giambattista Vico," in Harold Acton et al. (eds.), *Art and Ideas in Eighteenth-Century Italy,* pp. 156–236. Rome: The Italian Institute of London.

Bertillon, Jacques (1876). "La théorie des moyennes en statistique." *Journal de la société de statistique de Paris,* 17: 265–71, 286–308.

Bevington, Merle Mowbray (1941). *The Saturday Review 1855–1868.* New York: Columbia University Press.

Bouglé, C. (1905). "Un Sociologue individualiste: Gabriel Tarde," *Revue de Paris,* 3: 294.

Caffentzis, Constantine George (1989). *Clipped Coins, Abused Words, and Civil Government: John Locke's Philosophy of Money.* New York: Autonomedia.

Canetta, Rosalba (1985). "Beccaria economista e gli atti di governo," in *Cesare Beccaria: Atti di governo,* pp. 11–27. Milan: Mediobanca.

Cantù, Cesare (1862). *Beccaria e il diritto penale.* Florence: Barbèra.

Chadwick, Owen (1981). "The Italian Enlightenment," in Roy Porter and Mikulás Teich (eds.), *The Enlightenment in National Context,* pp. 90–105. Cambridge: Cambridge University Press.

Chevalier, Louis (1973). *Laboring Classes and Dangerous Classes in Paris During the First Half of the Nineteenth Century,* trans. Frank Jellinek. Princeton, N.J.: Princeton University Press.

Clark, Terry N. (1968). "Gabriel Tarde," *International Encyclopedia of the Social Sciences,* pp. 509–14.

Clark, Terry N. (1969). *Gabriel Tarde on Communication and Social Influence.* Chicago: University of Chicago Press.

Clark, Terry N. (1973). *Prophets and Patrons: The French University and the Emergence of the Social Sciences.* Cambridge: Harvard University Press.

Clark, Terry N. (1973). *Prophets and Patrons: The French University and the Emergence of the Social Sciences.* Cambridge: Harvard University Press.

Clark, Terry N. (1967). "Social Research and Its Institutionalization in France: A Case Study," *Indian Sociological Bulletin,* 4: 235–54.

Clinton, Katherine B. (1975). *"Femme et Philosophe:* Enlightenment Origins of Feminism," *Eighteenth-Century Studies,* 8(3): 283–99.

Cohen, Albert K. (1966). *Deviance and Control.* Englewood-Cliffs, N.J.: Prentice-Hall.

Cohen, Patricia Cline (1982). *A Calculating People.* Chicago: University of Chicago Press.

Cohen, Stanley (1974). "Criminology and the Sociology of Deviance in Britain: A Recent History and a Current Report," in P. Rock and M. McIntosh (eds.), *Deviance and Social Control,* pp. 1–40. London: Tavistock.

Cole, Stephen (1972). "Continuity and Institutionalization in Science: A Case Study of Failure," in Anthony Oberschall (ed.), *The Establishment of Empirical Sociology,* pp. 73–129. New York: Harper and Row.

Coleman, William (1982). *Death Is a Social Disease.* Madison, Wis.: University of Wisconsin Press.

Collard, Auguste (1934). "Goethe et Quetelet," *Isis,* 20: 426–35.

Collini, Stefan (1979). *Liberalism and Sociology.* Cambridge: Cambridge University Press.

Constant, J. (1961). A propos de l'école Franco–Belge du milieu social au XIXième siècle," in J. Léaute (ed.), *La responsabilité pénale,* pp. 303–15. Paris: Dalloz.

Cournot, Antoine-Augustin (1843). *Exposition de la théorie des chances et des probabilités.* Paris: Hachette.

Cousin, Victor (1829). *Cours de l'histoire de la philosophie,* 3 vols. Paris: Didier.

Cowan, Ruth Schwartz (1985). *Sir Francis Galton and the Study of Heredity in the Nineteenth Century*. New York: Garland.

Cullen, Michael J. (1975). *The Statistical Movement in Early Victorian Britain*. Hassocks, Harvester.

Darnton, Robert (1979). *The Business of Enlightenment: A Publishing History of the* Encyclopédie, *1775–1800*. Cambridge: Harvard University Press.

Darnton, Robert (1982). *The Literary Underground of the Old Regime*. Cambridge: Harvard University Press.

Davis, M. M. (1909). "Gabriel Tarde: Psychological Interpretations of Society," *Columbia Studies in History, Economics and Public Law*, 33(2): 84–336.

Doerner, Klaus (1981). *Madmen and the Bourgeoisie: A Social History of Insanity and Psychiatry*, trans. J. Neugroschel and J. Steinberg. Oxford: Basil Blackwell.

Donkin, Bryan (1917). "Notes on Mental Defect in Criminals," *Journal of Mental Science*, 0045: 16–35.

Donkin, Bryan (1919). "The Factors of Criminal Actions," *Journal of Mental Science*, 0063: 87–96.

Donovan, James (1981). "Justice Unblind: The Juries and the Criminal Classes in France, 1825–1914," *Journal of Social History*, 15(1): 89–107.

Douglas, Jack D. (1967). *The Social Meanings of Suicide*. Princeton, N.J.: Princeton University Press.

Driver, Edwin D. (1972). "Introductory Essay," pp. v–xiv, in Goring (1913).

Du Cane, Edmund (1879). "Discussion," *Journal of the Anthropological Institute*, 8: 142–43.

Ducpétiaux, Edouard. (1827). *De la justice de prévoyance, et particulièrement de l'influence de la misère et de l'aisance, de l'ignorance et de l'instruction sur le nombre des crimes*. Brussels: Cautaerts.

Dupréel, Eugene (1942) (ed.). *Adolphe Quetelet: Pages choisies et commentées*. Brussels: Office de Publicité.

Elmer, M. C. (1933). "Century-old ecological studies in France," *American Journal of Sociology*, 39(1): 63–70.

Farrall, L. A. (1969). *The Origins and Growth of the English Eugenics Movement, 1865–1925*. New York: Garland.

Fauré, Fernand (1918). "The Development and Progress of Statistics in France," in John Koren (ed.), *The History of Statistics*, pp. 217–329. New York: Burt Franklin.

Forrest, D. W. (1974). *Francis Galton: The Life and Work of a Victorian Genius*. London: Paul Elek.

Forster, Robert, and Orest Ranum (eds.) (1978). *Deviants and the Abandoned in French Society*. Selections from the *Annales, économies, sociétés, civilizations*, vol. 4, Baltimore: Johns Hopkins University Press.

Foucault, Michel (1979). *Discipline and Punish: The Birth of the Prison*, trans. Alan Sheridan. New York: Vintage.

Foucault, Michel (1980). *Power/Knowledge: Selected Interviews and Other Writings 1972–1977*, trans. Colin Gordon et al. New York: Pantheon.

Foucault, Michel (1988). "The Dangerous Individual," in *Foucault: Politics, Philosophy, Culture (Interviews and Other Writings 1977–1984)*, pp. 125–56. Ed. Lawrence D. Kritzman; trans. Alain Baudot and Jane Couchman. London: Routledge and Kegan Paul.

Fréchet, Maurice (1955). "Réhabilitation de la notion statistique de l'homme moyen," pp. 317–41 in M. Frechet, *Les mathématiques et le concret*. Paris: Presses Universitaires de France.

Funkhouser, H. G. (1937). "Historical Development of the Graphical Representation of Statistical Data," *Osiris*, 3: 269–404.

Funkhouser, H. G., and H. M. Walter (1935). "Playfair and His Charts," *Economic History*, 3: 103–9.

Garland, David (1985a). *Punishment and Welfare: A History of Penal Strategies*. Aldershot, Hants.: Gower.

Garland, David (1985b). "Politics and Policy in Criminological Discourse: A Study of Tendentious Reasoning and Rhetoric," *International Journal of the Sociology of Law*, 13(1): 1–33.

Gatrell, V.A.C, and T. B. Hadden (1972). "Criminal Statistics and their Interpretation," in E. A. Wrigley (ed.), *Nineteenth-Century Society: Essays in the use of quantitative methods for the study of social data*, pp. 336–96. Cambridge: Cambridge University Press.

Gay, Peter (1966). *The Enlightenment: An Interpretation*. New York: Alfred A. Knopf.

Giddens, Anthony (1965). "The Suicide Problem in French Sociology," *British Journal of Sociology*, 16: 3–18.

Gillis, A. R. (1989). "Crime and State Surveillance in Nineteenth-Century France," *American Journal of Sociology*, 95(2): 307–41.

Gilman, Sander L. (1985). *Difference and Pathology: Stereotypes of Sexuality, Race, and Madness*. Ithaca, N.Y.: Cornell University Press.

Gorecki, Jan (1985). *A Theory of Criminal Justice*. New York: Columbia University Press.

Green, Thomas Andrew (1985). *Verdict According to Conscience: Perspectives on the English Criminal Trial Jury 1200–1800*. Chicago: University of Chicago Press.

Gross, Hanns (1990). *Rome in the Age of Enlightenment*. Cambridge: Cambridge University Press.

Guyon, Bernard (1969). *La pensée politique et sociale de Balzac*. Paris: Libraire Armand Colin.

Hacking, Ian (1990). *The Taming of Chance*. Cambridge: Cambridge University Press.

Halévy, Elie (1928). *The Growth of Philosophical Radicalism*. London: Faber and Gwyer.

Haller, Mark H. (1963). *Eugenics: Hereditarian Attitudes in American Thought*. New Brunswick, N.J.: Rutgers University Press.

Hankins, Frank H. (1908). "Adolphe Quetelet as Statistician," *Studies in History, Economics and Public Law*, 31(4): 443–567.

Hankins, Frank H. (1939). "A Comtean Centenary: Invention of the Term 'Sociology'," *American Sociological Review*, 4(1): 16.

Hankins, Thomas L. (1970). *Jean d'Alembert: Science and the Enlightenment*. Oxford: Clarendon Press.

Hankins, Thomas L. (1985). *Science and the Enlightenment*. Cambridge: Cambridge University Press.

Harris, J. Arthur (1920). "Charles Buckman Goring," *Science*, 51(1310): 133–34.

Harris, Ruth (1985). "Murder under Hypnosis in the Case of Gabrielle Bompard: Psychiatry in the Courtroom in *Belle Epoque* Paris," in W. F. Bynum, Roy Porter, and Michael Shepherd (eds.), *The Anatomy of Madness*, 2: 197–241. London: Tavistock.

Hart, H.L.A. (1982). *Essays on Bentham*. Oxford: Clarendon Press.

Hélin, E., and G. Kellens (1984). "Quetelet, la morale et la statistique," *Déviance et société*, 8(1): 1–12.

Hickox, M. S. (1984). "The problem of early English sociology," *Sociological Review*, 32(1): 1–17.

Hindess, Barry (1973). *The Use of Official Statistics in Sociology*. London: Macmillan.

Hirst, Paul Q. (1986). *Law, Socialism and Democracy*. London: Allen and Unwin.

Houchon, Guy (1976). "Lacunes, faiblesses et emplois des statistiques criminelles," *Etudes relatives à la recherche criminologique*, 14: 7–29.

Humphries, Drew, and David F. Greenberg (1981). "The Dialectics of Crime Control," in David F. Greenberg (ed.), *Crime and Capitalism: Readings in Marxist Criminology,* pp. 209–54. Palo Alto, Calif.: Mayfield.

"J. B." (1857). *Scenes from the Lives of Robson and Redpath.* London: W. M. Clark.

Jenkins, Philip (1984). "Varieties of Enlightenment Criminology," *British Journal of Criminology,* 24(2): 112–30.

Jones, David A. (1986). *History of Criminology: A Philosophical Perspective.* New York: Greenwood Press.

Kent, Raymond A. (1981). *A History of British Empirical Sociology.* Aldershot: Gower.

Kidder, Frederic (1870). *History of the Boston Massacre.* Albany, N.Y.: Joel Munsell.

Klang, Daniel M. (1984). "Reform and Enlightenment in Eighteenth-Century Lombardy." *Canadian Journal of History/Annales Canadiennes d'Histoire,* 19(April): 39–70.

Knapp, G. F. (1872). "A. Quetelet als Theoretiker," *Jahrbücher für Nationalökonomie und Statistik,* 18: 89–124.

Knight, Isabel F. (1968). *The Geometric Spirit: The Abbé de Condillac and the French Enlightenment.* New Haven: Yale University Press.

Konvitz, Josef (1987). *Cartography in France, 1660–1848: Science, Engineering and Statecraft.* Chicago: University of Chicago Press.

Kurella, Hans (1911). *Cesare Lombroso: A Modern Man of Science.* London: Rebman.

Lacassagne, Alexandre (1904). "Gabriel Tarde, 1843–1904," *Archives de l'anthropologie criminelle,* 19: 501–34.

Landau, David, and Paul Lazarsfeld (1968). "Adolphe Quetelet," in *International Encyclopaedia of the Social Sciences,* pp. 247–57. New York: Macmillan and Free Press.

Landry, Eugenio (1910). *Cesare Beccaria: Scritti e lettere inediti.* Milan: Ulrico Hoepli.

Langbein, John H. (1976). *Torture and the Law of Proof: Europe and England in the Ancien Régime.* Chicago: University of Chicago Press.

Le Roy Ladurie, Emmanuel (1969). "A. d'Angeville: Un théoricien du développement," in d'Angeville (1836), *Essai sur la statistique de la population française, considérée sous quelques-uns des ses rapports physiques et moraux,* pp. 5–39. Paris: Mouton.

Lieberman, David (1989). *The Province of Legislation Determined.* Cambridge: Cambridge University Press.

Lindesmith, Alfred, and Yale Levin (1937). "The Lombrosian Myth in Criminology," *American Journal of Sociology,* 42(5): 653–71.

Lodhi, Abdul Quaiyum, and Charles Tilly (1973). "Urbanization, Crime, and Collective Violence in Nineteenth-Century France," *American Journal of Sociology,* 79(2): 296–318.

Logue, William (1983). *From Philosophy to Sociology: The Evolution of French Liberalism, 1870–1914.* Dekalb: Northern Illinois University Press.

Lottin, Joseph (1912) (1967). *Quetelet: Statisticien et sociologue.* New York: Burt Franklin.

Lukes, Steven (1973). *Emile Durkheim: His Life and Work.* Harmondsworth, U.K.: Penguin.

Lukes, Steven (1982). "Introduction," in Durkheim, *The Rules of Sociological Method,* pp. 1–27. London: Macmillan.

Lukes, Steven, and Andrew Scull (1983). "Introduction to Durkheim," in Steven Lukes and Andrew Scull (eds.), *Durkheim and the Law,* pp. 1–32. New York: St. Martin's.

Maestro, Marcello T. (1942). *Voltaire and Beccaria as Reformers of Criminal Law.* New York: Columbia University Press.

Maestro, Marcello T. (1973). *Cesare Beccaria and the Origins of Penal Reform.* Philadelphia: Temple University Press.

Mailly, Edward (1875). "Essai sur la vie et les ouvrages de L.A.J. Quetelet," *Annuaire de l'Académie royale de Belgique,* 41: 109–297.

Mannheim, Hermann (1936). "Lombroso and His Place in Modern Criminology," *Sociological Review,* 28: 31–49.

Mannheim, Hermann (1972) (ed.). *Pioneers in Criminology,* Montclair, N.J.: Patterson Smith.

Marsh, Frank H., and Janet Katz (eds.) (1985). *Biology, Crime and Ethics.* Cincinnati: Anderson.

Matza, David (1964). *Deliquency and Drift.* New York: Wiley.

Maugham, Frederic Herbert (1928). *The Case of Jean Calas.* London: William Heinemann.

Maury, Alfred (1867). *Guerry (André-Michel).* Paris: Baillière.

Mueller, G.O.W. (1990). "Whose Prophet is Cesare Beccaria? An Essay on the Origins of Criminological Theory," in William S. Laufer and Freda Adler (eds.), *Advances in Criminological Theory,* 2: 1–14.

Newman, Graeme, and Pietro Marongiu (1990). "Penological Reform and the Myth of Beccaria," *Criminology,* 28(2): 325–46.

Norton, B. (1978). "Karl Pearson and Statistics: The Social Origins of Scientific Innovation," *Social Studies of Science*, 8:3–34.

Nye, Robert (1982). "Degeneration and the Medical Model of Cultural Crisis in the French *Belle Époque*," in Seymour Drescher, David Sabean, and Allan Sharlin (eds.), *Political Symbolism in Modern Europe*, pp. 19–41. New Brunswick, N.J.: Rutgers University Press.

Nye, Robert (1982a). "Heredity, Pathology and Psychoneurosis in Durkheim's Early Work," *Knowledge and Society*, 4: 103–42.

Nye, Robert A. (1984). *Crime, Madness, and Politics in Modern France*. Princeton, N.J.: Princeton University Press.

O'Brien, Patricia (1982). *The Promise of Punishment: Prisons in Nineteenth-Century France*. Princeton, New Jersey: Princeton University Press.

Paolucci, Henry (1963). "Translator's Introduction," in Beccaria, *On Crimes and Punishments*, pp. ix–xxiii. Indianapolis: Bobbs-Merrill.

Parmalee, Maurice (1912). *The Principles of Anthropology and Sociology in Their Relations to Criminal Procedure*. New York: Macmillan.

Pasquino, Pasquale (1980). "Criminology: The Birth of a Special Savoir," *Ideology and Consciousness*, 7: 17–32.

Perrot, Jean-Claude, and Stuart J. Woolf (1984). *State and Statistics in France, 1789–1815*. London: Harwood Academic.

Perrot, Michelle (1975). "Délinquance et système pénitentaire en France au XIXe siècle," *Annales: Économies, société, civilisations*, 30(1): 67–91.

Perrot, Michelle (1976). "Premières mesures des faits sociaux: Les débuts de la statistique criminelle en France (1780–1830)," in Jacques Mairesse (ed.), *Pour une histoire de la statistique*, pp. 125–37. Paris: Institut National de la Statistique et des Études Economiques.

Perrot, Michelle (1978). "Delinquency and the Penitentiary System in Nineteenth-Century France," in Roberts Forster and Orest Ranum (eds.), *Deviants and the Abandoned in French Society*, pp. 213–45. Trans. Elborg Forster and Patricia M. Ranum. Baltimore, Md.: Johns Hopkins University Press.

Petit, Jacques G. (1984). "The Birth and Reform of Prisons in France," in Pieter Spierenburg (ed.), *The Emergence of Carceral Institutions: Prisons, Galleys and Lunatic Asylums 1550–1900*, pp. 125–47. Rotterdam: Erasmus University.

Phillipson, Coleman (1923) (1975). *Three Criminal Law Reformers: Beccaria / Bentham / Romilly*. Montclair, N.J.: Patterson Smith.

Phillipson, Nicholas (1981). "The Scottish Enlightenment," in Roy Porter and Mikulás Teich (eds.), *The Enlightenment in National Context*, pp. 19–40. Cambridge: Cambridge University Press.

Piccone, Paul (1983). *Italian Marxism*. Berkeley: University of California Press.

Pick, Daniel (1989). *Faces of Degeneration: A European Disorder, c.1848–c.1918*. Cambridge: Cambridge University Press.

Porter, Theodore M. (1985). "The Mathematics of Society: Variation and Error in Quetelet's Statistics," *British Journal for the History of Science*, 18: 51–69.

Radzinowicz, Leon (1962). *In Search of Criminology*. Cambridge: Harvard University Press.

Radzinowicz, Leon (1966). *Ideology and Crime*. New York: Columbia University Press.

Radzinowicz, Leon, and Roger Hood (1986). *The Emergency of Penal Policy*, vol. 5 of *A History of English Criminal Law and its Administration from 1750*. London: Stevens and Sons.

Robbins, Caroline (1968). *The Eighteenth-Century Commonwealthman*. New York: Atheneum.

Roberts, John M. (1960). "Enlightened Despotism in Italy," in Harold Acton et al. (eds.), *Art and Ideas in Eighteenth-Century Italy*, pp. 25–44. Rome: The Italian Institute of London.

Robertson, John (1983). "The Scottish Enlightenment at the Limits of the Civic Tradition," in Istvan Hont and Michael Ignatieff (eds.), *Wealth and Virtue: The Shaping of Political Economy in the Scottish Enlightenment*, pp. 137–78. Cambridge: Cambridge University Press.

Robinson, Arthur H. (1982). *Early Thematic Mapping in the History of Cartography*. Chicago: University of Chicago Press.

Robinson, Arthur H., and Helen M. Wallis (1967), "Humboldt's Map of Isothermal Lines: A Milestone in Thematic Cartography," *Cartographic Journal*, 4: 119–23.

Roshier, Bob (1989). *Controlling Crime: The Classical Perspective in Criminology*. Chicago: Lyceum Books.

Sarton, George (1935). "Preface to Volume 22 of *Isis* (Quetelet)," *Isis*, 23: 4–24.

Savitz, Leonard, Stanley H. Turner, and Toby Dickman (1977). "The Origin of Scientific Criminology: Franz Joseph Gall as the First Criminologist," in Robert F. Meier (ed.), *Theory in Criminology*, pp. 41–56. Beverly Hills, Calif.: Sage.

Schumpeter, Joseph A. (1954). *History of Economic Analysis*. New York: Oxford University Press.

Scott, William Robert (1900). *Francis Hutcheson*. Cambridge: University Press.

Searle, G. R. (1976). *Eugenics and Politics in Britain 1900–1914*. Leyden: Noordhoff.

Searle, G. R. (1978). "Eugenics and Class," in *The Roots of Sociobiology*, pp. 1–22. London: Past and Present Society.

Sellin, Thorsten (1931). "Charles Buckman Goring," *Encyclopedia of the Social Sciences*, 6: 703.

Sellin, Thorsten (1937). "The Lombrosian Myth in Criminology—Letter to the Editor," *American Journal of Sociology*, 42: 897–99.

Shackleton, Robert (1972). "The Greatest Happiness of the Greatest Number: The History of Bentham's phrase," *Studies on Voltaire and the Eighteenth Century*, 90: 1461–82.

Shaw, Clifford R., and Henry D. McKay (1942). *Juvenile Delinquency and Urban Areas*. Chicago: University of Chicago Press.

Silvani, Franco (1976). "Lavori recenti su Lombroso," *La Questione criminale*, 2(1): 194–205.

Skelton, R. A. (1972). *Maps: A Historical Survey of their Study and Collecting*. Chicago: University of Chicago Press.

Stead, Philip John (1983). *The Police of France*. London: Macmillan.

Stigler, Stephen M. (1986). *The History of Statistics: The Measurement of Uncertainty before 1900*. Cambridge, Mass.: Belknap.

Swingewood, Alan (1970). "Origins of Sociology: The Case of the Scottish Enlightenment," *British Journal of Sociology*, 21(2): 164–80.

Tilly, Charles, Louise Tilly, and Richard Tilly (1975). *The Rebellious Century: 1830–1930*. Cambridge: Harvard University Press.

Todhunter, Isaac (1865). *A History of the Mathematical Theory of Probability*. London: Macmillan.

Tombs, Robert (1980). "Crime and the Security of the State: The 'Dangerous Classes' and Insurrection in Nineteenth-Century Paris." in V.A.C. Gatrell, Bruce Lenman, and Geoffrey Parker, (eds.), *Crime and the Law: the Social History of Crime in Western Europe since 1500*, pp. 214–37. London: Europa.

Treiber, Hubert, and Heinz Steinert (1980). *Die Fabrikation des zuverlässigen Menschen*. Berlin: Ernst.

264

Van Ginneken, Jaap (1989). *Crowds, Psychology and Politics 1871–1899.* Amsterdam: University of Amsterdam.

Van Kan, Joseph (1903). *Les causes économiques de la criminalité. Étude historique et critique d'étiologie criminelle.* Paris: A. Maloine.

Venturi, Franco (1963). "Elementi e tentativi di riforme nello Stato Pontificio del Settecento," *Rivista Storica Italiana,* 25: 778–817.

Venturi, Franco (ed.) (1965). *Cesare Beccaria, Dei delitti e delle pene. Con una raccolta di lettere e documenti relativi alla nascita dell'opera e alla sua fortuna nell'Europa del Settecento.* Turin: Giulio Einaudi.

Venturi, Franco (1971). *Utopia and Reform in the Enlightenment.* Cambridge: Cambridge University Press.

Venturi, Franco (1972). *Italy and the Enlightenment,* trans. Susan Corsi. New York: New York University Press.

Venturi, Franco (1983). "Scottish Echoes in Eighteenth-Century Italy," in Istvan Hont and Michael Ignatieff (eds.), *Wealth and Virtue: The Shaping of Political Economy in the Scottish Enlightenment,* pp. 345–62. Cambridge: Cambridge University Press.

Vine, Margaret S. Wilson (1972). "Gabriel Tarde," Hermann Mannheim (ed.), *Pioneers in Criminology,* 2nd ed., pp. 292–304. Montclair, N.J.: Patterson Smith.

Vold, George B., and Thomas J. Bernard (1986). *Theoretical Criminology.* New York: Oxford University Press.

Westergaard, Harold (1932). *Contributions to the History of Statistics.* London: King.

Wills, Garry (1978). *Inventing America: Jefferson's Declaration of Independence.* Garden City, N.Y.: Doubleday.

Wines, Frederick Howard (1910). *Punishment and Reformation.* New York: Thomas Y. Crowell.

Wolfgang, Marvin E. (1972). "Cesare Lombroso," in H. Mannheim (ed.), *Pioneers in Criminology,* pp. 232–91. Montclair, N.J.: Patterson Smith.

Wood, P. B. (1989). "The Natural History of Man in the Scottish Enlightenment," *History of Science,* 28(1): 89–123.

Woolf, Stuart (1979). *A History of Italy, 1700–1860.* London: Methuen.

Worms, René (1905). "La philosophie sociale de G. Tarde," *Revue philosophique,* 60: 121–56.

Wright, Gordon (1983). *Between the Guillotine and Liberty: Two Centuries of the Crime Problem in France*. New York: Oxford University Press.

Young, David (1983). "Cesare Beccaria: Utilitarian or Retributivist?" *Journal of Criminal Justice*, 11(4): 317–26.

Young, David (1984). "Let Us Content Ourselves with Praising the Work While Drawing a Veil Over Its Principles': Eighteenth-Century Reactions to Beccaria's *On Crimes and Punishments*," *Justice Quarterly*, 1: 155–69.

Young, David (1986). "Property and Punishment in the Eighteenth Century: Beccaria and His Critics," *American Journal of Jurisprudence*, 31: 121–35.

Zehr, Howard (1975). "The Modernization of crime in Germany and France, 1830–1913," *Social History*, 8: 117–41.

Zehr, Howard (1976). *Crime and the Development of Modern Society*. London: Croom Helm.

Index